# EXPLORING ADHD

Attention Deficit Hyperactivity Disorder (ADHD) is the most commonly diagnosed psychiatric condition of childhood worldwide, yet the medical and psychological perspectives that dominate our understandings of ADHD present problems in their reductive understanding of the condition. *Exploring ADHD* incorporates Michel Foucault's notions of discourse and power into a critical ethnographic framework in order to analyse ADHD in terms of both the historical conditions that have shaped understandings of the disorder, and also the social conditions that build individual diagnostic cases in today's schools and families.

In this ground-breaking text, Simon Bailey also:

- acknowledges the necessary work of classrooms, schools and families in contributing to a social order;
- examines the problem of teacher autonomy and the constraints placed on schools to 'perform';
- describes the role of nurture groups in governing the emotional conduct of children;
- presents a unique gender analysis of ADHD.

This fascinating new book will be of interest to researchers and academics in the fields of early childhood education and special and inclusive education, and will illuminate and spark new debate in the arena of ADHD.

**Simon Bailey** is Research Fellow at the University of Manchester, UK.

# EXPLORING ADHD

## An ethnography of disorder in early childhood

*Simon Bailey*

Routledge
Taylor & Francis Group

LONDON AND NEW YORK

First published 2014
by Routledge
2 Park Square, Milton Park, Abingdon, Oxon OX14 4RN

Simultaneously published in the USA and Canada
by Routledge
711 Third Avenue, New York, NY 10017

*Routledge is an imprint of the Taylor & Francis Group, an informa business*

*British Library Cataloguing in Publication Data*
A catalogue record for this book is available from the British Library

*Library of Congress Cataloging in Publication Data*
Bailey, Simon, 1978-
  Exploring ADHD : an ethnography of disorder in early childhood / Authored by
  Simon Bailey.
    pages cm
  Includes bibliographical references and index.
  1. Attention-deficit hyperactivity disorder.   2. Attention-deficit hyperactivity disorder—
  Social aspects.   3. Attention-deficit-disordered children—Psychology.   I. Title.
  RJ506.H9B344 2013
  618.92'8589—dc23

                                                                              2013003207

ISBN: 978-0-415-52581-7 (hbk)
ISBN: 978-0-415-52582-4 (pbk)
ISBN: 978-0-203-11972-3 (ebk)

Typeset in Bembo
by RefineCatch Limited, Bungay, Suffolk

MIX
Paper from
responsible sources
FSC
www.fsc.org   FSC® C013056

Printed and bound in Great Britain by
TJ International Ltd, Padstow, Cornwall

# CONTENTS

# ACKNOWLEDGEMENTS

I would, first, like to thank Pat Thomson. This book began life as a doctoral study, conducted at the University of Nottingham under Pat's supervision. She was and remains a fantastic source of knowledge and support to me and I thank her for her wisdom and friendship.

I would also like to thank my PhD examiners, Roger Slee and Kay Haw, for all their constructive comments and for their encouragement in taking the project forward to publication. Thanks also to Gwynneth Lloyd and Valerie Harwood for making their expertise in this area available to me and providing me with opportunities to find my own space within it.

I am very grateful for the support and encouragement I have received from Alison Foyle, Rhiannon Findlay and Philip Mudd at Routledge, who between them have guided me safely through my first book.

I am also very grateful to Taylor & Francis for permitting me to use previously published material, co-authored with Pat Thomson: Bailey, S. and Thomson, P. (2009) 'Routine (dis)order in an infant school'. *Ethnography and Education*, 4, 211–27. This work is available from the Taylor & Francis website: http://www.tandfonline.com.

Lastly I would like to thank my wife, Sarah, for her unfailing patience.

# ABBREVIATIONS

**ADD:**    **Attention Deficit Disorder.** An older term for ADHD, before hyperactivity became part of the core diagnosis, those with hyperactivity were sometimes labelled ADD-H.

**ADHD:**    **Attention Deficit Hyperactivity Disorder,** described by the American Psychiatric Association, replaced previous nomenclature in 1994. ADHD refers to the 'combined' diagnosis of hyperactivity and attention deficit, also available are diagnoses of predominantly inattentive (ADHD-I) or hyperactive/impulsive (ADHD-H).

**APA:**    **American Psychiatric Association.**

**CD:**    **Conduct Disorder.** Another of the DBDs, has large overlap with ADHD and ODD.

**DBD:**    **Disruptive Behaviour Disorders.** Defined by the APA, the group of disorders to which ADHD belongs.

**DSM:**    **The Diagnostic and Statistical Manual for Mental Disorders.** Diagnostic criteria published by the APA, current version is DSM-V, published in May 2013.

**EBD:**    **Emotional and Behavioural Difficulties.** Umbrella term for a range of socio-psychological difficulties.

**HKD:**    **Hyperkinetic Disorder.** Alternative conception of similar problems to ADHD, as described by the World Health Organization. Thought to represent a particularly severe form of ADHD.

**ICD:**    **International Classification of Diseases.** Diagnostic criteria published by the World Health Organization, it includes HKD.

**MBD:**    **Minimal Brain Dysfunction.** Older term for ADHD, based on the action of stimulants on the brains of disruptive boys.

**NICE:**    **National Institute of Health and Clinical Excellence.** NICE produce evidenced-based practice guides for a range of mental and physical health problems. They published the most recent guidance on ADHD in 2008.

**ODD:**    **Oppositional Defiant Disorder**. Another of the DBDs, it overlaps with ADHD and CD.

# 1

# INTRODUCING ADHD

Attention Deficit Hyperactivity Disorder (ADHD) has become the most commonly diagnosed psychiatric condition of childhood worldwide (Timimi, 2005b). In this book I offer a sociological perspective on ADHD, and its place in the life of the school and family. The prevalent professional viewpoint on ADHD in the UK is that it is a biologically based disorder, with causal factors in genetics and neurochemistry (Kutcher *et al.*, 2004). This perspective goes on to claim that impairing symptoms of impulsiveness, hyperactivity and attention deficit will present in sufferers from an early age and will continue in some form into adulthood. One of the most controversial claims of this argument is the need for pharmacological intervention, and the trend whereby more and more young people are being placed on some form of psychoactive drug has attracted much contestation (Miller and Leger, 2003). This contestation has fuelled a politically charged and polarised debate about ADHD, circling around the somewhat intellectually stale question of its existence. ADHD also has an increasingly successful life in popular images; Bart Simpson has it, popular films and songs reference it, a new magazine in Liverpool, UK, adopts it as a name and mission statement: 'ADHD – Attention Deficit in High Definition – magazine is a free arts and culture publication, with few words, where you can let your mind wander free' (King, 2012).

My focus here is on the process of diagnosis and the production of the medical perspective on ADHD through the school and family. I will argue that everyday practices shape the social coordinates required for the application of a diagnosis. A simple analogy for this argument would be the preparation of ground ready for the ideal growth of a crop. Pursuing this analogy a little further, I argue that such practices derive from embedded assumptions concerning growth and development, and well-intentioned attempts to nurture robust and healthy crops. Such practices, assumptions and attempts can become concealed beneath names such as ADHD, and what follows in this book is an attempt to attract attention to some of these everyday means of ADHD production.

One of the key places I will locate this analysis is in the representations made of ADHD and of those personally and professionally associated with it. This focus on representation derives from Foucault's (1972) use of the term *discourse*, through which he analysed what we know and how we come to know it. I follow Hall (1997) in using the term *representation* to talk about discourse in terms of practices which signify a certain 'mode of seeing' (p. 65). I will begin the analysis with a recent example of ADHD representation in the popular media.

## Popularising ADHD

On the 13 August 2008, the US swimmer Michael Phelps became the most decorated Olympian in the modern history of the games; much media attention followed. The only article I read on the subject was printed in the *Guardian* the following day (Kelso, 2008). I might not have read the piece at all if my eye had not been caught by a striking photo of Phelps in mid-butterfly stroke taking up much of the page. Beneath the photo was stated: 'Phelps was diagnosed with attention deficit disorder as a young child. He competed in his first Olympics at age 15.' Eager to know the significance accorded this particular piece of information I read on, however the one further mention I found merely restated the photo sub-line: 'Diagnosed with attention deficit disorder as a young child, he became an Olympian at 15 and now stands as the athlete with more golds than anyone in history.'

Given such little information only questions remain. What is the significance of this particular piece of information, which made it worth selecting from Phelps' personal history? What point is the newspaper trying to make? What knowledge must the paper be assuming of its audience in order to print this information in this obscure way? How well and widely known must ADD/ADHD have become in order for these assumptions to be made?

When I first came to know about ADHD, over 20 years ago, it was not at all well known. I know now that there was still a significant research literature at this time, but I do not think the popular media would have been able to assume audience knowledge in the manner implied by the Phelps example. Even when I started studying ADHD academically, almost 10 years ago, I still had to explain what the four letters stood for to the majority of people. That is no longer the case. Now ADHD, hyperactivity and Ritalin are common parlance: if we read about an Olympian with a diagnosis of ADD we should all know what that means.

Bourdieu (1984) wrote that, 'the power to impose recognition depends on the capacity to mobilise around a name' (p. 481). The Phelps example suggests that a considerable capacity has mobilised in the name of ADHD, but what recognition is being imposed through such a mobilisation?

It could be speculated that the newspaper is using the diagnosis to emphasise the magnitude of the achievement: these gold medals mean that much more because of the past adversity faced by the athlete. The image of the proud, patriotic, disciplined Olympian is held up against its own real-life abject, the disaffected, disruptive, anarchic youth: this one came good. But then, the opposite could be speculated, perhaps the diagnosis is being used to tame the out-of-this-world achievement: the athlete was pre-conditioned toward Olympic success through his hyperactive, obsessional *nature*. All he required was the right outflow for all that excess energy, a place where a pathological inability to pay attention would not be a problem.

Foucault (1996a) argued that focusing on 'the play of the true and false' should divert attention away from such speculations, instead questioning the manner in which something becomes known as *true* or *false*. This line of questioning will be pursued in greater detail in the following chapters, for the purposes of introduction, it seems that ADHD represents *something* and that it is conceived as *something important* regarding Phelps' historic achievement.

If this is the case then surely I should not be required to speculate upon this subject. I have spent much of the last ten years studying ADHD, surely I should know by now what people with ADHD represent and why that should be important for the attainment of Olympic swimming medals? That I really should know what all this means is further shaped by the fact that Phelps and I share more than a love of swimming: I was also diagnosed with ADHD as a young child. Yet I am putting this information forward here as a means to disrupt these assumptions of representation and meaning. According to these assumptions, Phelps and I must share some essence; I should be able to look at the newspaper article and feel solidarity. If anyone should be allowed to get sentimental about Phelps' achievement then it should be me (and others of our kind) because *we* understand what it is he's been through. Yet of the two known similarities between us, *vis-à-vis* swimming and pathologisation, I am undecided as to which is the more coincidental and devoid of deeper meaning.

This is not to say that I accord ADHD an insignificant role within my current occupation. It is to say that I am perpetually unsure of what the precise meaning of this role is. I see this as a strength; a 'privilege' as Haraway (1988) might describe it. My experiences, first at home and school, later at work, in relationships, and in academia, have had much influence on my choice of topic. I do not use my experience to suggest that I represent any particular group; indeed the idea that I do makes me distinctly uncomfortable. I do not wish to wage war on the medical profession. Nor do I use it to suggest I have some unique formula; *the ADHD kid come good*, carries with it a conceited and hypocritical sentimentality I do not wish to replicate here. I do, however, wish to question the cultural assumptions implied by the Phelps example in a way that goes beyond deconstructing the superficial binaries of the mass media.

Four years on, the 2012 Olympics, and Michal Phelps won a further four Olympic gold medals, making him the most decorated Olympian in history with 22 medals in total, 18 of which are gold. He has since retired. This time the *Guardian* ran a piece which asked: 'What can athletes with ADHD teach us about the condition?'

(Barkham, 2012). Along with Phelps, two more Olympic athletes, Louis Smith and Ashley McKenzie, are introduced to us as having ADHD:

> Suddenly, a condition that is hugely stigmatised and still controversial, is unexpectedly in the spotlight. It raises several interesting questions. Does ADHD hinder or help sporting success? And can the Olympics offer a positive legacy for people suffering from it?
>
> *(Barkham, 2012)*

Interesting questions indeed. The article continues, describing the young Phelps seeking 'sanctuary' from his condition in the swimming pool; how Louis Smith learned 'discipline' via gymnastics; and how McKenzie 'credits judo with saving him from prison'. Of the three athletes discussed, McKenzie is presented as the one with the greatest struggle; unable to take medication for his ADHD because it is banned in judo, the story tells how he struggles to 'control his behaviour'.

While it certainly flirts with a dualism of good and bad, embodied by Phelps and McKenzie respectively, the newspaper article progresses with some more balanced reasoning, via the thoughts of Andrea Bilbow, founder of ADDISS, a charity and support service for ADHD. She states: 'Your ADHD isn't going to get you there, it's hard work that will. ADHD is not a contributor towards success but equally it is not a barrier to success.' Having realigned Olympic success with hard work, Bilbow goes on to state that many children find sport a constructive means of 'managing the condition', and criticises the prevalent norms in many schools, who 'scoff at the disorder, believing there are only naughty children – and bad parents', a scenario which often results in sporting opportunities being taken away from children with ADHD as a punishment for bad behaviour. The article concludes optimistically, suggesting that athletes such as Phelps and McKenzie should be used to inspire children 'who are having a miserable time at school'.

I have spent a little time going through this article, not because I believe it to be a particularly outstanding piece of writing, but because it offers a succinct way in to many of the issues presented by the existence of this *thing* called ADHD, which are to be the subject of further exploration throughout this book.

First, there is the assumed existence of the *thing* itself. This is an independent force called ADHD which exerts particular pressures on the bodies and minds of children, producing particular expressions, utterances and behaviours from them. It is something that people 'suffer from' and 'live with'; it becomes the 'bad person within'. There is much contention around this issue and yet it has become a stale and polarised debate between those who claim that ADHD is *real* and those that claim it is a *myth* (Laurence and McCallum, 1998; Bailey, 2008). Though intellectually stale, this is a highly political debate with many stakeholders and many interests: the professional interests of psychiatrists and other mental health practitioners, the financial interests of pharmaceutical companies, and the interests of the social and economic order as embodied by governments, teachers and parents.

A *thing* like ADHD does not have an existence independent of all these other *things* any more than a domestic cow has an existence independent of the production of milk and beef. This is not to say, however, that either cows or ADHD have no reality at all. Certainly the behaviours associated with ADHD are real enough, as is the distress frequently caused to, and by, those who are so labelled. Rather, what it means to destabilise the reality of a *thing* in this manner is to prompt a questioning of the social and cultural structures beneath which lie assumptions and expectations which shape the perceived nature of *things*.

The sociologist Howard Becker (1963) advanced this premise in the simplest of terms with his argument in *Outsiders*: creating a norm creates positions on both sides of it, it creates those on the inside and those on the outside. Therefore, rather than talking about a 'delinquent', 'deviant', or 'criminal' as a set of more or less essential characteristics, as independent forces in themselves, we might instead talk about them in terms of their position according to the social norms which have produced the categories of 'legal/illegal', 'good/bad', 'normal/abnormal' and so forth. The liberatory potential of this premise is that rather than there being a *thing* such as a criminal, with essential and largely unchangeable characteristics, there are instead norms, rules and codes which are socially defined and which can be changed. To do so, however, requires the assumptions that keep them in operation to be disturbed.

It is very difficult to make these argument in relation to ADHD without it being perceived by many of those stakeholders mentioned above that you are siding with the *myth* makers: understood as denying the very existence of ADHD, and that you have no capacity to care for the suffering it produces, that you are a radical, a theorist with no interest in empirical realities, only a political agenda (Barkley, 2002). In the past decade I have worked with many different stakeholders in the world of ADHD, and I have been called many of these things in one form or another. Yet I reject the very terms of the debate. I am well aware of the *realities* of what is perceived to be *abnormal* behaviour and the sense of alienation that accompanies it. I do not seek to undermine or deny such experiences in anyone labelled with ADHD. One of the attempts I make in this book is to seek a language that can *inhabit* (Derrida, 1967) this dichotomy of myth/reality, that can acknowledge the multiple realities and the multiple myths that surround, shape and give meaning to ADHD, and that can seek to disturb certain myths without making accusations of falsehood at children, parents, teachers and doctors. This attempt has been described as providing *critical support* (Lloyd et al., 2006).

The second issue the article presents is *discipline*, which it invokes in two senses: the discipline of sport which the Olympian must subject him or herself to in order to achieve success, and the disciplinary practices of schools, in this case the exclusion of children from sporting activities as a punishment for bad behaviour. Discipline is also of fundamental importance to the arguments in this book, channelled via the work of Michel Foucault, which will be introduced in more detail in Chapter 2.

The two variants of discipline in the newspaper invoke the use of discipline as both an object and an action, and as both a means of external control and self-regulation. The aspiring athlete attempts to discipline him or herself through the discipline of sport – the first usage is the verb, the action: I discipline myself, you discipline yourself – the second usage is the object: the discipline of sport, which is separated into many separate disciplines: swimming, athletics, gymnastics and so on, each constituted by a set of practices. Practice, like discipline, can be both object and action, and discipline and practice are deeply embedded in one another: in order to discipline oneself, one must practise, a set of practices makes up a discipline. Practice and discipline are therefore objects and actions that can be applied to bodies in order to achieve particular things, and to produce particular outcomes.

These distinctions are semantic, but they are more than this as well. The distinction between object and action in the use of discipline and practice, draws out the more difficult distinction between self and other. In the newspaper article, this distinction is drawn with relative clarity. Regarding the self, there is the discipline that the aspiring athlete *subjects* themselves to in the interests of achieving Olympic success. Regarding the other, there is the punitive practice of the school through which the badly behaved child is made an *object* of discipline. Within the context of the newspaper article, the fact that it is *about something*, ADHD, makes the distinction very easy to break down: the athlete sought the discipline of sport as a means to discipline the behaviour that was not sanctioned by the school. The active self-subjection was therefore presupposed by the objectifying social expectation. Though it is not always so easy to embed the self and social within each other in this way, it is from the first moment of self and social awareness always the case that no movement of the one can occur without a movement of the other (Lacan, 1966). There are many implications to this statement, in the chapters that follow these implications will be pursued through the everyday dramas of choice, agency, resistance and oppression in schools and families.

Does oppression belong in that last sentence? It stands out, it shouts. It conjures up dramatic images of collective power and domination, surely too melodramatic for this subject matter? Perhaps the distinction between those with power and those without is not always so clear as with conventional images of oppression such as slavery. Perhaps the language of oppression can be useful in drawing out the experiences of stigma described in the newspaper article as acting on children diagnosed with ADHD, as well as the stigma that attaches to their mothers, who are blamed for the existence of *mental disorder* in their children. Who is the powerful in this situation? Who is 'the stigmatiser'? Who promotes the assumptions on which the stigma is based? Convention implies that mothers have a certain power over their children, but it is clear just from this brief newspaper snippet that mothers might be made objects of greater powers in their enaction of this role. And is the child the lowest common denominator, the powerless one at the bottom of the pile? Certainly it seems that others have authority over them, that they resemble the tennis ball of Laing's (1969) analogy; 'served, smashed, volleyed, lobbed' (p. 15). Yet they are also 'the centre of the game and the spectacle' (p. 15); simple changes in a child's behaviour forces these authorities to mobilise resources: time, energy, money, labour, in an attempt not just to control or quash this behaviour, but to shape it, through discipline, into something more socially acceptable and economically productive: an Olympic athlete is certainly an extreme example; newsworthy to say the least. Yet who is the powerful one in this scenario? The *real* power seems to lie not with individuals, but with the material practices of discipline which transform and with the ideals of social acceptance and economic productivity which are the goal of transformation.

Drawing on Foucault's (1982) understanding of power as 'the ability to act on the action of others', the argument can be made that social institutions such as schools and families make up part of a disciplinary apparatus through which power operates in the interests of securing social order; through which individuals come to bind themselves to networks of social relations, forge kinships, learn cultural mores of behaviour, become responsible for themselves and others, participate in labour exchange, and contribute to collective wealth. Understanding discipline as both object and action means that it cannot simply be stated that this is either a punitive process of social control or a voluntary means of socialisation. Rather it is a messier, more integrated process through which individuals might aspire to achieve certain things and in so doing might reinforce a more secure sense of social order. Yet, in aspiring to do certain things and be certain people, the notion of social order might very well be far from our conscious objectives.

This is the terrain I intend to explore in this book through the everyday work of schools and families, and the labels and practices of psychiatry. In order to try and explore this terrain, several questions will run implicitly throughout the following chapters:

- How do schools and families go about this work of social governance? How are individuals who threaten ideals of social order identified, and what are the means employed to attempt to realign them to it?
- If there exists a certain meeting of coercion and voluntarism in an individual's developmental path, then what can the everyday worlds of schools and families tell us about what we as a collective social order see as an acceptable, ethical, balance of these?
- What do psychiatric disorders such as ADHD contribute to this play of order and agency?

## Personalising ADHD

One question that has remained particularly elusive throughout my research in this area concerns the nature of my own thoughts and feelings about ADHD. When I began my doctoral thesis on the subject in 2005, I thought it possible to draw a distinction between what I thought and felt about the disorder personally and what my research position was. Whether or not this personal/professional distinction was ever particularly meaningful has been progressively cast into some doubt and I now find that the two positions are thoroughly intertwined. These thoughts and feelings are important contingents to what follows here, so it is worth spending a little time on them.

I am critical of the diagnosis and treatment of ADHD, just as I am critical of much in the contemporary worlds of psychiatry, psychology and their allied schools of thought; the *psy disciplines* as N. Rose (1998) terms them. As described above, according to many popular and professional opinions on ADHD, this perspective positions me within the acceptable narratives on ADHD as someone who believes it a *myth*. If I am to be pigeon-holed as such the I would like to disrupt that position first by acknowledging some personal *realities* of ADHD.

I cannot argue that I do not tick all the diagnostic boxes, or that the *symptoms* associated with these boxes do not impair me in my ability to fulfil various everyday activities to my own full satisfaction. Conceived within a narrow medical paradigm, I cannot argue that I do not *have* ADHD as defined by the *clinical correlates* of inattention, impulsiveness and hyperactivity. I find this reality reinforced when I look through the list of *outcomes* that we are told are associated with the disorder: frequent casualty visits, poor driving record, educational under-achievement and drop-out, many relatively short-lived jobs and relationships, anti-social behaviour, substance misuse, criminality (NICE, 2008). I have encountered many of these *outcomes* and they often contributed to the feelings of alienation and exclusion which were a consistent personal reality for some time.

One of the principal problems I have with such *clinical* realities is that they mask socially produced phenomena. However, within the given medical terms there is a certain reality of ADHD that I must accept; as a set of deficits the existence and consequences of which I have often found it difficult to escape.

ADHD has given rise to many unanswerable questions for me. Would I have focused on or even noticed these deficits if it had not been for this description being made of me? Would I find it easier or harder to deal with my various weaknesses as a person if I did not have this diagnosis with which to think about myself? Are these weaknesses such that I am significantly more impaired by them than most other people? Clearly I cannot think about any of these questions free of the idea of ADHD, or free of the idea of myself as an inattentive and overactive person who once posed many problems to my parents and teachers. I might be able to offer various examples of ways in which I have managed to step outside the limits of this reality and achieve things I once did not believe I could, but I cannot step completely away and renounce it entirely. *It* still sits there, waiting for me to fall back into it like a default setting that requires my conscious bypass.

The *it* in the previous sentence troubles me. *It* speaks of *things*. *It* comes, perhaps, from having accorded ADHD a certain internal existence, in the interests of reflecting on *its* possible effects on my thoughts and feelings about *it*. In collecting these behaviours together and labelling them as *something* in my past that I attempt to step outside, I have given them a reality of their own which prior to me undertaking this reflection they did not have. The more I think about ADHD, the more a certain reality of *it* is likely to come into being. The psychoanalyst Jacques Lacan (1966) suggested that this is an inescapable product of the fact that our consciousness creates the external reality of which it is itself a part. I cannot talk about ADHD without reinforcing the reality of that particular acronym, even if I seek to criticise it to the point of displacing its *reality*.

## Studying ADHD

My personal association with ADHD has had much influence on the way in which I conceptualise it and the choices I have made in trying to build a research project around it. However, it is not the case that I had this view of ADHD ready formed and merely wished to gather what evidence I could to support it. This project has been exploratory from the start, and my personal and research views have developed a dialogic relation with one another through this exploration. Overall my research work has moved them closer together and tried to align them with one another, but this has only happened partially, and through repeated abrasions. If my research ends up portraying ADHD as a thoroughly perplexing phenomena, which cannot be reduced to simple labels or dualisms and about which I am somewhat ambivalent, then this is a result of a reflexive confrontation between my own experiences and the experiences of those with whom I have worked.

One influential set of experiences was my time working for the National Institute of Health and Clinical Excellence (NICE), as a member of their Guideline Development Group for ADHD. I participated as a 'service user representative', contributing to monthly meetings and to the research and writing of the guideline, though I resigned a year before the guideline was published. My experience at NICE was always overshadowed by an uncertainty about my role, insecurity about who or what I represented and guilt about my rights to generalise, speak on behalf of, and make recommendations based on my own partial experiences. My resignation derived from a combination of these factors as well as my despondency concerning the seeming impossibility of re-making certain institutional languages and creating an *inclusive* document. On reflection there were positives to take away from this process; in the uncomfortable but productive identity work it forced me into which contributed to the dialogue between the *me* and *I* of ADHD, which I continue to reflect upon in the interests of achieving a dynamic and situated perspective on it.

The present study is situated within an emerging corpus of critical and philosophical perspectives on ADHD and other behavioural disorders (Graham, 2007c; Harwood, 2006; Laurence and McCallum, 2009; Lloyd *et al.*, 2006; Prosser, 2006; Tait, 2010). One of the key attempts made by these authors is to move beyond the dichotomised intellectual inheritance of behavioural disorders: 'an intellectual territoriality characterised by struggles over whose knowledge is of most worth and the subsequent size and strength of each knowledge domain' (Graham, 2007c, p. 12). The stated objective of one collection of authors is to grapple with the balance between providing support for children, families and schools associated with ADHD while continuing to criticise the assumptions, theories and practices which serve an increasing diagnostic rate, an attempt it calls *critical support* (Lloyd *et al.*, 2006). This ideal is one I ascribe to and this book can be read as an exploration and problematisation of it. Following Foucault, this ideal can be pursued through the attempt to describe the processes that define and limit legitimate understandings of order/disorder, real/unreal, normal/abnormal. The attempt made in subverting these everyday assumptions is to displace notions of individual blame and responsibility, choice and consequence, to instead develop an account of active yet constrained actors situated in and contributing to particular cultural contexts. This attempt is therefore concerned with deconstructing our understandings of the present, and the means employed to fashion such an understanding. However, this is not simply an academic exercise in disconnecting individuals from accepted certainties and truths: 'such a cartography would not so much seek to destabilize the present by pointing to its contingency, but to destabilize the future by recognizing its openness' (N. Rose, 2007, p. 5).

My focus in this book is with the process of diagnosis. The achievement of a diagnosis requires a concerted arrangement of actors and institutions and I would like to gain some insight into these arrangements. I view diagnosis as the official point at which an identity is made other, in the sense that it becomes a new means through which identity can be positioned on an individual and social level. However, I believe that this process of othering might extend far back before the official point of diagnosis. Put another way, were it not for prior othering to have occurred there would not be sufficient grounds on which to base a diagnosis.

Such institutional arrangements are in turn supported by ways of thinking and knowing about children and the appropriate *direction* they should take (Laurence and McCallum, 2009). ADHD is predicated upon a developmental model of childhood, which aligns it with the prevalent assumptions of psychology and education (Tait, 2010). Developmentalism seeks to demarcate normative levels of acceptability according to age. Aspects of achievement, behaviour, cognition, personality, speech and interaction are used as indicators of whether the child is appropriately advanced/delayed/normal for their age:

> Developmental psychology capitalizes, perhaps not artfully but certainly effectively, on two everyday assumptions: first, that children are natural rather than social phenomena; and secondly, that part of this naturalness extends to the inevitable process of maturation.
>
> *(James et al., 1998, p. 17)*

Normal development prescribes thinking in terms of a pre-ordained grid of normality, creating what Jones *et al.* (2008) refer to as 'constitutive circularity': 'child behaviours come to be read as signs of deviation from the normal path; yet the integrity of the normal path is consolidated by the identification of deviations' (p. 6). Within school, the child with ADHD is one example of the *developmentally inappropriate* child. This psycho-cognitive description of the disordered child feeds into much of the guidance made available to schools and teachers (e.g. Cooper and O'Regan, 2001). In this literature, the presence of the internal other of ADHD is assumed and recommendations concern ways in which the afflicted child might be contained within *inclusive* educational settings (Tait, 2010).

For a diagnosis of ADHD to be made, one is required to show that the child in question is marked by their difference from their peers on various *ordinary* classroom tasks to a degree that the American Psychiatric Association (APA, 2000) describes as *significantly impairing*. This rather vague term represents the point at which the internal and external worlds of ADHD collide, for it refers to the severity of the physical symptoms which is gauged through comparison with peers and through their immediate social consequences (S. Rose, 2005). The APA would presumably not be the teacher's first point of reference for bad behaviour, therefore it seems reasonable to assume that a child who is marked in such a way has already been through some prior othering: situated or official disciplinary action might have been used; the child might have been excluded from certain activities; parent meetings might have been arranged; school counsellors, nurses, social workers, or educational psychologists might have been consulted.

Goffman (1968) argued that identities become positioned in multiple ways according to different social contexts. To take the category of *special educational need* as an example: the interaction of labelling and identity leads one to understand oneself as someone who is *special*, and further that this is a debilitating status casting one as *in need* (Corbett, 1996). Teachers and assistants at school are likely to pitch their expectations lower for a *SEN child* than for a *mainstream child* (Slee, 1997). The child will have joined one of the school's problem populations and they will be made more visible and accountable as a result of this new membership (Allan, 1996). Particular categories of need, such as ADHD, are associated with 'emotional and behavioural difficulty'; EBD (Cooper, 2003) and new positions are constituted for such children based upon more *appropriate* approaches to learning (Saltmarsh and Youdell, 2004). Such judgements are made according to a rhetoric of *support* and *protection*; for the deficient child, support, for the social order they threaten, protection. The combination of these twin ideals is represented through inter-agency policies concerned with *safeguarding children* (DFES, 2004; DCSF, 2010).

Problematic behaviours and characteristics of childhood are interpreted through medical perspectives as representing something within the child (Conrad and Schneider, 1980), and more precisely, within the child's brain. This *neurocentric* perspective risks emptying children of the capacity to think and act for themselves (S. Rose, 2005). Increasing levels of diagnosis such as ADHD and the increased recourse to pharmacological intervention imply that more and more this neurocentric perspective is governing the ethics of child education and care, creating *neurochemical citizenship* (N. Rose, 2007). Actors within these domains aspire to these forms of citizenship as a way of making sense of themselves in socially and culturally acceptable ways, in so doing reinforcing the integrity of neurocentric assumptions of normality and pathology. Different behaviours and characteristics, the availability of fitting descriptions underscored by legitimate forms of knowledge and the correct institutional arrangements can therefore be understood as the conditions upon which a diagnostic case rests. They are the necessary contingents upon which a diagnosis bases its authority. Yet the application of a diagnosis conceals the productive process of social positioning upon which it is built, leaving only a model of individual deficit and organic pathology.

## Structure of the book

Including this introduction, *Exploring ADHD* is set over eight chapters. In this chapter I have used news reports to introduce some of the themes around ADHD to be discussed, while also introducing something of the theoretical framework to be used. I have also used my own relevant subject positions in relation to ADHD to introduce my perspective on the contingent nature of *being someone with something* (Haraway, 1988; Bailey, 2009). This perspective engages one of the guiding epistemological assumptions followed here. It immediately undermines the notion that a set of biological or psychological coordinates can produce an account of being or that a group of people collected together on the basis of such coordinates could be said to represent a particular *kind of being*, a particular *thing*, known as ADHD.

Chapter 2 develops the notions of discourse and power introduced in this chapter through a discussion of Foucault's use of these terms, and connects them to the theory and methods of ethnography. It is argued that discourse provides *ways of being* according to subject positions, which are distributed through institutional channels of communication and shaped by historically derived power relations. Discourse is embodied in the everyday through *texts*, of which people, behaviour, timetables, lifestyles, intentions and actions are all examples. Though people are not merely empty vessels for the enaction of discourse and power, existing relations do partially determine the extent to which individuals might act autonomously, however, Foucault (1980) claimed that individuals can always resist, responding 'to every advance of power by a movement of disengagement' (p. 138). These individual disengagements create spaces for action; 'micro emancipations' (Alvesson and Willmott, 2002) through which new possibilities can be imagined.

Chapter 3 introduces each of the settings where research was carried out, situates them in context, and describes the steps taken in carrying out the research. Critical ethnography (Carspecken, 1996) was used in this study to produce an account that is both *thickly* descriptive (Geertz, 1973) and sensitive to power relations, both as an object of analysis, and a product of the research process itself. I provide critical reflection on the relationship between the methods I adopted and things I found, and my own engagement of power and the practices I adopted to try and negotiate and *disengage* these.

Chapter 4 presents the first piece of fieldwork, in which I adopted the role of a teaching assistant in Years One and Two of Kilcott Infants.[1] The analysis develops the notion of 'routine' as a productive rationale in disciplining children and adults into the regime of the school. Through the ascription of order and norm to the times, spaces, utterances, action and conduct of the school day, the routine constructs the categories of normal/abnormal and order/disorder against which individuals can be made visible. Routine, therefore, works to make disciplinary inscriptions of otherness on to individuals. It is argued that this individual inscription is one of the necessary first stages in creating *diagnosable objects* (Graham, 2007c), with the notions of dis/order and ab/normality holding particular significance for the clinical definition of psychopathology.

Chapter 5 presents the first piece of data from my second research site, Alderley Primary. This chapter seeks a gender analysis of ADHD predicated on the fact that at least five times as many boys than girls are diagnosed with the disorder. I critique a common-sense explanation for increasing diagnosis whereby failing and disruptive boys are drugged into conformity via a feminised primary school regime. Through the presentation of data I argue that masculine subject positions are privileged in school through the sanctioning of male dominance in classrooms, leading to *special* resources and interventions being targeted almost exclusively at boys. Observations of children with ADHD are then used to argue that a diagnosis produces a loop through which male dominance is perpetually re-enacted.

Chapter 6 presents the interview data from work with the two families who made up the third research site. Parents of children with ADHD are discursively positioned within cultures of blame and responsibility (Carpenter and Austin, 2008; Singh, 2004). Each parent in this account attempted to take up an active opposition to these representations of them. However, while they might have been successful in negotiating particular forms of recognition there were incidental effects to this activation. In each case, the means to recognition came through the progressive submission to the internal, biological account of ADHD. This led to the progressive effacement of the agency that each parent sought as well as to the reinforcement of their children's deficit in narrowly medical terms.

Chapter 7 presents the second piece of data from Alderley Primary. The focus here is on nurture groups, which were the principle means at Alderley for the management of children with ADHD outside the mainstream classroom. I argue that the groups represent a problematic place in early years schooling, through their contradictory nature/nurture assumptions and through their enactment of a combination of exclusionary discourses of routine, risk, gender, class and family. The philosophy of the nurture group is centred on notions of growth and empowerment, however it is argued that the practice of the groups within school has a primary objective of administration over empowerment.

Chapter 8 concludes with a return to the notion of routine and its relation to culture. Within this relation lies both the current means of ADHD production as well as the potential means for re-opening possibilities in the everyday worlds of school and family.

In making an argument about the social production of ADHD I am not arguing that medical and psychological understandings of children hold no validity or that they have no therapeutic value. I do argue that such understandings tend to conflate organic and social pathology and that this enacts a counter-productive subjectivisation, reinforces existing divisions and inequalities, and defers the ideal of change. Neither am I blind to the need for classrooms, schools, families, and other social worlds to function according to some notion of order. I do argue that such an order should be the product of participation not prescription. Currently I do not believe this is the norm and I believe ADHD to be one symptom of this.

# 2

# TIME, SPACE AND POSSIBILITY

The research presented in this book subscribes to the ideal of 'critical ethnography' (Carspecken, 1996), the 'critical' implying an engagement with power relations through the method, to involve participants meaningfully in the research process, and to reflexively examine the production of selves among others. Both this chapter and Chapter 3 are concerned with providing a theoretical and descriptive framework for interpreting the ethnographic analysis which begins in Chapter 4.

The theoretical point of orientation here is Foucault's related notions of *discourse*, *power* and *subjectivity*, which I shall introduce here before explaining how I attempted to connect this 'tool box' (Foucault, 1996c, p. 149) to the objectives of ethnographic fieldwork. Both theory and method offer an anchor to the ideal of reflexivity, in which researchers attempt to set up a dialogue between their own positioning and the positioning of those they encounter through their research.

To do this is to acknowledge the sense of 'partial perspective' (Haraway, 1988) which is the condition of all actors in complex social situations, in which the governing relations of knowledge and power are partially obscured from view. By exploring these relations the arguments presented in this book aim to describe and open up *conditions of possibility* (Foucault, 1974) in the everyday work of children, schools and families grappling with ADHD.

## Foucault's pendulum

That was when I saw the Pendulum.

The sphere, hanging from a long wire set into the ceiling of the choir, swayed back and forth with isochronal majesty.

I knew – but anyone could have sensed it in the magic of that serene breathing – that the period was governed by the square root of the length of the wire and by $\pi$,

that number which, however irrational to sublunar minds, through a higher rationality binds the circumference and diameter of all possible circles.

(*Eco, 2007.* Foucault's Pendulum, *p. 3*)

Although the 'Foucault' that Eco wrote about in the above quote was not the same Foucault I will discuss here, the idea of the pendulum is a very useful point of departure for thinking about Foucault's ideas, and their place in contemporary institutions of governance. The pendulum, as described above, tells of time, but also of space – time passes according to the movement in space of the pendulum. It is these two related concepts, time and space, and their productive work, in combination with ways of knowing (Eco's π) which produce particular rationalities, binding 'all possible circles'.

The world that Michel Foucault described can be usefully analogised by picturing a clock. We – individuals, groups, societies, our world – are the hands moving around the clock. The spaces between the hands, the minutes and hours, collected into days and weeks, these are *discourses*, embodiments of meaning through which we make sense of this time/space, making it measurable and governable. The mechanism that keeps the whole thing moving, the pendulum, this is *power*, which combined with *knowledge* of the discursive movement of the hands, constitute the twin forces which keep the hands moving regularly and rhythmically, and keep the clock ticking. The combined effect of power, knowledge and discourse therefore is to *discipline* the hands, to keep them on track.

A quaint analogy, and one that can only be taken so far. Individuals, clearly, are not hands on a clock. They do not move in such predictable, patterned, ordered ways. Therefore, our individual agency, our active sense of being, our *subjectivity*, can be expressed by our usage of this space of the clock face as a means to order ourselves as individuals and societies. Although we might not believe we move with the rhythmic order of the hands on a clock, we cannot transcend the ordering functions of time and space, to do so would be a state of non-being, but we can *take time, make time, save time* and *waste time*, just as we can *maximise space, make room, carve out a niche* and *expand our horizons*. So, the extent to which we are able to gauge time, and its effects upon us, to interrogate the mechanisms that make us and move us, is a measure of our capacity for *resistance*, for the *practices of freedom*, which constitutes our *ethics*, our *ways of being*.

The logic that holds this system in place, a product of power and knowledge carried by discourse, is the means by which we use time and space to regulate ourselves into a functional, productive and self-governing order. This logic is *governmentality*; the art of government *from a distance* (Foucault, 1979) in the sense that we do not necessarily think of our everyday actions, movements, choices and utterances as self-government, yet this is the effect of them.

Therefore, in the rhythms and routines that we develop using this apparatus of time and space are contained both the means of our *subjection* to the logic of governmentality, and concurrently our *practices of freedom*; our expression, creativity, imagination and individuality.

In terms of drawing Foucault's thought down into an ethnographic schema, discourse becomes the primary point of interest, as it is discourse, carried into the present by *texts*, which it is the task of the ethnographer to describe. The work of discourse is to provide logical footholds for thought and action; textual spaces on which particular inscriptions of time and space can be made. The next section moves towards a fuller description of this *textwork* (McWilliam *et al.*, 1997); the description and interpretation of texts.

## Textwork

Discourses are signs or *statements*, they carry messages, they carry embodiments of meaning. Discourse analysis, therefore, proceeds according to the description, interpretation and problematisation of signs and statements, which are referred to as *texts*. Text here refers not only to words, written or spoken, rather it borrows language as a metaphor for describing the manner in which discourse becomes inscribed on everyday action. The texts themselves might range from the material to the symbolic. Referring back to the last chapter, we might talk about a particular organisation of time and space, as in the practices that make up a sporting discipline, or a particular understanding of masculinity, as in the Olympic athletes, as texts which convey particular messages about ourselves and our society. These messages are not easily or unproblematically read, for certain, but they tell us something about the logics by which they have been fashioned, the buried assumptions of everyday life. It should be noted here that in taking on this language of texts, this account is littered with such metaphors borrowed from the governing metaphor of language; thus things referred to as 'written' or 'spoken' are more often than not making use of this rhetorical device.

Discourse offers insight into historical relationships between thought and action, and the material, political circumstances of the time. Incorporating discourse analysis into a critical ethnographic framework implies an inversion of this historical analysis, to instead attempt to trace historical narratives via their signalling in the texts of the present. Foucault (1972) referred to his earlier historical work as 'archaeology', which presents a useful entry metaphor for the ethnographer, digging around in the present to construct their narrative. Of course, transposed on to the social world there are a range of problems associated with taking the minutiae of everyday life as the basis for the expression of more general rules and logics, and it is the work of this chapter to present some of the ways in which these problems might be tackled.

Ethnographic work following Foucault presents a combination of *textwork* and *fieldwork* (McWilliam *et al.*, 1997). The 'critical' inserted in the ethnographic framework implies an interest in the workings of power. For Foucault (1980) power is not something that is held by one individual over another, but rather it is the totality of relations of force between people, what he described as a *microphysics* of power (Foucault, 1977). Discourse is the means through which power is given voice, the 'means of its exercise' (Foucault, 1981b, p. 32). If power is understood as productive and relational, then the texts which carry discourse into the present are the means by which sets of governing rules are written on to the present. These rules might apply to a great array of phenomena; among those described by Foucault are the classificatory systems of medicine (1973) and the natural sciences (1974). For Foucault what was important was not the supposed validity or otherwise of these systems of thought, but rather the manner in which they had emerged and been given credence, and the mechanisms they produced for ordering subjects and objects. The systems he referred to as *discursive formations*, akin to 'schools of thought'. 'School', much like discipline and practice in the previous chapter, can be taken as both noun and verb; not only a place of learning, but also the action of learning on bodies. Britzman's (2000) description of discourse as 'communities of consent and dissent' (p. 36), evokes this dual notion of schooling, and also presents one of its fundamental implications; inclusion and exclusion. Being a member of a school of thought, following its rules of inclusion and exclusion, saying things in the manner defined by that school, will likely imply exclusion or only partial membership of other schools.

Different processes of schooling, therefore, produce different objects of knowledge. Sometimes schools are able to hold on to their objects, retain their ownership of them. Special languages and processes are constructed around these objects, with high barriers to entering the discourse, such as lengthy and demanding educational processes. Yet these objects of knowledge are not always exclusively owned by the schools which fashion them, some objects have tendency to *leak* (Brown and Duguid, 2001) out of their confines in a certain school of thought and shift into more public arenas, producing categories such as 'expert', 'popular' and 'lay' knowledge.

Discourse analysis is often concerned with the political arrangement of texts, which is where discourse connects with power relations creating 'generative mechanisms' (Cherkaoui, 2005) which shape *conditions of possibility* (Foucault, 1974). These mechanisms are described by Fairclough (1992) as 'the institutional and organisational circumstances of the discursive event' (p. 4), and by Judith Butler's (1997) situated notions of address and autonomy. The former draws attention to structural conditions of the possible, the latter to the wedge that agency can drive between these conditions: we are addressed by discourse and our autonomy is expressed in our ability to mediate this address.

Fairclough (2000) has brought this style of analysis to bear on the language of New Labour, in which he describes the rhetorical shift occurring in the move from the language of 'poverty' to that of 'social exclusion'. The discursive shift is in the move from conceiving marginalisation as a given economic circumstance to thinking of marginalisation as a moral choice. New Labour thus achieved 'cultural governance' (p. 61) by making claims about the *deficiencies* of certain groups; individualising and essentialising difference and advocating the Government's right to intervene.

Fairclough's (2000) study illustrates well the constitutive nature of discourse. By taking individual fragments of text which bear certain rhetorical relations, he is able to make a more general comment about the way in which a population might be managed. He is able to do this because this is the action of discourse; 'what seems accidental from the viewpoint of words, phrases and propositions becomes the rule from the viewpoint of statements' (Deleuze, 1988, p. 9). Descriptions constitute subject positions, ways of being, and these positions are negotiated and enacted through everyday action. Ian Hacking (1995) has coined the term 'looping effects' (p. 351) to describe the continuous historical process of distribution and mediation. Individual agency might be able to loop back, resist and re-negotiate the terms by which a certain way of being is understood, however, in Foucault's (1980) terms, what they are attempting to re-negotiate – power relations – are 'always already there' (p. 141) as a product of hierarchical historical processes.

This sense of discourse as an embedded process of address and mediation has been emphasised by Dorothy Smith (1990) in her adaptation of Foucault's discourse:

> The notion of discourse displaces the analysis from the text as originating in writer or thinker, to the discourse itself as an ongoing intertextual process … Analysis of the extended social relations of complex social processes requires that our concepts embrace properties and processes which cannot be attributed to or reduced to individual 'utterances' or 'speech acts.'
>
> *(D. Smith, 1990, pp. 161–2)*

Here, Smith wants to move beyond a static or structural notion of discourse, as passing through action, casting individual agency as transparent and empty, while still retaining the sense in which discourse is productive and constitutive. For Smith, macro socio-historical processes must first be understood through a close reading of individual action in the everyday world. Action in the everyday is connected to broader structures through social relations and through institutional and organisational processes. These, in turn, are fashioned according to the available descriptions concerning given groups of people. Therefore, while Smith is concerned with these textual relations, her emphasis is on the means through which they are put to work in the everyday: 'though discourse, bureaucracy, and the exchange of money for commodities create forms of social relations that transcend the local and particular, they are constituted, created, and practiced always *within* the local and particular' (D. Smith, 1987, p. 109).

The connection made here by Smith in referring to bureaucracy and monetary exchange as *creating* forms of social relations, works according to the same logic as Foucault's (1991) concept of *governmentality*, which describes the means by which actors become participants in their own governance. With governmentality Foucault argues that the social body is driven toward self-management through multiple and diffuse forms of governance. Bureaucracy and monetary exchange are two examples of mediants in this process. Monetary exchange mediates relations of production and consumption; fundamental sources of disciplinary power in capitalist societies where individuals are socialised to value capital accumulation and collective wealth. Combined with laws and codes defining legitimate monetary exchange, these values create a moral order defining those who make legitimate and illegitimate contributions. Therefore, in gaining employment, in earning a wage, in buying a house, in starting a family, we are all contributing to our own self-governance as well as the governance of social order: a distanced and motivated regulation. Those who are considered to be 'unmotivated' to regulate themselves, who deviate from the legitimate order and cheat, steal and defraud, are subject to intensified external means of control; fines and prison sentences, which acts both to remove an individual from, and reinforce the legitimacy of, the order.

Foucault (2004) referred to this dual working of disciplinary power in his distinction between the 'seizure of power over the body in an individualising mode' and power that is 'massifying, that is directed not at man-as-body but at man-as-species' (p. 243). By valorising the needs of the social, discursive forms of the family (Donzelot, 1979), the school (Hunter, 1994) and the therapeutic state (N. Rose, 1989) become naturalized forms of social governance, which Smith (1987) describes as 'relations of ruling' (p. 214). These relations affect what Foucault (1981b) describes as an *optimisation* of individual forces toward the regulative ideal of efficient social exchange; 'a "biopolitics" of the human race' (Foucault, 2004, p. 243).

Therefore, governmentality alerts us to the disintegration of the structure/action divide, as the optimisation of individual forces aggregates through institutional relations to produce structural governance. Although the model disintegrates the divide, it still relies on an analytical separation of the two to remain in thinking about the production of certain institutional arrangements as *governing* and certain subject positions as *governable*. The next section seeks to understand further what might contribute to an individual's capacity to govern and to be governed, and applies this thinking to the present object of enquiry.

## Power and subjectivity

In questioning the discursive processes at work in the formation of objects, Foucault's primary concern was with the dominance of some objects over others and the means by which that dominance had been produced. He states this in the form of a question: 'What has ruled their existence as objects of discourse?' (Foucault, 1972, p. 45). He then offers three points of departure for such an analysis: first, to describe the '*surfaces* of their emergence'; second, 'the authorities of delimitation'; third, 'the *grids of specification*' (pp. 45–6; emphasis in original). These three movements, emergence, delimitation and specification, can be read as mapping, respectively, the historical conditioning of a way of knowing, the shaping of an object of knowledge and the application of this object to an administrative function.

In terms of applying these points to childhood behavioural disorder, two analyses, which also draw on Foucault, offer some useful insights. The first I will discuss is *Schooling Attention Deficit Hyperactivity Disorders* (Graham, 2007c), the second is *Diagnosing 'Disorderly' Children* (Harwood, 2006).

Graham has adapted the notion of the *grid of specification* to produce a highly visual tool for the investigation of discursive formations. In place of the grid, Graham (2006) offers a '*net* constructed with many intersecting threads, which is woven tightly enough to capture an object but allows permeability for the non-object to pass through' (p. 6). The net is depicted by two axes. The vertical works by 'enunciating otherness' and the horizontal by 'objectifying otherness' (p. 6).

The *other* for Foucault (1982) is 'the one over whom power is exercised', where power is understood to be the 'total structure of actions brought to bear on possible actions' (p. 220). Given that Foucault saw discourse as the vehicle for the action of power, the *enunciation* axis of the net can be seen as combining the first two of Foucault's analytical points – emergence and delimitation, with the *objectifying* axis contributing to delimitation and specification. Graham (2006) separates the two by referring to 'discursive practices' and 'disciplinary technologies'; one is concerned with asking what it is possible to *say*, the other is concerned with how that might be *said* in practice. In Chapters 4 to 7, I will attempt to trace both enunciation and objectification, describing the subject positions made possible by ADHD, and by the related contexts of the school, the teacher, the pupil, the family, parent and child. This is an analysis of what Bourdieu (1990) called 'political mythology' (p. 70), which is concerned with the conflation of the natural and social in relations of status and inequality. Each chapter attempts to map some of the ways in which such mythology might be 'realised, embodied, turned into a permanent disposition' (p. 70).

If this is the strategy according to which this study is organised, then further specification is required as to the techniques by which this strategy will be pursued. Foucault (1982) has further specified this description of 'action upon action' (p. 220) according to five analytical points:

> [1] The system of differentiations which permits one to act upon the action of others ... [2] The types of objectives pursued by those who act upon the action of others ... [3] The means of bringing power relations into being ... [4] Forms of institutionalization ... [5] The degrees of rationalization.
>
> *(Foucault, 1982, p. 223)*

In terms of the strategy, points [1] and [2] map more on to the conditioning of enunciations and the remainder on to the disciplinary specification, though there is much overlap.

The second work on ADHD I wish to introduce here, that of Valerie Harwood (2006), takes up this analysis in order to interrogate the 'power to diagnose disorderly children' (p. 62). Harwood's analysis proceeds according to the relations at work in producing 'the truth of the disorderly child' (p. 32). Alongside power, truth is one of the most enduring themes around which Foucault envisaged his *problematisations*: 'the set of discursive or nondiscursive practices that makes something enter into the play of the true and false, and constitutes it as an object for thought' (Foucault, 1996a, 456–7). Harwood's focus on *truth* follows Foucault's (1981a) description of truth as 'the instrumental investments of knowledge' (p. 55), and the *will to truth* as the primary function of discourse. Truth is concerned with knowledge which above all *does* something. Harwood is interested in what truth does in terms of individual identity. In pursuing this she draws on the concept of *subjectivisation*:

> my problem was not to define the moment from which something like the subject appeared but rather the set of processes through which the subject exists ... I would call subjectivization the process through which results the constitution of the subject, or more exactly, of a subjectivity which is obviously only one of the given possibilities of organizing a consciousness of self.
>
> *(Foucault, 1996b, p. 472)*

Where *other* was used above, Harwood (2006) uses the term *subject* 'to describe the focus of subjectivization' and takes 'subjectivity to be one of the many products of this process of subjectivization' (p. 6). In so doing she attempts to describe the process whereby discourse constitutes certain subjectivities, which when enacted through power relations produce certain truths about certain people.

Harwood also provides an elaboration of how Foucault's (1982) five point analysis of power might be put to work, which I have drawn on to produce the following schema according to which this study proceeds:

1  *The system of differentiations*, which is the means by which a body of knowledge constitutes subject positions. Psychiatric knowledge is ordered according to several categories of expert and lay knowledge, with psychiatrists, research scientists and other mental health practitioners at the expert end, and the general public via the popular constructions of ADHD in various media situated at the lay end. Actors, such as teachers who become associated with ADHD, occupy ambiguous spaces somewhere between these two positions, with the responsibilities of their social role defining and limiting their autonomy regarding this knowledge. Constituting these limiting subject positions has consequences for these actors, in their constrained take up of them, and in the consequences for them of being marked 'risky' for adopting positions which threaten the order of the discourse.

   The rhetoric of risk is an important intermediary between abstract descriptions and everyday life (Beck, 1992; Giddens, 1991; Lupton, 1999). In a related mode to that in which Fairclough (2000) critiqued New Labour's language of social exclusion, risk individualises notions of choice, obscuring from view the constraints of a given circumstance and interrogating individual morals. Once a subject is understood as risky then further interrogations are justified by the attempt to subvert future truths, *impairments* and *outcomes*.

2  *The types of objectives*, which is concerned with the political ordering of a body of knowledge. Chapter 1 has introduced the *regime of truth* (Foucault, 1980) made up by the competing perspectives on ADHD, organised according to a dualism of *myth/reality*. One objective of introducing my own subject position with regards ADHD was to 'disturb the scientificity of the relations of power'

(Harwood, 2006, p. 43) making particular statements about ADHD *more true* than others.

Chapter 6 describes the multiple truth regimes in operation for parents of children with ADHD, which define their responsibilities as 'good parents', creating binds by which their active subjectivity becomes effaced and their children's behaviour becomes bound to narrow psychiatric perspectives.

3   *The means of bringing power relations into being*, which is concerned with the institutional conditions that constitute certain ways of being and knowing. This notion crosses both textwork and fieldwork, and is one of the general empirical concerns here. It is particularly applicable to Chapter 4, a study of discipline in the infant classroom. The structure of *routine* is offered as the means by which power relations are 'actualized' (Gore, 1993, p. 63) in the everyday to produce subject positions.

Following Foucault's (1977) analysis of the action of power through the systems and structures of distribution and surveillance, routine is viewed as the principle means by which integration is achieved through schooling, and therefore, also the means by which the non-integrative other becomes known. Gore's (1995) observational classroom study provides several categories through which some of the structural conditions of this integrative script are analysed for their constitutive force.

4   *Forms of institutionalisation*, extends the institutional thinking to map some of the ways in which naturalised historical dispositions are reproduced through organisational discourses. Again this point cuts across several chapters, however Chapters 5, 6 and 7 all aim to 'raise awareness of the multiple levels at which the relations of power function' (Harwood, 2006, p. 63) in both school and home through prescriptive notions of gender and familial responsibility.

Chapter 5 uses gender relations to enact the notion of discourse as performance in the primary classroom. Fragments of discourse are presented which constitute different forms of masculine domination, contingent on certain truths of masculine/feminine, which implicate further dichotomised truths of good/bad, normal/abnormal and order/disorder, and which form an unequal distribution and re-distribution of financial and intellectual resources.

5   *The degrees of rationalisation*, is concerned with the principles by which individuals are drawn into self-governance. Chapter 7, the final piece of fieldwork, offers an analysis of the 'principles that substantiate the actions made on the actions of young people' (Harwood, 2006, p. 63), through the theory and practice of nurture groups and their place within the core values of the educational project. The therapeutic ethic of the nurturing formula is analysed for its constitutive effects in various forms of subjectivisation according to routine, risk, class and gender. Governmentality is then used to explore the role of nurture in education and the role of education in society.

In moving now to the task of accomplishing these objectives within an empirical project I am making the move towards fieldwork. First it is necessary to provide a rationale for the choice of ethnography as the preferred means with which to see discursively. Following this, Chapter 3 then moves to a description of ethnography, and the actual steps taken in carrying out the fieldwork.

## Connecting textwork to fieldwork

In thinking about how to *do Foucault* (MacNaughton, 2005) via an empirical project, ethnography offered a promising way to me of trying to map some of the process of discourse; the archaeological dig around in the present, witnessing the constitutive force of discourse in everyday action. I was interested in the processes by which a diagnostic case might be constructed. I wanted to see whether action and interaction in the present might offer some indication as to the means by which the future othering of diagnosis could be achieved. Therefore, the sense in which Foucault spoke of discourse and power as productive, in the formation of objects of knowledge, seemed to offer the means to enter into this process.

With promise inevitably comes danger. Two issues were high in my mind: first, Foucault is sometimes cast, rightly or wrongly, as painting the subject out of his problematisations (Smart, 1986). Second, his thought is often considered a template for which reality is shaped to fit (Habermas, 1981); employing the theory as an 'overly certain moral economy' (Marcus, 1998, p. 19). I hoped that ethnography would force me to confront both of these issues, and in fact doing the first one properly should imply that the second one had also been subverted.

In striving for Geertz's (1973) ideal of *thick description* the ethnographer is compelled to focus initially on the individual subject: their everyday, every-moment action and interaction. This action can then be contextualised according to similarly everyday processes, systems and relationships. This action–relation–system model is how Smith (2005) conceptualises 'institutional ethnography' according to the mutually constitutive interplay between everyday action, social relations, institutional knowledge and systemic relations of ruling.

Clifford (1983) argues that a shift has occurred in ethnography since Geertz's (1973) interpretive paradigm towards more dialogically based constructivist models. However, the notion of thick description and its importance in producing authoritative accounts has remained in the minds of many contemporary proponents of the method. Marcus (1998) tackles this precise issue in talking about the potential *thinness* of ethnography:

> The space of potential discovery and increased understanding of processes and relationships in the world (which requires a bedrock of very thick description indeed) is taken over by a discourse of purpose and commitment within a certain moral economy ... Ethnographic projects ... must be allowed to 'breathe', especially in terms of their descriptive accounts of things, before the theory kicks in.
>
> *(Marcus, 1998, p. 18)*

In a world of anthropology marked by postmodernism and bearing close relations with terms like *discourse* and *reflexivity*, Marcus feels able to talk in terms of *discovery* as the potential for which ethnography should strive. Perhaps it is in this optimism that ethnography's greatest guile and greatest danger lies; also Derrida's (1967) critique of Foucault's (1967) history of madness, this concerns representation of the other:

> Foucault, in rejecting the psychiatric or philosophical literature which has always imprisoned the mad, winds up employing – inevitably – a popular and equivocal notion of madness taken from an unverifiable source . . . everything transpires as if Foucault knew what 'madness' means.
>
> *(Derrida, 1967, p. 49)*

Part of the reason I felt my brief *confession* in the first chapter was an important move to make was to disrupt the sense of silence which Derrida reads in Foucault's account of madness. It was an attempt to give voice to a partial truth of disorder, which is one among many other truths. Foucault (1980) argued that we are all othered by discourse and power; 'one is never outside it' (p. 141). Therefore, our freedom is constituted by our ability to respond 'to every advance of power with a movement of disengagement' (p. 138). Though he might have wished it otherwise, Foucault (1981a) was forced to concede that we are required to find a place within discourse; a place the space for which is already inscribed within that discourse: 'I wish I could have slipped surreptitiously into this discourse . . . I should have preferred to be enveloped by speech, and carried away well beyond all possible beginnings, rather than have to begin myself' (p. 51). Far more than an informal way in to his inaugural address at the *College de France*, this speaks directly to the notion of representation. We cannot slip surreptitiously into discourse, because we are to some extent already known by discourse. If power is understood as some kind of *grid* or *net* in which we are all mutually constrained, then othering is a product of our understandings, descriptions, perceptions and expectations of each other. So, I acknowledge that in writing a text I will be involved in 'making up people' (Hacking, 1986, p. 222) according to the discourses that are made available to me. Therefore, I saw it as ethically compelling and theoretically interesting to make clear the way in which I was other also, in so doing emphasising the extent to which the textual process authored me, as well as those I authorised. This is the condition of all authors, regardless of *meaningful* childhood experiences.

What opening up representation in this manner tells us is that the very term *representation* is deeply problematic. In short, it is impossible to *re-present*. We cannot step outside discourse with either our description or our interpretations, thus there is no authentic object to capture and no neutral lens with which to capture it. Stephen Tyler (1986) attempts to disrupt the sense in which ethnography is necessarily involved with representation of the other through his use of the term *evocation*: '[ethnography] transcends instead by *evoking* what cannot be known discursively or performed perfectly . . . it makes available through absence what can be conceived but not presented' (p. 130). Here, evocation is being used to try to subvert the Lacanian (1966) truth that language will always leave a separation between the sensory and the textual; between what is *imagined* and what we are able to *re-present* (Kenway and Fahey, 2009). In this attempt to voice without words, Tyler finds himself constrained by other customs and assumptions, such as the linear fashion in which Western grammar produces a bind whereby:

> '*x* evokes *y*' must mean that *x* and *y* are different entities linked by a third rather peculiar 'process-entity' called 'evoke', and that, moreover, *x* must precede *y* in time, and consequently *x* must be a condition of *y* or *y* a result of x.
>
> *(Tyler, 1986, p. 130)*

Thus Tyler finds his discourse already to some extent *known* by these governing relations, and unable to fashion entirely new means of speaking he can only seek to disrupt the means by which he is being spoken. He cannot stop discourse being coterminous with the enaction of power relations, he can only hope to respond with 'a movement of disengagement' (Foucault, 1980, p. 138) and make his enaction a subversive, resistant and reflexive process, described by Marcus (1998) as a 'bold attempt at endless self-parody' (p. 185).

The uses of discourse and power outlined in this chapter introduce an ethical commitment to self-parody in the performance and representation of ethnographic work. If Lacan's (1966) separation between feeling and sense leaves what he called *endless desire* in our frustrated attempts at representation, then perhaps Marcus's (1998) *endless self-parody* is required to effect an ongoing and continuous disengagement of power. At any rate, Marcus's image is a useful heuristic for the integration of subjectivism into ethnographic work because it requires one to think beyond the meta-approach so far outlined into the more situated strategies and techniques by which the integration might be attempted. In order to discuss these issues further, it is first necessary to provide an account of ethnography as methodology, and the approaches I have taken in making use of it.

## Ethnography as methodology

Conventionally, the ethnographer seeks to embed themselves in their chosen field of study, that is, collective life, for a prolonged period of time; upwards of around a year. The method pays close attention to the accomplishment of the seemingly mundane, the *doing* of social organisation and interaction (Solberg, 1996). Though the term *culture* can take on various meanings, at its most material, culture could be described as the regular patterns by which people *do* collective or institutional life. Clifford Geertz developed a very influential framework with his *interpretive ethnography*, from which came his ideal of *thick description*. Geertz considered thick description to be a process of making sense of doing through 'thinking and reflecting' and 'the thinking of thoughts' (1973, p. 6). Describing something thickly implies describing it contextually, getting inside tacit assumptions and elaborating action according to the codes which are meaningful to those who embody them. Geertz captures the attempt as one of moving *from twitch to wink*; on the surface very similar, yet one is unembedded, involuntary, meaningless, the other is acculturated, symbolic, knowing and communicative.

Ethnography is contested on a number of counts; for charges of *micro* unimportance (see Noblit *et al.*, 2004 for a discussion), for the underhand or deceitful manner in which the ethnographer appears to ingratiate themselves to their society (Fine, 1993) and for its contribution to colonialism (Said, 1978). Revision in ethnography has sought to address these concerns, openly discussing the problem of representation through literary as well as academic narratives (Clifford and Marcus, 1986), fusing with critical theory to provide more *macro relevant* disciplines, critical and post critical ethnography (Noblit *et al.*, 2004; Carspecken, 1996), and by seeking the means to embody power relations in an ethical and participatory manner, embracing post-colonial theories (Cannella and Viruru, 2004) and the reflexive voice (Behar, 1996; Pillow, 2003). Nevertheless, these attempts can only acknowledge the relativising and subjectivising dangers of ethnography, which cannot be eradicated, only opened to awareness and negotiation.

In terms of incorporating ethnography into a critical discursive framework, the work of Mauss ([1936] 1973) provides a useful illustration of the dialogue that can be created between individual dispositions and collective logics. Mauss described techniques of the body, claiming that behaviour was not a naturally occurring phenomena, but an acculturated process of symbolic limitation. Following Mauss, Douglas (1970) stated that: 'the social body constrains the way the physical body is perceived. The physical experience of the body, always modified by the social categories through which it is known, sustains a particular view of society' (p. 72). In a statement which bears a striking resemblance to the discussion of governmentality above, the conclusion reached here is that people's actions and behaviours bear the imprint of the rules and customs of their society, with the limits of bodily expression enunciating the limits of social acceptability.

The rise of ADHD is symptomatic of an epistemological primacy given to biology over culture in the interpretation and management of problems of everyday life. Statements from within the medical perspectives conceive of the behaviours associated with ADHD as arising from deficiencies in mental abilities which it views as natural and universal; that is, 'all humans normally would be expected, regardless of culture, to have developed that mental ability' (Barkley, 2002, p. 89). The contradictions inherent in combining universality with what would 'normally' be expected, illustrates the mis-representation of culture contained within this particular medical discourse and the primacy of biology, in relation to which culture is conceived as some kind of blockage or distraction, which I aim to invert in this study. This attempt is certainly not without precedent, as Geertz (1973) persuasively argued for the constitutive nature of culture in relation to biology through his description of the Australopithecines, an evolutionary pre-cursor to *Homo sapiens*, with much smaller brains, but with the beginnings of a simple cultural system, which separated them from apes:

> In the Australopithecines we seem to have ... an odd sort of 'man' who evidently was capable of acquiring some elements of culture ... but not others ... as the *Homo sapiens* brain is about three times as large as that of the Australopithecines, the greater part of human cortical expansion has followed, not preceded, the 'beginning' of culture.
>
> *(Geertz, 1973, p. 64)*

The facile nature of a statement which posits the universality of mental development, immaterial of the practices and relations that body and mind have developed through, is made quite clear by this argument. Following this understanding of culture, I seek an embedded analysis of a social phenomena – ADHD – understood to have physiological origins. I aim to describe the lines of acceptability drawn by the existence of ADHD, and what unexamined rules have conditioned such an existence. Having situated this attempt within the *thinking of ethnographic thoughts*, I will now move to situate it in the *doing*, retaining the focus on the conditions of the possible, by turning this analysis on my own research practices and the possibilities enabled and limited by them.

## Ethnography as method

The choice of methods for this study reflects the objective to theorise a pre-diagnostic space for ADHD, a space which is *enunciated* by certain ways of conceptualising children, schooling, families and social order, and *objectified* according to the everyday disciplining of school and classroom. I want to map the construction of a diagnostic case according to the social coordinates that are required, in order to consider the possible application of a diagnosis. Within this rationale ethnography finds its distinct place in offering the researcher the chance to witness and embody in moment-to-moment fashion the language and practice of the classroom order based on the inclusion and exclusion of certain ways of being. The attempt is to de-naturalise the physiological narrative of ADHD by focusing on the means by which objects of knowledge are formed through everyday social and cultural codes.

My objectives centre on the notion of power relations and the manner in which they condition interactions and relations, and hence thought and knowledge, between adults and children. I use the ethnographic method to disturb these relations, to try and get inside the conceptual frameworks ordinarily employed in interpreting and representing the action and enunciation of children. Yet I could never hope to eradicate these altogether. While the image of the *least-adult role* (Mandell, 1991) was a productive heuristic for me in carrying out my fieldwork, I certainly did not consider the distinct relations between adults and children in schools and families to be 'inconsequential' (p. 40). Rather I saw these relations as shifting but essential objects of analysis and self-analysis, to be acknowledged, embodied and reflected upon in an ongoing manner.

In pursuing ethnography as 'a way of looking' (Wolcott, 1999, p. 41), I was concerned with investigating the social worlds of the classroom in an embedded and exploratory manner, primarily through participant observation, or *observant participation* (Moeran, 2009) to draw on the more active conception. Here the ethnographer attempts a dual role in which their observation is facilitated by their participation in the ordinary life of the society. Although it is not possible to separate out completely these two aspects, participation-observation, it is possible to experiment with different combinations of them, reflecting on the differences in the kinds of data produced.

Reflexivity is used within ethnography in an attempt to create a sense of 'mobile positioning' (Haraway, 1988, p. 585), which in turn aids the production of contextually thick description. The following consideration of the productive effects of my different ways of working in each school featured in this study offers a way into this reflexive process.

In conducting the data collection for the arguments presented in Chapter 4, I took the role of a teaching assistant in a Year One class at Kilcott Infants. I took the work voluntarily and had I not been there then no teaching assistant would have been present in the classroom. Nevertheless, offering to fulfil a particular role carries the responsibility of doing it properly. It was not simply that participation was prioritised over observation, rather, taking on this role meant that the needs of the role were prioritised over the needs of the research. On reflection I find that this can be broken down to individual interactions and a set of choices; for example, as I was often tasked with supporting children who were struggling with the task in hand, I spent a good deal of time in the company of the children who most interested me. Yet, my role required that my interactions with them were task oriented. This meant that not only could I not *follow my nose* in the manner valued in ethnography (Wolcott, 2002) but also that I was often required to deliberately embody the regulative structures that I was seeking to disrupt. Though this relation was something I was more overtly aware of due to the particular research strategy employed here, it is a relation that any work with children within institutional contexts must acknowledge as culturally conditioned and only ever partially negotiable (Alderson, 1995; Mayall, 2000).

These relations also played out in the manner in which I recorded my fieldnotes and in the content of those fieldnotes. The notes would be scribbled down during a break time, in an empty classroom, or in my car with my lunch on my lap. They were privatised; they were the work of someone who found themselves in an ambiguous role, somewhere between researcher and staff member; inside and out. They were always already reflective; based on past events. They lacked the level of detail that I might have achieved if I had been recording live observations, yet, they compensated for this in the felt experience of participation, the embodiment of the processes of the infant classroom that I attempted to channel into a reflection on the possibilities both opened and closed by the enaction of these processes, an attempt that was my *practice of freedom*, my response to my engagement of those objectifying relations of power. The novelty to me of this environment, and this role, gave rise to a set of observations which returned me to one of the first principles of ethnography, and the first questions which the researcher takes into their participation:

- What are the rules of this game?
- What do the players do?
- Who is in charge?

For the data presented in Chapters 5 and 7, I sought a new environment, a new role, and a different balance. I entered Alderley Primary as a researcher, not to offer my services as any role ordinary to that environment, but in order to conduct research which required me to sit, watch and write in a Year One and a Year Two classroom. A new set of relations emerged with teachers; I was no longer a support, even a confidante, as I had sometimes been to the Year One class teacher at Kilcott. Now precisely because I was in a role unconventional to the environment I was in, precisely because there were not a clear set of conventions governing my possible actions, I was viewed with a mixture of intrigue and suspicion, and it must be said, the only participants who tended to the former were children.

That teachers should view me with suspicion, even as a threat, was hardly surprising. I was not, am not, and never have been, a teacher. I hold no teaching qualifications, nor any experience of teaching in those environments. Yet, I appeared to them as being in a position of passing judgement on their actions; scribbling away in the corner of their classroom. As is required of such research processes, I had gained access to the school via the head teacher, who then introduced me to the class teachers; in itself a process conferring a certain authority on me. As is also usual in research, I had told each teacher *something* of my research interests, but without giving too much away for fear that they would subsequently be responding to my interests through their actions. So, they knew I was interested in 'challenging behaviour' and 'inclusion', terms I had not discussed with them in any great detail when I began sitting in their classroom, watching. Therefore, with each instance of classroom disorder, each intensification of pen stroke on paper, perhaps each teacher thought: 'How am I being judged in this moment?'

My response to this in the manner in which I practised research at Alderley was to do everything as openly as I could. I wrote copious notes, but never in private, always a public act. I shared openly with teachers my reflection on what I was seeing, thinking and writing. Often I would arrive ten minutes early for a morning class in order to have some more open conversation with the class teacher, helping them set up the classroom, and then afterwards, perhaps during a break time, I would continue these conversations. When I came to the end of my time in each classroom, I shared my entire fieldnotes, completely unedited, with each teacher, and carried on the conversation; more on this experience later.

The fieldnotes themselves also changed radically.[1] They were 'live', scribbled in as much detail as possible, with regular markings of time, with as much detail, micro, moment-to-moment subtleties of interaction, as I could manage. These notes were then written into fuller accounts after school the same day, to include reflection and interpretations, to make up a daily document of around 5000 words.

But, what did this excess of words actually say? What was I actually looking for? I wanted to try and look at challenging behaviour in a manner that allowed me to look not at the behaviour itself so much as the challenge, or, rather, what it was perceived to be challenging. I did not see this as simply looking for the immediate triggers or apparent causes of behaviour that challenged, but more as an attempt to build up an account of the classroom that recognised both behavioural events and the notion of challenge as socially produced phenomena. Following the thinking of *Outsiders* (Becker, 1963) introduced in Chapter 1, I saw the most promising way in to this analysis to be in first understanding what was supposed to be happening in classrooms, in order to understand what was perceived to be challenging it. My initial work at Kilcott was a first attempt to describe the everyday norms of the classroom, the expectations placed on adults and children and the regulatory practices designed to shape reality towards those expectations.

This is one of the reasons I felt the more participatory role at Kilcott would be a good fit; not only did it mean I was taking on, embodying, some of those regulatory practices myself, but it was also a novel role to me, in a fairly novel environment. Thus I felt it might accomplish the necessary ethnographic act of *making strange* (Wolcott, 1999; Ybema and Yanow, 2009), a way of attempting to see things unclouded by tacit judgements, prompting questions which one more familiar with the setting might not think to ask:

- Why are all the children dressed in uniform but the adults not?
- Why is there a register?
- Why are desks and chairs organised in this way?
- What is the function of this timetable?

In pursuing these apparently infantile questions, I was able to develop an account of the normative structure of the classroom which disrupted the horizon of *the familiar and poorly known* (Foucault, 1997). The experience also showed to me the fundamental connection of time, space and possibility; between the theoretical framework I saw things through and the methods I employed to describe those things.

One difficult question attending this research concerned what it might have meant for me to be an adult in that time and space. In what ways was my presence shaping and shaped by the conditions of possibility I encountered? Certainly I acknowledged the need to think and plan carefully, and distinctly, in light of the age of some of my participants. However, at the conceptual level I did not see anything 'particular or indeed peculiar to children' (Christensen and James, 2000b, p. 2) that would involve a wholesale re-imagination of method. In fact, one of my objectives in choosing ethnography was so I might place children at the centre of an account of *doing* childhood (Comber, 1999; Solberg, 1996). Once again however, critical reflection was required in order to make an ongoing disruption and disengagement of these situated workings of power.

## Conditioning the possible

Prior to conducting the research at Kilcott, reflexivity was a research narrative I knew something about; it was interesting to me for its association with critical theories (Maynard, 1993; Pillow, 2003) and for its recommended use in studies involving children (Christensen and James, 2000b; Davies, 2008). Yet a previous research attempt to employ reflexivity had misfired, leaving me as keenly aware of its dangers as its promise. The work I have been describing here, which yielded the routine analysis, was initially designed to help me free myself of the self-conscious bonds the reflexive narrative had lent my previous project. Yet, this experience brought the reflexive directly to me through my everyday work, I still had to make the active choice to pursue it, but the need to do so seemed quite clear to me.

If reflexivity found an initially uneasy place in my own discourse, then this mirrors the uneasy reception it has been granted within research. For some, the 'endless self-parody' by which Marcus (1998, p. 185) describes the reflexive encounter spirals into introspective, confessional and narcissistic work, eradicating any political drive (Patai, 1994). I know that in choosing the subjectivism of the confessional in the opening chapter, and in extending it here into reflections on fieldwork, that I might well appear to many as conceited. However, in both cases, I felt it was a necessary step to making myself more aware of the effects of institutional logics on individual action, an essential step both in terms of the ethnographic method and in terms of the argument I wish to construct around ADHD. Therefore, rather than eradicating any political drive, the subjectivism I have employed has allowed me to position myself in order to move into a more direct and radical engagement with power, which is the foundation stone of all politics, big and small. Above all else, situated within my use of Foucault's discourse, reflexivity is an essential component in describing the possibilities which discourse has shaped, limited and ordered, inside/out.

Discourse has been introduced here as ontologically and epistemologically relevant to the understanding of social realities. Discourse suggests that what *is* has been made so according to the historical conditioning of possibility whereby particular pieces of action, involving particular agents, come to be understood according to derivative artifacts of knowledge and representation. Dorothy Smith's (1987, 2005) ethnographic approach readily fits this conditional manner of viewing the everyday. Smith is concerned with separating action in the everyday from the relations and systems which give meaning to it, which make it describable, knowable, possible. Foucault (1982) understood knowledge and action as not just interacting within the constraints of existing power relations, but as playing a productive role in their evolution. This is to acknowledge that the partially sighted actor, while not necessarily fully accountable for their action, nevertheless is involved in the engagement of power and knowledge relations, and should take this on in a responsible, reflexive and ethical manner.

These concerns collide head on with some of the abiding assumptions of ethnography. First, the micro and phenomenological nature of ethnography as a method enacts the notion of *partial perspective* (Haraway, 1988), which is furthered by the situated choices made in the field. Ethnography seeks to get beneath the natural progression of the everyday, with description of the sense-making that has gone into the construction of a given reality. Therefore, though ethnography seeks the *naturalised* experience, it does so in the hope that it can reveal something not ordinarily made visible. The work of ethnography is to use the everyday to produce new meaning, therefore the ethnographer self-consciously places themselves in the interpretation and re-enaction of power and knowledge relations, and has a commitment to make this positioning as ethical as possible. My aim with the reflexive work in this and the following chapter has been to illuminate an example of the productive nature of power relations within an established institutional setting and the conditions, both active and received, that have shaped the analysis to come. In the following chapter I move to describe in detail the settings that I encountered in this research and situate them in their political and theoretical context.

# 3

# CHILDREN, SCHOOLS AND FAMILIES

The research presented in this book was carried out in two schools and with two families over a period of approximately two years, commencing September 2005. Before describing these settings as I encountered them, it is first necessary to situate them in their political and theoretical context.

The arguments presented here should be understood within a specific socio-historic context. The recent history of the English state school is one of progressive commodification according to the market forces of competition and performative credentialism (Gerwitz *et al.*, 1995; Gleeson and Husbands, 2001). This context has productive effects on the disciplinary practices adopted within schools, with the neo-liberal image of the self-responsible citizen an important heuristic (Hunter, 1994). *Good schools* are taken to equate with routinised orderly schools, according to a de-politicised 'rhetoric of discipline' (Slee, 1995, p. 4). The schools in this project served predominantly working-class communities in ex-coalfield areas: because the New Labour government was particularly anxious to 'raise standards' in its traditional heartlands, schools such as these were under pressure to perform (Ball *et al.*, 1999). This was manifest in an anxiety to ensure prescribed standards of development and integral to these is a press for order. As infant and primary schools, Kilcott and Alderley were expected to take a pastoral approach to schooling, historically positioned as emotional, female work (Skeggs, 2003; Walkerdine and Lucey, 1989). The head teacher, teachers and assistants at Kilcott were all female, with one male member of staff at Alderley. This might be seen as indicative of a *feminised* approach to schooling and behaviour management (Miller, 1993), however, such conceptions can reinforce existing masculine dominance and risk an over-simplification of *being* gendered (Skelton and Francis, 2005).

While there has been a change of government since this research was carried out, there has been no slowing of the neo-liberal agenda in education, as illustrated by the Coalition government pushing the development of independent academies, privately financed and autonomously governed, with whom traditional state schools now have to compete for capital spending. Combined with the Coalition government's austerity spending programme, schools find themselves in the same vulnerable position as many other public services, which have moved on from the *pressure to perform* under New Labour to more of a *fight for survival*.

Education and its associated institutions were explicitly drawn into Foucault's (1977) account of institutional knowledge and practices, unified by their shared objectives of discipline. An institutional space is at all times governed according to the rules of hierarchical observation and normalising judgement; the examination being the ever-present possibility of the intersection of these two vectors. Presupposing this state, and demarcating what could be understood through this observation and this judgement, lies discourse, which refers not only to everyday signs, symbols, utterances and practices, but also the systems (epistemes) of knowledge by which such symbols are known and accrue meaning (Foucault, 1972). The ideal state of discipline achieved through the examination therefore requires a set of narratives articulated via discourse and the means with which to observe and limit subjectivity according to these narratives. Foucault (1977) uses the term *panopticism* to describe this state of perfect transparency and translatability; 'a domain of clear visibility' (p. 105) through which the process of subjectivisation can operate.

Educational environments have stimulated much ethnographic work of relevance to the objectives of this project. In particular, Jackson's (1960) description of school's *hidden curriculum*, which defines the moral literacies required in 'learning how to live in classrooms' (p. 33). I also share Jackson's choice of the infant classroom for witnessing this embodiment of morality, as this is when 'the young child comes to grips with the facts of institutional life' (p. vii). Jackson *et al.*'s (1993) work on the moral significance of what goes on in classrooms meshes with ethnographic work in both the UK (Jeffrey and Woods, 1998) and US (Noblit and Dempsey, 1996) of some of the broader politics of performative classroom cultures, particularly the role of accreditation and inspection in undercutting the knowledge, experience and 'commitment of teachers to their profession' (p. 201).

The present account aspires to move beyond a description of social control in the primary classroom which emphasise *teachers' ideologies* (King, 1978; Pollard, 1985) in the control of learning and behaviour. This assumes a knowing and transparent relationship between the individual and the institution which is problematic within a critical account of reality, in which actors are partially sighted and constrained within a given moral and political frame. Extending more discursive ideals, Fine (1991) provides a sophisticated textual analysis that seeks to understand 'how it is that public schools contain the ironies of social injustice through what and how they teach, and what and how they won't' (p. 9). Related, though set in a very different context, Benjamin (2002) maps the moral terrain upon which the politics of social exclusion become individualised, producing 'students as inherently unable to aspire to reach the prestigious grades that count as success for the majority' (p. 108). If the progressive ideal or emancipatory 'vision fails to "trickle down"' (Fine, 1991, p. 149) then this result has been shaped by structural and systemic disempowerment, and it is the task of critique not to further encroach on individual choice, but to trace the varying levels of regulation at which disempowerment occurs.

## Kilcott Infants

The research presented in Chapter 4 was carried out at Kilcott Infants, a village school in England's rural East Midlands. I spent ten weeks during the Autumn term 2005 as an unpaid teaching assistant, working primarily with two classes from Years One and Two. Kilcott schooled just over 100 children from the age of three to aged seven. The two classes that feature in this analysis each held around 25–30 children of between five and six (Year One) and six and seven (Year Two). Informed consent of all participants and their parents was obtained before commencing work in school. The data consists of daily ethnographic fieldnotes which contain descriptions, recorded speech, maps and reflection.

Kilcott Infants was the school at which I had conducted the research for my Master's dissertation, and had that not been the case or had that been a more fulfilling research experience I might not have undertaken the latter term's work. I first learned of the school through a colleague and made contact through the head teacher, Margaret, who introduced me to the deputy head, Sarah, who was head of Foundation and whose class I would work in as a teaching assistant. Following my initial month at Kilcott for my Master's dissertation I arranged a further term's work to start from September, which I planned as a pilot study for the more prolonged period of my PhD research to be conducted at Alderley Primary. However, the Kilcott study became a formative part of the main body of the research because of some distinct features of its design, as discussed in the previous chapter. To repeat the same work at Alderley appeared superfluous, however, the findings from Kilcott guided the design of the work at the subsequent site, the routine construct offered an epistemological and material point of departure for the remaining research, also providing a consistent heuristic to help negotiate the *multi-site* ethnography (Marcus, 1998).

Part of my interest in Kilcott was based on some of the demographics of the school and immediate area, particularly the sort of characteristics often associated with marginal social status. Kilcott served a small ex-coalfield community, the town had been built as a colliery village in the 1920s, and when the pit closed in the 1990s it lost its central economic resource. This immediate economic circumstance is one shared by many communities in the local authority, county and broader geographic area.

According to the office of national statistics (ONS), Kilcott's local authority had higher than average unemployment as well as a higher than average *economically inactive* population, as Table 3.1 shows:[1]

**TABLE 3.1** Kilcott economic activity as a percentage by local authority

|  | LA | District | UK |
| --- | --- | --- | --- |
| Economically active: unemployed | 3.10 | 3.27 | 3.35 |
| Economically inactive: sick/disabled | 5.73 | 5.29 | 5.30 |

Almost 40 per cent of those in full-time employment worked in manufacturing or retail. In terms of socio-economic status, these industries feed mainly into what the ONS calls 'routine' or 'semi-routine' occupations. It should be noted, however, that the figures in Table 3.1 show quite marginal percentage differences. In terms of more qualitative economic experiences, the village of Kilcott was associated with considerable efforts at community regeneration, through various projects such as the redevelopment of former pit sites into arts centres.

According to the OFSTED report current at the time of the research, the pupil population at Kilcott entered Foundation at below average attainment levels and with a higher than average rate of learning difficulties and disabilities.[2] By Key Stage One OFSTED notes that achievement was 'broadly average' with average numeracy and slightly lower than average literacy levels at Year Two. The report goes on to note Kilcott's strong ethos towards personal, social and emotional development, with creative approaches to curriculum and good opportunities for pupils to contribute to the school and wider community through pupil councils and mentoring schemes. Attendance rates are described as 'satisfactory' with a 'significant minority' recording 'well below average' attendance. In all other areas the school is described as 'good' with particular mention made of 'strong leadership' and 'purposeful vision'.

Though learning difficulties and disabilities were described by OFSTED as above average, very few children had statements of special educational needs. The local authority had a reputation at the time for being resistant to statementing, and had far fewer children with statements that neighbouring authorities, with similar populations. This meant that there was a lack of resources available for special needs support in schools such as Kilcott. Extra support was minimal; one teaching assistant assigned to the Year Two class, mainly to support two children with Down's Syndrome. There were no extra assistants assigned to the Year One group and assistants would only usually be brought in as cover for teacher group planning time.

The Year One class that I worked in was made up of 26 children: 14 boys, 12 girls. Though no children had statements of SEN there were six who had individual education plans, which were designed to focus on particular areas of weakness. The deputy head, Sarah, was also the Year One class teacher. Though I had not previously worked in class with Sarah, she had been my main point of contact for the previous research project and we were on good terms. She was very enthusiastic about my return to her class, not least I suspected because I would be providing valuable assistance for her. Beyond this, Sarah seemed to have a genuine concern for issues of behaviour and inclusion, and also for the development of my research.

Before commencing the research for the previous project I had adhered to accepted standards of informed consent. For this I provided detailed information for teachers and parents about my planned research and gave all participants the opportunity to withdraw at any time.[3] Upon commencement of the first project I also spoke to the children in the classes where I would be working, describing myself as someone who wrote stories about what goes on in classrooms. Once I had completed the first project, the planning and permission for the second project was relatively unproblematic. I provided parents with further information concerning my new role as acting classroom assistant, offering a new opportunity to withdraw. I was able to speak to staff individually within school. By the end of the first project I was also on familiar terms with many of the children, which meant they were more likely to ask questions about what I was doing and also meant I was better equipped to answer them.

My growing familiarity with both the assistant role and the children whom I was assisting offered the possibility of staying sensitive to issues which the children might have had but found difficulty voicing. The fact that my role responsibilities matched my research interests meant that the children I got to know best were the ones I wrote most of my notes about. This meant I was given good opportunities to explore their impressions of what a researcher's job might be and what I might be looking for. The notion of informed consent with children this young is problematic because of the difficulty of explaining ideas and intentions in a meaningful way (Billington, 2006; Johnson, 2000). Even with these conversations, I am not sure if the children fully appreciated what I was doing there, but I did try to secure their willingness to appear in my stories – in fact this sometimes turned out to be an effective prompt to engage with an activity.

I had regular conversations and discussions with Sarah. This gave us both a chance to think and reflect on what was happening in the classroom. Sarah would often suggest individuals I might look out for and offered me ways of moving forward with my competence in the assistant role. In return I shared my thoughts and perceptions on the work. The dialogue was open, respectful and constructive. Though my note taking was privatised, I was open and honest about my impressions with Sarah, and she returned this with her own impressions as well as encouragement and support.

To move to more *situated* notions of ethical decision making (Simons and Usher, 2000), the role I took required me to adopt a different protocol of ethics than I would derive from personal or educational research resources. I became quite critical of the way in which the classroom effectiveness might only be supported by siphoning off a selection of children to the teaching assistant, and yet I was required to actively participate in this segregation.

The regular conversations I had with Sarah also presented some dilemmas. From the perspective of information gathering they were extremely useful. However, Sarah knowing my research interests and offering me 'ones to watch' and work with, might well have reinforced these children's marginal positioning. If it had not been for my presence in the classroom then there would have been no assistant there and so segregations occurred that might not have otherwise.

I acknowledge that this was an artificial effect of the research, directly the result of my intervention on this social setting. Such effects are an inevitable product of naturalistic enquiry, but attention is required for their impact on the validity and reliability of the analysis (Hammersley and Atkinson, 1983). Rather than thinking in the somewhat conventional and rigid terms of 'validity' and 'reliability', it might be better to think about an ethnographic research strategy 'in terms of what brings fieldworkers into a setting in the first place and whether they are well situated to observe what they hope to observe' (Wolcott, 2005, p. 81). Doing so brings meaning to the design of the work and justifies the artifice. Part of the objective with the research was to gain insight into the everyday work of schooling *challenging behaviour* in the context of a local authority with a low record of statementing. If there had been an assistant in class then there would have been less reason to pursue that classroom on the basis of under-resourcing. Additionally, schools and classrooms are highly structured environments where interactions are in part determined by systemic codes; therefore, the fact that I enacted institutional codes which otherwise might have remained dormant does not alter the fact that those codes were and are available and their use quite acceptable and commonplace within that context.

Taking a more humanist perspective on this artifice results in no such easy justification. I cannot escape the fact that my presence, via the role of the teaching assistant, led to a reinforcement of extant power relations between adults and children at Kilcott Infants. This is a perennial problem for researcher participation, particularly in research involving children (Christensen and James, 2000a) to which I could only respond with an ongoing attempt to create spaces through which children could experience more equal participation in the research, and to reflect carefully on the disciplinary structures I reinforced in the interests of developing a more potentially empowering argument.

For my own sense of ethics the most consistent abrasions I experienced were in the disciplining aspect of the role. There was so much that I didn't think warranted drawing specific attention to the children involved through verbal or physical reprimands, and yet these were the requirements of the job and the resources available with which to do it. In other ways however the adoption of a relative *insider* role was empowering, particularly in terms of access and participation: I have never, before or since, been given the opportunity to work alone with *challenging* children while in school. In my interactions with staff I found my role management much easier than in my subsequent interactions at Alderley. Here, I was the one with the skills to acquire, who lacked the necessary knowledge, and who needed the guidance. This yielded more open and informative dialogue with other staff than can be easily produced when you are perceived to be either *expert* or *judge*.

Yet at the same time assuming a role meant that I was required to assume responsibilities regardless of my own sense of right and wrong. A memorable example of this came about halfway through the term. Sarah was commenting on the behavioural improvement she had seen in a Year One boy, James, which she ascribed to him having been put on Omega 3.[4] From this day onwards Sarah arranged for the whole class to be given Omega 3 supplements in the morning and it became my job to sit at the head of an orderly line of children spooning out the medicine one-by-one.

I was perhaps fortunate in never encountering any *crisis* incident that forced a serious clash between personal ethics and role commitments. For the most part I became adept at performing the disciplining role and, even with my own self-concept of inadequacy in the role, I cannot think of more than one or two occasions where I had to seek help. As I grew in confidence with the role so Sarah gave me more responsibility and I started to develop ways in which I might do my job in both an effective and personally satisfying way. I found my happiest home in this regard to be the Year Two class and their weekly drama sessions which I was drafted in to help with, more of which in Chapter 4.

Kilcott took up one corner of a larger site shared with a primary school, into which many of Kilcott's children fed. The school was all based in one oblong, apexed building with individual classrooms curtained off from one another. The only exceptions to this were the Foundation, which had windowed walls from the rest of the school at one end of the building, and the staff room and school offices at the other end. The small size of the school and this arrangement of classroom spaces gave Kilcott a very intimate feel which occasionally felt quite claustrophobic.

The library was one illustration of this. It was placed in the centre of the school partitioned from the three classrooms it bordered by curtains. It was to this room I was frequently sent with a small group of children from the Year One classroom, either to read or to use the computers housed there. The often disruptive and noisy behaviour of the children in the group I was given meant that frequently other teachers would look round the curtain to check that there was a supervising adult present. I usually read this outside interest as reflecting the fact that my group had disrupted other classes and they were concerned about me and the children in my care, however, at times it felt more regulative than concerned. My interpretation would depend on the circumstances and on the individuals involved, however, overall it fed the impression of Kilcott as a space where everyone needed to try and find a way of being very close to one another.

## Alderley Primary

Alderley Primary was the school where I carried out the most prolonged period of research; my work there ran from September 2006 until June 2007, one complete academic year. The first two terms I spent mainly in classroom observations in the Nursery, Foundation, Year One and Year Two, and the nurture group. The third term was spent mostly in the staff room in conversation with the special needs coordinator, arranging and conducting interviews with staff members, and providing general assistance as required.

Alderley Primary is located in the same county as Kilcott, but under a different local authority. The village of Alderley is older than Kilcott, and was not built specifically for industry. The village sits just outside a mid-sized town which is a historic site of interest, dating back to Anglo-Saxon times. Until the mid-1990s the town was also the centre of the local coal industry and home to one of the largest collieries in the area. Since the closure the town had attracted a reputation for drug use and anti-social behaviour, for which it was compared to much larger inner-city problem populations.

The ONS figures on the authority were a little worse than those of Kilcott, as Table 3.2 below shows:

**TABLE 3.2** Alderley economic activity as a percentage by local authority

|  | LA | District | UK |
|---|---|---|---|
| Economically active: unemployed | 3.95 | 3.27 | 3.35 |
| Economically inactive: sick/disabled | 7.60 | 5.29 | 5.30 |

While the active unemployed figure was marginally more than Kilcott and higher than the local and national rates, the figure that was striking was the economically inactive. These figures are included here because it is thought that within them are many of the long-term unemployed of industry shutdowns.

There is also more variation within the employment figures. This time the 'routine' and 'semi-routine' occupations combined to make up just under 25 per cent of the local population, compared to 40 per cent at Kilcott. The biggest single occupational group was 'lower managerial and professional' with just under 16 per cent, which implies a more mixed demographic than Kilcott.

The indication from these figures is that though there were more people within the authority unemployed or economically inactive, there was also a greater proportion in so-called 'white collar' occupations. Interestingly, the village of Alderley offers a highly visual illustration of this diversity. Alderley was very much a village of two halves, old and new. The old village was based around the main road which ran north from the nearby town. It had privately owned, period houses, a small church, several shops and pubs, and a small (and exclusive) primary school. Tucked away in the north west corner of the village was the *new* estate. The estate housed a larger proportion of the population than the old village, it was over 70 per cent council or housing association owned, and apart from Alderley Primary and a police station, had very few amenities. Though it made up most of the village population, a tourist map, printed a little before the time I worked in Alderley, which did not include the estate as part of the village at all, illustrated its marginal status. Alderley Primary was located on the edge of the new estate and was the product of an amalgamation in 2004 of a primary and infant school. While I was working there the school housed 244 pupils between the ages of three and 11. In their 2007 report of Alderley, OFSTED referred to the 'economically disadvantaged' local population, the 'well above average' number of children eligible for free school meals, with learning difficulties or disabilities, and with statements of special educational need.

The OFSTED report goes on to talk about the recent turbulence, particularly among staff, following the amalgamation, producing what it called 'inadequate achievement and exceptionally low standards'. The appointment of a new head teacher was reported to be improving the situation and standards were up to 'satisfactory'. Personal, social and emotional development was commended, noting the Healthy Schools Award achieved the previous year. Particular mention was also made of the Foundation stage which received praise for its 'stimulating and safe' environment. Teaching and learning, leadership and management, curriculum, and care and support are all described as 'satisfactory'. The report did not announce either notice to improve or special measures to be applied to the school, however, subsequent to this report the school was put on the new 'hard to shift' list, which is made up of schools causing concern for the significant 'barriers to improvement'. Additionally, the head teacher who was praised within the report has since left.

Once again I became aware of Alderley through a colleague, who put me in touch with the head teacher, Sue. I arranged to meet with her and discuss my plans as well as provide information for both staff and parents about my planned work. Once Sue had agreed to my working in the school I was introduced to the other staff with whom I would be working. At this time I also provided Sue with all participant information and withdrawal forms.[5]

In preparation for my work in Years One and Two I spoke to both the class teachers (Tina and Rachel) to make sure they were happy for me to observe their classrooms and to answer any questions they might have. Sue had introduced me as being interested in early identification, and I contextualised this a bit by talking about challenging behaviour and inclusion. There was some apprehension from both teachers about what kind of scrutiny they would come under. I told them that I was interested in the classroom as a social situation, and so while they would appear in my notes, I would not be holding individuals to account in the way they feared. I also reassured them that I was not there to judge their teaching practice, and that my findings would not feed back into any monitoring or evaluation process. Finally, I offered to share with them the notes I had made in their classroom, giving them the opportunity to question my judgements, and giving them exclusion rights over anything they were not happy with. Following this they both agreed to participate.

Upon commencement of work in a classroom the teacher would introduce me to the class and again I would use storytelling to explain my work in the class. Again, initially none of the children had any questions for me, but as my work in each class progressed I would attract interest from several of the children. I was always happy to talk to them about what I was writing and would always try and answer their questions. To the children I became an object of interest or amusement. They would find the speed and illegibility of my writing funny. On one occasion a Year Two boy produced a small hourglass of sand and challenged me to finish my page before the sand ran through, when I asked him what would happen if I failed, he laughed and told me something along the lines of: *you won't be allowed to write anymore and you might die*. These interactions were usually enjoyable for both parties and constructive for me in terms of developing good relationships. However, I was mindful of not causing a significant disruption. There were one or two children who showed a repeated interest in me, more often I felt on the basis of attempting to escape work. On such occasions I would attempt to guide them back to what they should be doing rather than engage them in conversation, and I became quite adept at performing these little disciplinary tasks.

Nevertheless, I felt the relaxed relationship I had with the children contributed to the uncertain view that the teachers in Years One and Two seemed to take of me. In contrast to the experiences with staff at Kilcott, both Tina and Rachel seemed to view me very much as an outsider, and as someone who was there to judge their performance, with material implications for them. I found this relationship management very difficult at the time; it was the source of considerable anxiety and personal feelings of guilt, regarding my rights to be there. On reflection I think I am more inclined to look to the means by which I accessed the school – via the head teacher, as is the legitimate means, as prompting the view of me as being someone there to monitor. With the passing of time I am also more inclined to see the context of the difficult recent history of Alderley as producing a kind of default sense of apprehension towards any outsider; this was a place all too used to being put under the microscope. I have already described how I attempted to gain the trust of both teachers before my work in their class commenced. The strategies deployed turned out to be only partially successful, and my experiences in each class compared and contrasted with each other in various ways.

I observed Tina's Year One class for a total of six weeks. Initially Tina seemed quite unnerved by my presence, so I did my best not to make myself more intimidating. I would always try to arrive early in the morning so that I could talk to her before the children arrived and could discuss things I had observed, or simply build up some kind of relationship. During my time in the classroom this developed into a stronger working relationship. I knew that she was very aware of my presence in the classroom, and so I kept my note taking as discrete as I could. While she knew I was not in the class to help her out or assist, there were occasions where I felt that it would be better if I combined my observation with an element of supervision. The only teaching assistant in the Year One classroom was a nearby high school student on a rather sporadic work-experience placement, and so when situations arose which were more problematic for one person to handle alone, I would help out. One example of this was when there was a division of activities between the indoor and outdoor spaces of the Year One classroom. It was simply impossible for Tina to be in both places at once and so I offered to supervise one side. This was primarily to check that nothing was going seriously wrong, and that children were safe. If anything serious had occurred I would have deferred straight to Tina, but it never did. Besides this, whenever the class was required to go from one place to another I would usually walk at the back of the line in order that I might survey the group. This was not something Tina asked me to do, I did it almost automatically, perhaps a response internalised during my time at Kilcott. At these times it seemed my role as an adult among young children was more powerful than my role as a researcher. Most of the time however, interaction within class between Tina and I would be no more than occasional eye contact, or an affirming smile, or when she required me as a prop to a conversation or activity.

When the six weeks came to an end as promised I gave my notes to Tina, with the caution that she might be a little surprised by the detail with which events had been recorded. She came to me very shortly afterwards having read the first week and feeling very upset by the poor light in which she felt I had portrayed her. She said that she felt 'betrayed' by some of the things I had written and she had already spoken to Rachel, who now had serious misgivings about having me in her class.

I explained to both that this was why I had agreed to show them the notes, so they could discuss any specific concerns. I said that if there was something specific they were particularly unhappy with then we could discuss it being taken out altogether. I also pointed out that nobody else in school would be reading these notes. In separate conversation with Tina I encouraged her to carry on reading, pointing out that the first week was really me trying to find my way around the place and made up very early and partially formed impressions, and that if she read on she would find that these impressions were open to change. In fact I could think of several places throughout the notes where I had considered the difficulties of Tina's role very carefully. Tina agreed to do this and was much happier after she had read the whole document. Eventually the kind of productive co-reflection was prompted by the notes that I had hoped for, and Tina did not have anything that she wanted to dispute or exclude.

My work in Rachel's class produced more of these sorts of problems and I did not feel they were resolved to the same mutual satisfaction. The incident with Tina's notes had reinforced Rachel's view of me as monitoring her performance and though we held regular conversations in the same way as Tina and I had, they were much more guarded, more defensive. Nor did Rachel ever seek my participation in class, even in the small, situated ways that Tina had, to the extent that we would barely even make eye contact. Adding to this was the fact that more of the children in Rachel's class took an interest in what I was doing, and more often in a search for distraction. This led to Rachel frequently becoming frustrated with my presence in the room. I tried to become firmer with children when I felt they were using me as a distraction and tried as much as possible to stay out of the way. Rachel had a large and quite disruptive class with a number of *known problem children*. One child had a teaching assistant every morning and the more relaxed norms governing his activities coupled with his frequent loud outbursts made the class very difficult for Rachel to manage. During our conversations Rachel would often refer to the amount of time taken up with preparation rather than delivery – her biggest frustration being the 20 minutes she had to cut the last class by in order to prepare to go home.

Rachel shared Tina's initial misgivings about my notes when I presented them to her, however she had more sustained problems with them. She did not see the relevance of many of the things that I had included, nor did she like the fact that I had taken note of the conversations we had held together. There were several occasions where our reading of events did not match, and while in some cases she was prepared to concede that this was down to differing perspectives, there were several items she asked me to take out, which I did. Nevertheless I felt that Rachel was not happy with having had me work in her class, and I have tried to use the notes I gathered there sparingly in my analysis, and have omitted anything that Rachel sought to question, including things she had not asked to be officially removed.

During my work in Years One and Two, the importance of the school's nurture group had become apparent to me for its role in the management of *problem children*.

During morning assembly the children from Years One and Two who were to go to the nurture group were kept back in the Year Two classroom. After a couple of weeks of attending assembly I decided to stay back in the classroom, and this is how I met Clare and Andrea, the two teaching assistants who ran the nurture group. During one of our conversations on such a morning, Clare suggested that I come and observe the group. My work in the nurture group required me to re-adopt a participant role similar to my Kilcott role. The room in which the group took place was very small and there were already two adults for about eight children. It was neither practically or ethically appropriate to sit, watch and write, and so I participated in activities instead, helping out where needed, talking to both the staff and children in the group, assisting break time supervisions, and working with the small amount of required literacy and numeracy work. Andrea and Clare had both encouraged me to participate with them in this manner, however, they were also very aware of the *vulnerable* position in which the children in the group found themselves, and after I had been in the group for six weeks they suggested I should bring my work there to an end. Once again I showed my notes to Clare and Andrea, they were both very interested in what I had written and had plenty to add. I decided to conduct an interview with them in which I would use some of the observations directly, as vignettes against which alternative possibilities could be explored, in which both teaching assistants engaged fully and reflectively.

My final six weeks at Alderley were mainly spent with Heather, the SEN coordinator (SENCO), in conversation in the staff room. Though informal these conversations were mutually informative. There seemed an unspoken agreement between us that there existed some very difficult problems which did not have perfect answers. We would each seek each other's opinions on these challenges and we found much common ground as well as occasions where we could challenge the other's assumptions. As researcher–participant relations went it was ideal, as to some extent these roles were dissolved. On occasion this meant that I had to check that I was not having too direct a hand in any intervention, or non-intervention, with a particular child, as I did not feel it was my place to have such direct influence. One notable occasion was during one of our regular conversations concerning a Year One boy, Chris. Chris had been diagnosed with ADHD and I knew from our previous conversations that neither Heather nor I saw this as a particularly helpful diagnosis. Chris had a review approaching, a multi-disciplinary meeting in which child, parents and school met together with social worker, school nurse and educational psychologist. Heather asked me if I would like to attend this meeting, and though my researcher's curiosity was certainly taken, I felt that this was not appropriate. In fact, I wondered if even in reaching the point where I had been asked, whether I had been giving slightly the wrong impression to Heather, and from here on I reined my opinion in a little. Happily this did not seem to detract from our continued constructive working relationship.

I spent approximately six weeks each observing Year One, Year Two and the nurture group. As with Kilcott, using routine as an initial guide to observations I would record the daily accomplishment of life in the classroom according to the

**TABLE 3.3** Alderley Primary: Years One and Two timetable

| Time | Activity | Location |
|---|---|---|
| 8.45–9.25 | Arrival and Registration | Classroom |
| 9.25–10.00 | Assembly | Hall |
| 10.00–11.00 | Lesson | Classroom |
| 11.00–11.15 | Morning break | Outside |
| 11.15–12.00 | Lesson | Classroom |
| 12.00–13.15 | Lunch | Dining hall |
| 13.15–14.15 | Lesson | Classroom |
| 14.15–14.30 | Afternoon break | Outside |
| 14.30–15.15 | Lesson | Classroom |
| 15.15–15.30 | Departure | Classroom |

normative expectations of the timetable and the explicit and tacit expectations of conduct. Both Years One and Two worked to the same demarcations of time.

Included in every school day was an hour each of literacy and numeracy activities, in line with then current UK government policy (DFES, 2005). This would usually proceed with Tina explaining an activity to the whole class on the carpet, perhaps offering some examples and asking a few questions. Then the class would be split up between tables to complete an activity based on Tina's instructions. Places at tables were another aspect of the classroom organisation which had been jointly agreed, though Tina reserved the right to move people around if they were causing disruption. During these work activities Tina would allow a certain level of 'conversational' noise for which there was no precise meter, however my impression was that she applied her standards quite consistently, which was illustrated by my ability to accurately predict when she was about to quiet things down. Movement that was related to the task in hand (i.e. fetching materials, checking something on the board, asking Tina something) was the only movement permitted, again, Tina seemed to apply this quite consistently.

Once Tina had the class all sitting at tables and settled in an activity then the class did not seem unusual in its levels of disruption. Tina showed me through the children's work folders, as one would expect the standard of work produced varied between individuals, however, the vast majority completed the work to at least a 'satisfactory' standard in the allotted times. There was a regular group of about four or five children who would require some extra help in completing this. Mostly they were boys, and Tina would either provide this extra help in class or sometimes individuals would be taken out of class for extra work to be completed with one of the teaching assistants. The extra work usually employed what were called 'five-minute boxes'. As the name suggests a box containing materials for a given set of tasks would be used for five minutes at a time with each child. These materials were either bright red or yellow in colour and usually had a 'fun learning' emphasis.

I was intrigued by the use of time they employed, apparently presupposing an encounter with a very short attention span.

Sometimes during, and frequently outside the structured activities, order maintenance in the classroom was more problematic. There was a core group of about six disruptive boys, some, though not all, were the same ones who regularly required five-minute boxes. Their regular disruption as well as the rough manner in which they interacted with each other was a source of great concern to Tina. The boys' impact on the class was very noticeable. Within a week I was writing about *the usual group of boys* in my notes. Whole class activities would be punctuated with frequent admonishment for the regular infractions the boys would make: usually excessive noise or movement or some other breaching of routine regulative norms. During structured activity time this behaviour would sometimes force Tina to make dispensations to these norms: allowing the boys to choose their own activities, for example. This contrasted to whole-group activities where Tina was much more persistent in trying to internalise rules like raising hands before speaking. Such admonishment would sometimes be so regular as to make the whole-group activities break down altogether. In moving from the more holistic impressions I gained at Kilcott and through the use of the routine lens to identify *others*, I developed a more individualised focus at Alderley, and I will now describe some of the individuals who became of interest to me, and who feature in Chapters 5 and 7.

Two of the core members of the dominant group of boys were Greg and Kyle. If I were to pick one ringleader for the group of boys then it would be Greg. He was both older and bigger than most in the class. He was boisterous and loud, he answered back to adults with cocky comments, and was prone to shouting things out in whole-group activities without first raising his hand. Yet for all his boisterousness and disruption, he seemed good-humoured. I did not observe him behaving in an openly malicious manner. On the occasions when I witnessed Tina having a more serious word with some of the boys about fighting or bullying then Greg was not usually involved. Therefore, while on a typical day Greg's name would be among the most heard in anger, he did not have a particularly problematic status attached to him. He was understood to be a 'little boy' who, like lots of little boys, liked to run and play and shout. My impression was often that he was perhaps over enthusiastic, but innocently so. I remember a conversation with Tina after she had read my notes; she said that she shared this impression of Greg, and that she tried very hard to include him in activities, but that his persistent failure to raise his hand before shouting something out made this very difficult. Significant perhaps in the maintenance of this impression was the fact that when Greg could be persuaded to perform an activity in an acceptable manner then he displayed very competent levels of ability.

Kyle was another boy for whom the routine regulation of the classroom was clearly a problem, however, in contrast to Greg, he pushed the normative boundaries in ways which over time had acquired him a more severe *problem* status, requiring specific interventions of various kinds. He was young for the class and smaller than most. He was known to lack patience, and staff spoke of the 'unpredictable' nature of his behaviour. Like Greg, he had failed to internalise various routine conduct norms. He was very active and fidgety and would frequently shout out. Like Greg, he would enjoy a cocky response to an adult, however, just as often as not, his outbursts would be entirely unrelated to the activity in hand. His speech was basic and delivered in a stuttering manner, and his literacy and numeracy levels were described as 'well below average'. Within a problematic group of boys he had acquired a particularly *troubled* status, and if he was involved in some disruption then he was generally considered to be the root of it. Tina found Kyle very difficult to manage; she felt that if she allowed him some dispensations then he would push further, forcing her to either relax the rules further or admonish him. If she consistently did the former then the integrity of the norm would be threatened, if she did the latter then he would often become petulant and non-participative.

One of Kyle's older brothers was two years ahead of him at school, was in a special class, and had a diagnosis of ADHD. Kyle was suspected to be 'going down the same road', as was his younger sister, who at that time was in the Nursery. Each child's behaviour was understood to be the likely, even inevitable, consequence of a 'difficult' family background. The term I started work in the Year One class, Kyle began attending the Years One and Two nurture group. This intervention was targeted at his perceived *EBDs* and required him to be out of the mainstream class for four mornings per week.

Separate from the main group of boys, and often from the rest of the class, was a third boy of interest to me, Chris. Chris was one of the youngest; small and wiry, with a very pale complexion, ordinarily he was very shy. In the whole time I was in the Year One class I did not hear more than a few fragments of barely audible speech from him. Like Kyle, Chris was understood to have a 'difficult' family background. Unbeknown to me at the start of my work in Year One, Chris had been diagnosed with ADHD. He also attended the nurture group four mornings per week. When he was in the Year One classroom, Chris was made immediately visible by the fact that none of the ordinary rules seemed to apply to him. He did not have to sit on the carpet with the whole group, nor did he have to join any activity. Instead he was allowed to roam freely, and as long as he was not causing any disturbance then he would likely be left to his own devices. Chris would regularly demand attention from Tina in the form of physical contact; frequently he would be at her side, holding her hand, often he would request a hug. Chris's speech was the most obvious sign of his academic difficulties. His speech was mumbly, often inaudible, and it was very unusual to observe him applying himself to any of the tasks the rest of the class were involved in. In some respects Chris seemed very shy, he did not seem to like a lot of attention being focused on him, and frequently he would find a table to hide under and play quietly while the rest of the class continued in their work. In contrast to this seeming shyness, Chris also had a tendency to anger quickly if he did not get his way. He frequently lost his temper, sometimes becoming violent with both children and adults. As a result of this adults tended to tread very carefully around Chris, and while he was in the mainstream classroom, as long as he did not seem to be disruptive, he would most likely be left to his own devices, largely free of the learning agenda of the classroom.

Chris's difficulties with school were highly complex. Though he had a diagnosis of ADHD and took Ritalin three times a day, nobody really seemed to know under what circumstances this diagnosis had been made. Heather was meant to have copies of such documentation sent to her by the doctor, however in Chris's case this had not happened. Like Kyle, Chris's family was considered to be a big part of Chris's problems and there were several staff who thought that his mother had pushed for a diagnosis to give her medication to make him more manageable at home. From my early impressions of Chris as shy and untalkative, I was surprised when I heard about the diagnosis. The more I observed and worked with Chris, the more I came to perceive the extent to which the medication he was on contributed to the mumbly, shy and non-participative child I had initially come to know. When he was off the medication the effects were certainly discernible as he would run, shout, scream, disrupt and fight. I witnessed him hitting other children and members of staff on several occasions and without medication it seemed he was too much for the school to handle.

To move now to Year Two. The classroom was slightly smaller in size than the Year One class and did not have its own outdoor area. Its appearance in most other respects was very similar, with the same arrangement of desks and carpet space, the same wall displays, the same timetable and the same rules of conduct. The Year Two class was perceived around the school to be a 'problem' year, mainly for the presence of three children with ADHD, one with an additional diagnosis of Autism, another with an additional diagnosis of Conduct Disorder. These children did not make up a 'gang' as in the Year One class, in fact the opposite was true; one of the major challenges here was that they did not get along with one another to the extent that two of them had to be separated at all times. Rachel also showed me the children's work folders. Again there were gaps between higher and lower abilities in various tasks. However, there were several children who had not completed what Rachel considered a satisfactory amount of work, among whom were the aforementioned pathologised children. Rachel also showed me examples of work from some of these children where they had drawn violent images, and ripped or scribbled over the page, which she found a disquieting illustration of underlying problems.

While I chose not to use too much of the data that I collected in Rachel's class, one of the 'problem' boys with whom Rachel and I did concur in some of our perceptions does make up part of the analysis in Chapter 5. Ali was probably the biggest boy in the class, he was boisterous and at times very loud. He was not expected to obey the same rules of the class as everyone else, and he had his own very specific normative ideals concerning 'his' space and 'his' things. He had a diagnosis of ADHD and Autism, for which he received statemented funding for one-on-one support in class five mornings per week. In the afternoon he joined the rest of the class. He was described as quite a 'bright' boy, with a good vocabulary and with the ability to be very mature for his age in his interactions with adults, particularly his teaching assistant, Anna. At times Anna tolerated all manner of shouting, swearing, throwing, punching and kicking in the interests of getting him focused on his work. Frequently this paid off for Anna in the work that she was eventually able to motivate Ali to complete. Often I observed quite touching interactions between the two of them, where both parties would be proud of what they were achieving and some days laughter was the more frequent sound to be heard from them. However, Anna was only there in the morning and in the afternoon Ali's presence became more like Chris's in the Year One classroom. Persuading him into any kind of activity was likely to be an uphill task, and in the interests of the majority he was frequently left to his own devices. However, unlike Chris, more often than not Ali *did* want to get involved with activities, but on his terms, and this produced further management problems for Rachel.

Ali was made highly visible in class by the fact that he had his own assistant, sat at a separate table away from the rest of the class, and by the fact that he was given liberal reign on both noise and movement. The initial position I took up in the Year Two class was on the opposite side of the room to Ali's table, yet my attention was frequently taken by one of his regular shouts, yelps and screams. Though some children seemed to find it more of a distraction than others, it seemed at first that this noise was more normalised for the rest of the class than for me. However, Ali was capable of making it extremely difficult to hear what Rachel or anyone else was saying, he was also prone to getting up from his seat and running round the classroom, or joining in with the main activity, and in these cases he could cause the whole class disruption. In these ways his experience and the experience of those around him contrasted with two of the other three children in Year Two with a diagnosis of ADHD, who were removed from the classroom every morning to the nurture group.

Ross was the other child from this group who did not go to nurture group, and he received neither assistance in class nor an out-of-class intervention. Unfortunately Ross is largely absent from my notes. Part of not wanting teachers to guide me too much according to their own preconceptions of 'problem' children meant that I had not mentioned a particular interest in pathologised children, and therefore Ross had not been pointed out to me. Ross had a diagnosis of ADHD. He was quite a small boy and had a knack of slipping away from notice. His name was very rarely heard for any reason and during structured activities he sat at a desk on the far side of the room from me, out of my field of vision (unlike Year One where my own movement was a bit more free, part of attempting to minimise the distraction I caused in Year Two was placing myself much more out-of-the-way, and, consequently, with a more restricted gaze). It was not until one of my conversations with Heather towards the end of my time in the Year Two classroom, that I became aware of the concerns over Ross's schooling. What I had not observed in Ross was illustrative of his non-participative role at school. He had produced very little work and had very basic levels of literacy and numeracy. He did not seem to enjoy whole group activities or the collective nature of schooling in general. He had very few friends and his ability to 'wind other children up' was one of the reasons offered by both Rachel and Heather for the other two children with ADHD being removed from the class to the nurture group; it is to this intervention I now move.

Nurture groups are an out-of-class intervention designed to help re-integrate children with EBDs into the mainstream. At Alderley there were two nurture groups, one was a Years Four and Five group which was staffed on a full-time basis by a teacher (the only male member of the teaching staff) and an assistant. The other was a Years One and Two group staffed four mornings per week by two teaching assistants, Andrea and Clare. The latter was the group I worked with. About six children regularly attended the group, with two or three others who would attend more sporadically. The regular group contained three children with ADHD: Chris from Year One and the two remaining boys from Year Two, Paul and James. Not pathologised, though thought of as 'at risk' of being so, were Kyle from Year One and a Year Two girl, Lola. The last regular member was a Year One girl, Sam.

The theory and practice of nurture groups is discussed at length in Chapter 7, so I will give only a brief outline here. Nurture groups are designed to provide a 'safe and supportive' environment in which children can *nurture* their senses of *esteem* and *attachment*. Though there is a small amount of structured work time, the emphasis is on building up individual levels of self-confidence and on learning the kinds of skills needed to function in the collective environment of the classroom. A typical day consisted of the group eating breakfast together during which they discussed their previous day at home, then each described how they were feeling that day and why, and then each set themselves a target for the day. Following this there were group activities such as cooking. The group then had an outdoor break before coming back to complete some work before lunch. In the afternoon each child returned to their class, with the exception of James, who only attended school in the morning, and would be picked up, usually by his mother, just before lunch.

In the course of my day at Alderley I would also use the staff room as a space where I could write up my notes as well as talk with the other members of staff. In addition to this, for the last six weeks or so I was at the school, I spent the majority of my time there in conversation with Heather, arranging interviews and generally being available to any requests for assistance (being asked to coax Chris down from a tree providing one memorable example of such requests). I did not see the staff room as a research site in itself, more a chance to *hang about* and become more immersed in the social life of the school. I certainly did not want to be seen as a *spy* within the sanctuary of the staffroom, so, unless otherwise agreed, the conversations that I was part of in the staffroom did not make it into my notes or my analysis. Nevertheless these conversations fed into my perceptions and understandings of the experience of working at Alderley, as well as sometimes guiding my interests in particular children.

The most regular and productive conversations were with Heather. The staffroom and the small room next to it were the nearest things Heather had to her own office, and she was usually to be found there during the school day. Our conversations started with my interest in individual children I had observed in Years One and Two and the nurture group. Heather had been the school SENCO since the amalgamation two years earlier. In this time she had been on a series of professional development courses which she was in the process of combining into a Master's degree. Prior to amalgamation she had been a teaching assistant at one of the previous schools, where she had organised her own nurture group. She was also a mother of a child with special educational needs who had gone through the local school system. Through this personal and professional experience Heather had developed a distinct perspective into the schooling of *problem* children. She was committed to philosophies of inclusion and with her personal experience she had much insight into the *other* side of the derisive school–family discourse. This became a regular point of discussion for us, both of us acknowledging that it might represent a problem for individual children, but also both critical of the speed with which it could be jumped to as an explanation, the inescapable nature of it once reached, and the fatalistic attitude towards solutions that this produced.

It is to this *other* side of the home–school relation that I now turn, with a description of the work carried out with the two families featured in Chapter 6, and the several challenges which were associated with this piece of research. First, it is necessary to briefly situate the family in the context of the study.

## Situating families

Although the means for regulating families are perhaps more indirect than with schools, with no formal inspections or exams to pass, there is no lesser sense in which families are shaped by neo-liberal discourses of *performance* (Vincent, 2000). The New Labour policies around *Every Child Matters* and its associated 'outcome framework' (DFES, 2004, 2006) were part of a broader set of policy principles enshrined under the banner of *safeguarding* (DCSF, 2010). Safeguarding is a discursive formation in its own right; it has become one of the assumed logics upon which new policy can be written, and this has remained true through the most recent change of government. Safeguarding is an interagency network of regulative policies which seek a dual protection; ostensibly the *vulnerable* individual or group of individuals: the mental health or social care *service user*, the *at risk* family, the child with *special educational needs*. Yet benevolent as it might seem, within an economy of power which reproduces vast inequalities in the distribution of financial, social and symbolic forms of capital (Bourdieu, 1984; Bourdieu and Passeron, 1979), the *protection* comes only at the price of the closer regulation of the *vulnerable* according to the needs of social and economic order. Ultimately this results in a deepening *vulnerability*. *Every Child Matters* illustrates this reproduction through its equation of 'being healthy' and 'staying safe' in childhood, with the attainment of future 'economic stability' (see Chapter 7). The *correct* family should therefore be the first line of defence in this guard. The work with families in this study attempts to raise awareness of this *invisible work* (D. Smith, 1987).

As introduced in the previous chapter, institutional ethnography makes people's everyday worlds the point of departure and proceeds by exploring 'the social relations individuals bring into being in and through their actual practices' (D. Smith, 1987, p. 160). The method was first advanced by Smith to bring attention to the many forms of women's work which dominant sociological paradigms tended to conceal; 'in this literature mothers appear in a peculiar way as necessary links in a causal process, but without agency' (pp. 163–4). The objective is to trace this invisible work through the action, intention and rationale of the individual within the context of the social relations which connect the individual world to institutional ideologies and discursive *relations of ruling*. In such a way research of this kind aims to cut through the forms of social knowledge in which mother's work, 'their thinking, the effort and time they have put in, and the varying material conditions under which their work is done do not appear' (D. Smith, 1987, p. 164).

While institutional ethnography was originally conceived as a 'sociology for women' (p. 49), its aim, 'to find the objective correlates of what had seemed a private experience of oppression' (p. 154), does not limit it only to this group. Smith's own concerns have broadened in this regard, stating that the method: 'has to work for both women and men. It has to be a sociology for people' (2005, p. 1). This point is important for the research presented in Chapter 6, where though the mother's voice is often the dominant one, and where it is mothers who are perhaps more tightly regulated by naturalised images, it is also a story of fathers and their related *responsibilisation* (N. Rose, 1999).

## Accessing families

My interview work with families was perhaps the most challenging aspect of this project. This was first felt in relation to research design. In my initial designs I had not envisaged moving outside the school. However, in terms of my initial research objectives, which were concerned with the production of a diagnostic case, there was only a very slight possibility that I would be present in school while an individual child was actually going through such a process. Even if I had been there my access to such sensitive environments would have been problematic. Therefore, I planned the work with families on the basis of exploring individual diagnostic cases. Though these cases would be in the past and, therefore, open to some retrospective *biographical illusion* (Bourdieu, 1987) in their telling, I felt this was a safer strategy than potentially becoming involved in a diagnostic process, expected to mediate some struggle for recognition between home, school and doctor. Once I had done some work in schools I had also appreciated the importance of trying to get inside the other side of the home–school relation. By the time I came to plan my interviews I had completed my work at Kilcott, and the actual interviews themselves were conducted towards the end of my time at Alderley. Therefore, I knew something about what it meant in school to be a *good* or *bad* parent. However, I did not wish to contact families through the same schools in which I was conducting the rest of the research. This was partly because I did not want to be viewed by parents as a representative of the school, which could merely reproduce existing relations, but could also make unnecessary implications about their children's negative school experiences.

Challenges also arose out of the potentially sensitive nature of the material under discussion and the far more individualised and potentially invasive context of the interview. I have already discussed the notion of distance in relation to my work in schools in terms of the different levels of inside/out status I achieved. This relation was inverted with families; this sense of distance became a buffer, a comfort, which I would now be denied. Where my work in schools consisted of negotiating some kind of closeness to my participants, just the mere task of trying to contact families with a view to entering their lives and putting them under scrutiny made me feel uncomfortably close from the outset.

Lastly, there was a representative challenge via my own association with ADHD. This presented a certain challenge to many aspects of this project, however, I felt particularly limited here by the potential interaction of my personal and research world. I was diagnosed at a time when the disorder was not well known at all, and my mother was instrumental in the achievement of my diagnosis. I was certainly unhappy at school, but I did not feel I had any need for a psychiatric diagnosis, and I haven't ever felt that I have grown or been empowered by this description being made of me. Therefore, perhaps there is a sense in which I rather I was never diagnosed. This prompted some uncomfortable questions:

- Does this mean I 'blame' my mother for my diagnosis?
- If I represent mothers critically in this project do I compound this sense of blame?
- Conversely, might concern at this possibility drive me towards an overly sympathetic account?
- Does my own 'positioned rationality' threaten the trustworthiness of my account?

When I first posed the first of these questions to myself I was quite instinctively sure that the answer was 'no'. I was also resentful of being positioned according to these binary oppositions. Yet the remaining questions appeared to still be relevant. Regardless of the first question's status as truth I felt I was required to position myself in relation to them. I hoped that this discomfort could be turned into a more responsible and trustworthy representation, yet prior to actually doing the work, it resulted mainly in apprehension.

I was able to contact potential participants through a colleague at NICE. I arranged to have an email sent out on my behalf by the administrator of a national parent support group for ADHD, who I had been introduced to by one of the members of the guideline development group. In this email I invited respondents who would be willing to participate in a series of interviews discussing their experiences of diagnosis. Initially, those interested were invited to reply through the support group who then notified me and I would send out more detailed participant information.[6] A total of three families volunteered through this process, of these three I managed to arrange a total of three interviews with two families.

The information I provided to families contained a similar brief about my research interests that I provided to schools, with the same opt-out and the same proofing and exclusion rights for the transcript of the interview that I had offered teachers with my fieldnotes. In addition I provided more detailed information about what kind of questions I would be asking, including examples. I provided cautions about the sensitive nature of the subject matter and the potentially distressing circumstances which might be brought to mind. I also offered some details of my own background and my personal association with the topic. I did this for a couple of reasons, which I will now discuss.

First, as with my work in schools, my work with families aspired to a sense of authenticity in the word *participant* via the notion of *active* interviewing (Holstein and Gubrium, 1995). Here there is an attempt to break down the binary of authorised interviewer questioning vulnerable respondent, acknowledging and exploring instead the active co-construction of reality in the interview context. I felt that sharing some personal information from the start might pave the way for this more participatory style of research.

Second, I was attempting to manage my presentation of self. As already discussed there are limiting subject positions available within the various narratives on ADHD, which tend to equate any criticism of the disorder with blaming the family. I wanted to make sure that each of my participants did not perceive me as casting judgement on them in this way. What I perhaps did not appreciate fully at the time was the extent to which I might have been implying the opposite position: that I was there as advocate, and in one interview in particular I got the distinct impression that this was expected. Given that it was never my intention to take such a position, the fact that I might have unwittingly created the impression made me feel as though I had used my personal associations as a manipulative device with which to ingratiate myself with my participants. This threw my interview experience into some disarray, seeming to enact the representative issues that had made me apprehensive about conducting the interviews in the first place.

Through this analysis, I have attempted to inhabit this dichotomy of judge and advocate, in which I enact neither; instead attempting what might be called *critical consciousness raising* (D. Smith, 1987). I think it important to highlight here the extent to which this eventual position was shaped by the difficult process of access I went through with each family.

To move to the more practical challenges of access, one result of the attempt to separate families from schools in my research design was that there was no geographical restriction over where families might have been located. As it turned out the two families with whom I did manage to arrange interviews could not have been much more geographically spread either from each other or from my home, which did limit the number of times I was able to travel to each family. However, I was fortunate in that one family was located in an area that shared several of the features I have posited here as contextually important. Interestingly, the other family, though located in a more affluent area, was the one who felt the most limited by their geography. Below I introduce each family.

The first family I interviewed was made up of mother and father, Louise and Mike Bartlett, and their three sons. Their middle son, Liam, was seven years old at the date of the first interview (30 November 2006) and had been diagnosed with

**TABLE 3.4** Kenard economic activity as a percentage by local authority

|  | LA | District | UK |
|---|---|---|---|
| Economically active: unemployed | 6.64 | 3.94 | 3.35 |
| Economically inactive: sick/disabled | 12.41 | 7.89 | 5.39 |

ADHD aged five. Liam was in a special class at school and his parents were waiting upon a decision about his statementing allowance. When I first met them neither parent was working in order to make time for childcare.

The Bartlett's lived in 'Kenard', a suburb of a large town in South Wales. Once again pit closures had had a major economic impact on this area. Since 1984 the area had seen 23 pits closed, leaving just one active colliery. In a minority of cases pits had been successfully regenerated into museums or conference centres. Table 3.4 shows the ONS figures for the Bartlett's local authority against the national averages.

As Table 3.4 shows, the district in which the Bartlett's lived was economically less active than the national average, and the local authority was significantly lower than this. Furthermore, these figures went well beyond the marginal percentages recorded for the two schools above. In terms of the ONS socio-economic classifications, only 9 per cent were employed in lower managerial occupations, with routine and semi-routine occupations making up over 35 per cent.

The Bartlett's lived on a large housing estate, which Louise described as 'working class', stating that most of the houses there were council owned. However, the Bartlett's had plenty to say in favour of the local area: they had extended family in the area who helped them out with childcare, and they were very happy with the local services available to them, their school, their General Practitioner (GP), and their Child and Adolescent Mental Health Services (CAMHS), from whom they received multi-agency support for Liam.

The second family I interviewed was made up of mother and father, Sian and Neil Hyland, and their two sons. Their eldest son, Charlie, had been diagnosed with ADHD at age seven, but had subsequently progressed to secondary school, and by the date of interview (14 March 2007) was approaching his GCSE exams. The Hylands lived in a village near a small town, 'Cooksam', in a remote, rural part of East England. Sian had not worked since prior to Charlie's diagnosis, though Neil was in full-time employment.

Economically, the area compared favourably to the other areas so far discussed, as Table 3.5 shows:

**TABLE 3.5** Cooksam economic activity as a percentage by local authority

|  | LA | District | UK |
|---|---|---|---|
| Economically active: unemployed | 3.23 | 2.60 | 3.35 |
| Economically inactive: sick/disabled | 4.32 | 2.91 | 5.39 |

As Table 3.5 shows, both the unemployed and the economically inactive figures, though above the local average, are below the national average. The socio-economic classifications also reflected greater economic affluence, with over 20 per cent in the lower managerial class, with routine and semi-routine making up just under 20 per cent between them. Sian considered both herself and the area to be broadly middle class. However, in contrast to the Bartlett's praise for the local area, Sian felt extremely cut-off from most of her family, she had also had many years of what she considered to be inefficient and unsupportive services from schools, GPs and CAMHS.

I originally intended to conduct at least two interviews of around one hour each with each family, with a possible third interview to involve children. The first two interviews would be concerned with exploring the before, during and after of diagnosis, first with just the principal carer and second with both parents. In addition to these interviews I was also keen to collect any documents related to the diagnostic process that the families were willing to share. These might have been in the form of letters between home, school and doctor, medical or psychological reports, individual education plans, report cards, disciplinary procedures and so on.

The actual experience of conducting the interviews did not fit this schedule, and I was required to make various departures from it as circumstance demanded, which I will now describe.

Both the interviews I conducted with the Bartlett's involved both parents. Both parents had given up work and as they were both at home it seemed to go unsaid that they would both be involved. I did nothing to question this, and in analysis some interesting dynamics emerged in having both parents there. While they usually presented a unified voice, it was clear even in the moment that they had differences in perspective and approach, different ways of conceptualising difficult or hurtful situations, and different proposals for managing these. There were several times when Mike was out of the room either fetching refreshments or attending to their youngest son, who was also at home. One such occasion sticks in my mind very clearly for the slight discomfort which my questioning had just prompted. Louise had until this point presented herself as strong and determined; prepared to do whatever it took to gain the recognition she sought for her son. In this one moment this guard came down a little and she talked of the 'hopelessness' that she felt in the face of what she saw as a lifetime of suffering that Liam faced. A short silence followed in which Louise played nervously with the small silver cross she wore around her neck, and I wondered whether I could take this issue any further. Mike re-entered with tea and biscuits and the moment passed.

The second point of departure was in the material covered. As I was asking very open questions and trying to base follow-up questions from within the answers I was offered, I had not intended any great control over the material, preferring to be driven by those things that seemed significant to participants. This combined with the fact that I had not predicted how much each interviewee might have to say about a given topic. Louise and Mike were both very keen to open up and share everything they could, and they both had a perspective to offer on everything I asked of them. Originally planned for one hour, the first interview lasted over two, in which time most of the ground I had planned for the first two interviews, and more, had already been covered.

This left me feeling very positive about the experience, but also unsure of where to go next. I decided to conduct the second interview around a joint reflection on what had already been said, as well as hearing about the intervening experience with the Bartlett's statement application for which they were awaiting a decision with guarded optimism.

However, by the time I returned for the second interview, Louise and Mike knew that they had not received the funding they had applied for. This seemed to set the tone for the second interview experience, which was also beset by further problems. First, I had sent copies of the transcript from the first interview, along with some brief comments and reflections. When I asked, neither parent had anything to add; in fact Louise said she had not read beyond the first couple of pages. This of course was entirely their choice, however, it did not feed the discussion I had hoped for. Second, about two minutes into our conversation, my digital recorder malfunctioned and could not be recovered. This meant that on top of the usual practical demands of the interview I was required to notate as fully as I could. This means I produced only a five-page impressionistic report for the second interview compared to the 30-page transcript from the first.

The positive upshot of this was that with much of my attention devoted to noting what I could from their answers, Louise and Mike used the empty space to ask me questions about my experiences with the disorder, my schooling and what strategies I had developed to cope with the various deficits. Most of the questions that day moved in the reverse direction; I became the respondent, offering what I could from my experience that might have been valuable to them. It is extremely unfortunate that I do not have a transcript of what was the most *active* interview I have managed to conduct, or perhaps in this case, be conducted by – but if I did then the activation might not have occurred. It seems surprising to me now that at this time I had not thought at length about the things that Louise and Mike were asking me, as such I found the experience extremely challenging. This not only prompted some very productive self-identity work, but also offered me an indication of some of the demands that researchers are likely to place participants under.

The last departure from the original plans was that Louise felt that Liam was too young to be put in the interview context, however informal I might have made it. Though this was disappointing I of course respected Louise's wishes. In fact I did still get a chance to chat a bit more informally with Liam on both occasions as Mike offered to drive me back to the railway station on the way to which he would pick Liam up from school. On the second occasion Mike invited me in to the classroom and introduced me to the class teacher and the three of us spoke briefly together. Then I would chat with Liam in the car on the way to the station. These conversations lasted no more than five minutes in each instance; however, they contributed to that sense of quality *thickness* which I took forward into my analysis of the interviews. The difference in Liam's familiarity with me between the first and second encounters also left me feeling hopeful for future possibilities of engaging younger participants in research.

To move now to the experience of interviewing the Hylands: I was only able to conduct one interview, which just included Sian, as Neil was at work. I was also unable to arrange an interview with Charlie. Sian had initially been quite keen for me to talk to Charlie, as she felt sure that he would have an interesting perspective to offer. Unfortunately the fact that Charlie was approaching his GCSE exams, combined with the practical difficulties for me in getting to the Hyland's remote corner of the country foreclosed this possibility.

In terms of covering the material I had planned for the first two interviews, the fact that I only conducted one was not a limiting factor, as the interview lasted well over two hours. Additionally Sian had looked out every document she could find relating to the long process of Charlie's diagnosis. This process had involved several battles between Sian, various schools, GPs and specialist services, and I took home three large box-files full of information. This included three years of a diary which Sian had kept everyday, tracing the complete story from her earliest concerns over Charlie's behaviour. I have not used this diary directly in my presentation of data, as there was simply not room within my study design to do it justice. However, reading the diary gave me that same sense of immersed quality, in the moment-to-moment insight it gave me into Sian's personal struggle, which, as with Louise, might have remained well concealed beneath the strong image she presented through the interview.

The descriptive work of this chapter has been concerned with contextualising and providing a sense of what it was like to *be there* ahead of the analysis, which now follows and in which the data becomes more detached from these real life circumstances of its production. The time spent on this chapter is considered an essential component of ethnography in attempting to draw the reader close to the sense of the *everyday* in each context, and the aspirations and constraints experienced by both participants and researcher in its construction.

# 4

# ROUTINE CONDUCT

## with Pat Thomson[1]

ADHD is popularly understood to be a condition which resides in the person. In this scenario, the school is an innocent bystander, a container for the *maladjusted child*. To date, the school's potential complicity in the construction of the disorder has not been extensively explored (though see, Graham, 2007a, 2007d, 2008). Here, this argument is pursued empirically through the first presentation of ethnographic data, collected from Kilcott Infants. The focus here is on micro-integrating practices of routinisation. These practices, material manifestations of normative discourses of good behaviour, enact a medicalised episteme, including some children while excluding others. Those who fail to conform to the norms are singled out for *special education* or treatment, one form of which is a diagnosis of ADHD.

In investigating elements of what has been termed school's *hidden curriculum*, Jackson *et al.* (1993) offer two categories that seek to govern moral life in the classroom: moral instruction and moral practice. This chapter takes up this notion of moral practice, understood as the embodiment of certain moral subject positions through the regulatory activities of the classroom. Thornberg (2007) has taken these categories and applied them to the moral inconsistencies of everyday school rules. Here, we seek a prior discursive plane through an exploration of school routines, which function to distribute the subject positions which are enacted through regulative practices. For Thornberg (2007), 'everyday life is maintained by its manifestations in routines' (p. 403), here we argue that, beyond 'maintenance', routine has a prior, constitutive function in shaping the conditions by which moral regulation is experienced.

Routine has played a longstanding role in medical and pedagogical assumptions concerning *correct*, or perhaps *corrective*, approaches to schooling children with ADHD (Bailey, 2007; Hjorne, 2006; Laurence and McCallum, 2009). These approaches tend to make an assumption about the *normality* of the routine, against which is held the *abnormal* child incapable of internalising its demands. From this assumption the corrective solution is assumed to be an intensification of routine conduct. This illustrates the shared assumptions that exist in the management of conduct between such diverse social institutions as schools, hospitals, prisons and the armed forces (Foucault, 1977). While recognising that routine provides a set of management tactics essential to collective schooling, we wish to problematise this 'one size fits all' mechanism and its associated episteme, by highlighting their combined capacity to divide and internalise.

## Normative routines

This chapter focuses on the normative routines at work in the two classrooms where Simon was working. Normative routines are productive and essential. Ian Hunter (1994) argues that the pastoral power of schools is necessary for society and for individuals, but, through its ability to divide and exclude, it is simultaneously damaging to a minority. To find routines in classroom life is expected: what is at issue is the kind and degree of normative/exclusionary work they do.

Assumptions regarding the disciplinary function of schools are ground deep within expectations as to how a *good teacher* might react to disruption in the class. The *good teacher* is expected to enact pastoral and punitive disciplinary structures within the school as well as communicate with others, both within the school (other teachers, the SENCO, or head teacher), and outside (the parents, behavioural support teams). Far from unexpected, these activities constitute familiar everyday scenarios in schools.

The research for this study took place at Kilcott Infants (see Chapter 3), where Simon took on the role of teaching assistant, working mainly in the Year One classroom. The classrooms where Simon worked were dominated by routines. Routine prescribed a correct way to enter the class in the morning, to leave in the afternoon, to wash hands before lunch, and line up for assembly, to interact with other children, sit and listen to the teacher, speak in public, sit on chairs, use a pair of scissors, or read a book. As the following song, which the Year One children sang several times during a 'free moment' says:

> Only one can talk at a time; So what shall I do?
> Listen while you talk to me; And then talk back to you.
>
> *(fn 21–9)*[2]

This drill was an instance of young children being taught to *do school* (Comber, 1999). Their bodies and speech were to conform to teacher and school determined rules of conduct. However, more than simply regulating behaviour was involved, rather such instances were constitutive of dis/ordered subject positions. That is to say, that within these classrooms a secure and consistent knowledge of *who I am* was contingent on the production of a secure and consistent knowledge of *where I am*, *what I am doing* and *how I am doing it*. Gidden's (1991) suggests that 'the discipline of routine helps to constitute a "formed framework" for existence by cultivating a sense of "being", and its separation from "non-being", which is elemental to ontological security' (p. 39). Under this conception the rejection of, or failure to internalise, the routine is read as a *non-classroom-being* requiring intervention. However, routine does not just help one to constitute one's own 'formed framework'; routine is itself a *ready-formed framework*, an external form of discipline, predicated upon the needs of managing a population (Laurence and McCallum, 2009), which functions for others to know *where I am*, *what I am doing* and *how I am doing it*, thus invoking the normative order. Authoritative others such as teachers and teaching assistants not only know *what I am doing* but are also in a position to say whether or not what is being done is satisfactory; thus producing the norm.

Routines were established through the establishment of infinite, normatively regulated, miniature orders in the classroom which worked to create il/legitimacy in the times, places, movements and utterances of the school day. Routinisation emerged as the overarching strategy of classroom management, 'designed to permit the possibility of certain things considered "natural" and "normal" to children' (Walkerdine, 1986, p. 67). It was one of the 'general forms of domination', which create 'subjected and practiced bodies, "docile" bodies' (Foucault, 1977, p. 138).

The routines in the classrooms at Kilcott were marked by and through eight functions (see Table 4.1 below). Functions 1–4 and 6 are derived from a classroom observation study of power relations by Jenny Gore (1995), 5 and 8 from a study of discipline in the nursery by Chris Holligan (2000) and 7 emerged from the fieldnotes. The terms and definitions shown are those used in the original publications, except where stated in discussion.

Analysis begins with each individual category before looking at some of the ways in which the categories overlap and communicate with each other.

## Surveillance

Surveillance is a foundational routine and a component of all the others: for bodies to be acted upon they must first be made visible; one of the reasons to distribute, segregate and differentiate is to better survey.

**TABLE 4.1** Routine functions

---

1. **Surveillance:** Supervising, closely observing, watching, threatening to watch, avoiding being watched.
2. **Distribution:** Dividing into parts, arranging, ranking bodies in space.
3. **Segregation:** Setting up enclosures, partitioning, creating functional sites.
4. **Differentiation:** Normative classification of ability and difference amongst individuals or groups.
5. **Examination:** Checking, recording, measuring and displaying ability or progress.
6. **Self-regulation:** Regulative practices directed at the self.
7. **Authorisation:** Making an individual's authority legitimate, routinising an individual's presence.
8. **Docility:** Rendering bodies still and/or silent, invoking passivity.

---

Simon spent most of the fieldwork in a Year One class, and much time in conversation with the teacher, Sarah. Sarah knew his research interests in discipline and behaviour, and offered him a list of 'ones to watch', which contained the names of six children, five of whom were boys. Such children were often the focus of conversation, for example on one day a teaching assistant (Clare) talked on two separate occasions about a child (Andrew) who she said came from a family where 'the men ... were all quite aggressive and violent – and she saw this is a partial explanation for his disruption' (fn 14–9). Sarah shared this perspective on the harmful influence of the family: 'whilst on an outing to the forest ... Sarah [said] "well you do know his background don't you?"' (fn 14–9). There is a double surveillance at work here, both of the child's behaviour, and of the family circumstances. Such instances of surveillance were frequent, with the same operant 'discourse of derision' (Kenway, 1990) tying child behaviour to family circumstance, and providing a persistent example of the way texts can communicate with each other under particular conditions.

Several instances of surveillance often came together in the teacher's conversation:

> Christopher [a 'one to watch'] is the youngest child in the class ... Sarah and I had a chat about him ... Sarah described Rosa [Christopher's mother] as 'carrying a lot of emotional baggage', saying that she had 'broken down' during the meeting. Sarah clearly didn't think much of her as a parent and thought Christopher was probably spoilt.
>
> *(fn 21–9)*

Here developmentalism acted as a benchmark for surveillance, which then moved outside the classroom to the family. The authoritative gaze which her position as teacher gave her legitimated Sarah's evaluation of Christopher and Rosa.

These regular conversations about children marked a mutuality of surveillance between Sarah and Simon. Sometimes Simon would 'report back' to Sarah on the day's behaviour, which aided Sarah's surveillance. Frequently these same instances allowed Simon to survey Sarah as part of his research agenda. Both Simon and Sarah's descriptions: 'ones to watch' and 'on the lookout for', provide two everyday examples of speech which become less benevolent when viewed through the lens of surveillance.

The combined effects of surveillance in the classroom made an immediate impression on Simon; in only the second week at school reflecting that:

> the amount of attention that becomes focused on individual children ... is important ... The more intensely you scrutinize something the more likely you are to find a problem with it. Andrew has people – peers, teachers, parents, head teachers – always on the lookout for him to do something. He has reports written about him, IEPs [individual education plans] written for him, regular interviews between teachers and parent. A file seems to grow on these children.
>
> *(fn 21–9)*

## Distribution

Like surveillance, distribution is a continuous and generalised practice within schools. If surveillance is the primary strategy, then distribution is the primary technique for achieving it. This technique can be located at the most basic levels of school organisation: children and teachers are distributed within school into individual classrooms; children are distributed at most times throughout their school lives according to age, subject and ability; within the classroom, children are distributed according to various different spatial arrangements, separately on desks or all together on the carpet. Attention and assistance is also distributed, for example, in group work, where the teacher circulates around tables. Such distributed assistance is also simultaneously the means of keeping watch on what children are doing. The surveilling function of an effective distribution is also noticeable in its absence:

> if badgers [name of class grouping] were generally disruptive, rabbits were even worse – Marjorie [a teaching assistant] was called away to have her photo taken and two successive teachers then came and attempted to lead some sort of activity. The problem is that there is no routine to Wednesday afternoon, because of the PPA [teacher's protected planning time] splitting into groups and having different teachers and moving rooms – all provides plenty of scope for disruption.
>
> *(fn 21–9)*

When teachers were distributed away from their routine places into the staffroom for the PPA time, the disruption that this might cause had to some degree been predicted; classes had already been distributed into groups and each child was wearing a name badge.[3] Additionally, extra staff had been drafted in to offer Drama and French classes. However, as noted, the routine distribution had been disrupted and this, in turn, produced more disruption. The proposed solution was as follows:

> What has now been decided is that the teachers who come in to do French and Drama are going to have the whole group of badgers while rabbits are split between the two classes and then swap over.
>
> *(fn 21–9)*

Where the ordinary means of distribution have not been effective, this new solution proposed an intensification of distribution, based on a *divide and rule* strategy, involving smaller groups of children split between more adults.

## Segregation

Segregation shares strategy and tactic with distribution through the assignment of bodies to particular spaces. Gore (1995) uses the term 'space' to describe this function, however, in order to distinguish from 'distribution' we use 'segregation'.

While distribution uses space to confer a generalised authority, for example, of adults over children, segregation denotes a more individualised practice and carries a more immediate and recognisable degree of exclusion than distribution, in which a 'normal' and 'marginal' begin to emerge.

The responsibilities of the teaching assistant were frequently associated with practices of segregation; drawing out a small group of children to be partitioned away from the main group. With this segregation came implicit notions about the child's ability levels. Usually, though not always, this had a negative implication. The following excerpt is taken from a whole-school assembly:

> I alone stayed in assembly with Margaret [the head teacher]. I soon inherited Cameron [a Year Two boy] from Susan's class who requires pretty much non-stop attention and pays little notice to what's going on. Margaret also brought another disruptive influence to sit by me.
>
> *(fn 14–9)*

Such segregating practices were commonly seen in activities involving large groups, as in the example above; individualised segregations were the result of a judgement having been made about the child's suitability for the main social group. In these situations the child was physically and visibly marginalised.

Segregation does not always come with such a socially visible connotation; it might be a way in which the teacher uses the resources available to offer variety and get the required work done:

> This morning I've been doing mainly computer work again, with a small group ... in the library looking for pictures on the national portrait gallery website.
>
> *(fn 5–10)*

The library was in the centre of the school, partitioned from the classes it adjoined by curtains. Even though segregation was present the activity was a relatively appealing one, it was certainly not a punishment. However, there was still some order maintenance going on in terms of the *difficult* selection of children Sarah had chosen.

As this scenario progressed, the library's relative seclusion from the classroom might well have worked to temporarily lower the net of surveillance on these children: the challenge of the task required Simon to guide children one at a time, which caused disruption amongst those waiting their turn. Simon's authority was also clearly not considered equivalent to Sarah's, which he discovered through the effective use of Sarah as a threat if good behaviour were not restored; surveillance by proxy. Eventually, Simon was forced to complete most of the task himself in order to 'get the job done' on time. As such, this scenario underlines fundamental connections between the school's need to perform and the kinds of disciplinary apparatus it employs to do so, while also providing an indication of the potential paucity of educational experiences driven primarily by disciplinary considerations.

## *Differentiation*

Performance and accountability in schooling, working towards Key Stages, exami-nations, and inspections, makes a necessity of practices that differentiate children, teachers and schools from one another. The point at which the *tail* of performance *wags the dog* of schooling is the point at which we can refer to these environments as *performative* (Jeffrey and Troman, 2012). The principle focus in this study on pedagogy should not eclipse the extent to which pedagogy has been re-defined by the curricular changes that have come about since the extension of market forces into schools (Gerwitz *et al.*, 1995; Gleeson and Husbands, 2001). In setting up an image of the future *normal* or *able* school child via a list of curricular achieve-ments, the need to construct environments that are conducive to generating this future image is also produced. 'Getting the job done' for the teacher and assistant is intimately tied up with mandated attainment and accountability, and forces the need to differentiate. This is in line with the then current Primary National Strategy in England, which positively highlighted the need for differentiation, interpreted as necessary for inclusion (DFES, 2005).

> This morning I was assigned to helping each child in turn to design their 'special person badge' on the computer. Each week one child is chosen as the special person and they get to take the badger diary home and write about their week. Helping children do this was great because I got them one at a time to do something they enjoyed and the various tasks involved gave me some idea of the spread of 'ability levels'. Most of the children displayed good mouse control – which Sarah had asked me to take note of. When it came to writing their name using the keyboard, levels of ability were much more mixed. Lorraine, Laura and Gina were the most confident, Christopher and Leo were the only two who really struggled.
>
> *(fn 21–9)*

Several differentiations were in operation here. The 'prize' of the 'special person award' for those judged as performing the best was not restricted to curricular achievement, but was about the ways in which they produced this achievement: conduct in class, involvement in group activities, helpfulness, politeness, sociability. The special person award, therefore, encapsulates the image of the well-adjusted, *uniform* school child (Meadmore and Symes, 1996).

In designing the badge children were further differentiated according to their 'fine motor skills'; micro-level bodily control. This differentiation was made possible for Simon through the 'enjoyable' notion of having pupils segregated 'one at a time' in order to assess their ability levels better. Tellingly, this was early in Simon's time at school and such a differentiation was one of the ways he sought to gain familiarity and 'know' certain things about certain children. He then spontaneously embodied the differentiating discourse, when beyond the mouse control he had been asked to observe, he also ranked children according to their ability to use the keyboard. Given that Simon's interest in behaviour only mirrors one of the most continuous everyday responsibilities of the teaching assistant, such differentiating opportunities are key to the ways in which assistants' responsibilities are organised, according to 'ones to watch'.

Through surveillance and differentiation, the 'file' that was previously observed to 'grow' on these children works to inscribe the inter-relation of power and knowledge upon them, in a self-reproducing process. In many instances, Sarah's prior knowledge of her class, the prior differentiations that she had made, guided her decisions regarding efficient distribution and segregation.

Sarah would segregate a small group with Simon to attempt to raise these children's 'rating' on a particular task. On one occasion Simon reports having been able to successfully re-enter one child into the main group, which left just one child, Christopher:

> He really struggled with both the task itself and paying attention to it. His number understanding is seriously behind the majority – unable to identify individual numbers up to ten, let alone teens. The other major problem is his attention which is, in Sarah's words, 'that of a gnat'.
>
> *(fn 5–10)*

While Simon has drawn attention to Sarah's description of Christopher's attention span, in the moment this did not prompt him to reconceive as 'distracted' or 'disinclined' Christopher's 'inability' to identify numbers. The one-on-one segregation had increased Simon's authority and allowed him to confer further differentiation upon Christopher in which both his poor ability and Sarah's prior knowledge reinforced one another. The extent to which Simon was able to progress at all with the task was limited by Christopher's restless behaviour:

> he was very bored ... kept looking round, playing with things on the table and knocking his chair – to the extent that he knocked it over and ended up on the floor.
>
> *(fn 5–10)*

Eventually, frustrated by this behaviour, Simon invoked his authority through a harsh statement:

> I said 'If you can't get this then you won't get anything else!' which I was later appalled at really.
>
> *(fn 5–10)*

Here, Simon came up against the reality of the low achieving, inattentive and fidgety child: a more and more frequent player on the classroom scene if medical diagnostic rates are to be believed. This reality is important; Simon failed to 'get the job done' even under the 'ideal surveillance' of the one-on-one segregation. Simon interpreted this failure partly through a self-perception of relative non-expertise, before visiting his frustration on the child in what can be seen as a manipulative and deficit-ridden comment. This comment 'appalled' Simon for two reasons: first, he had unreflectively been spoken by the discourses of the school of which he was most critical, second, the continuous cycle of differentiations that we have been describing through which the unruly child must become the literate pupil, give the comment a discomforting resonance of *truth*.

## Examination

Examination plays a fundamental and well-acknowledged role within contemporary schooling. It also has a relatively obvious place within the discussion of the functions so far. The image of 'school exams' illustrates this. Under 'exam conditions' pupils are segregated from the rest of the school, distributed on individual tables row-by-row, at all times under the surveilling gaze of both invigilator and clock, made docile by the requirement for silence, and differentiated according to their performance – both in their conduct while being examined and in the results of that examination.

In one lesson the children listened to a magic story, and then were tasked with creating their own spell inspired by it, writing it down, and then presenting it to the rest of the class. In a 'typical' classroom strategy, Sarah distributed children into a number of groups informed by prior differentiations which allowed her to 'spread' ability levels. Previous examinations had indicated the need for some children to be taken out of class for extra work on literacy or numeracy. In such instances Simon was responsible for the 'pool' of children from which this segregation was taken, giving him responsibility for a rolling group of individuals. This segregation allowed Simon to attempt to achieve the task's aim through a differentiation and delegation of the group. Simon's own examination, namely what he was accountable for, was to 'get the job done' and this had particular challenges given the 'lower ability levels' and constantly changing personnel of this group:

> I had a major breakthrough with Christopher, who having seemed characteristically detached and disinterested in the exercise so far, suddenly came out with a full two line spell to write down. As this was such a major breakthrough I really wanted to get the whole group involved in writing it down and saying it together.
>
> *(fn 2–11)*

Prior differentiations of Christopher had informed both Simon's judgement of this 'breakthrough' and his desire for the group's 'successful' examination. Here he had given Christopher a dominant role in the group, however, Christopher was then removed from the group. Perceiving an impending 'failure', Simon manipulated both group and task:

> With or without the sentence written, we had to get it together to read the spell out. I went through it about ten times, but felt that it wasn't really

going in with anyone except Anthony. So when it came to do it in front of everyone else I did it with them – whispering prompts where needed.

*(fn 2–11)*

The task was judged a success, but Simon was only to fabricate this 'pass' (for himself and the group) on the basis of an implicit pre-failure of the children, whereby he judged them incapable of performing the task on their own. Once again this presents as problematic the pre-ordering of achievement by examination.

## Self-regulation

This category is the most problematic in terms of its distinction from others. In the examination example, above, Simon was attempting to regulate himself according to the position of authority he had been given, and the examination that this implied. However, he had only fabricated his self-improvement; coercing the children through numerous instances of differentiation, segregation and examination, culminating in his implicit failure of them.

Self-regulation uses Gore's (1995) 'self' category, which she reserved mainly for private self-directed reflection. Because of the reflexive relation between researcher and object in this chapter, the category has been given a more formative position. The new category offers the opportunity to introduce some distinction into the movements of regulation and normalisation so far discussed. In doing so we hope to develop some contrast to the negative implications of segregation and examination.

'Self-regulation' is generally preferable to external regimes of discipline. For Foucault (1977) external discipline is manifest in prisons and the asylum. In Iris Young's (1990) terms, this form of discipline *dominates* subjectivity to the extent that alternative conditions are not available. Heuristically speaking, self-regulation provides opportunities for a motivated participation. Instead of *dominating* it attempts to *optimise* (Foucault, 1981b), though for children in school this still occurs according to received definitions of acceptable conduct. In demarcating some space for self-regulation, Simon's experience in a Year One and Year Two drama group is offered.

Drama was one of the subjects, along with French, which Kilcott introduced to provide some cover for teacher PPA time. The strategic part played by these subjects was, therefore, to regulate through distribution; a strategy made very clear after the first week's failure to maintain order, when the two subjects were used to divide and rule the most difficult groups. Within the drama group the teacher, Amy, introduced a regulative technology which combined several of the functions already described. More than any other group, however, she also introduced opportunities for children to perform a motivated self-regulation.

For the first few weeks Amy would begin each session with a rundown of the rules which she hoped would ensure the smooth running of the drama and allow the class to complete the session in the relatively short time available. There were signals which denoted when a child should be sitting in a circle, freezing on the spot, or instantly silent. There were positive incentives for good behaviour in gold stars and a chance to hit the metal gong, which Amy would bring in at the end of each session. There was a traffic light system to sanction behaviour, where after being given a 'sad face' and 'cloudy sad face' the third warning would be a trip to the 'sad chair', visibly excluded from the drama until told otherwise. Amy also had a tactic she used quite regularly to maintain low noise levels: she talked so quietly that were there any noise her instructions would not be heard. So far, this seems little different to many other sanction/reward systems of regulation, however, the effectiveness of the 'whispering tactic' hints at what Amy was also attempting to do, in persistently referring to 'the drama' as the ultimate rationale for good behaviour, in so doing attempting to enact a motivated self-regulation.

As a subject which gives more freedom of movement and mind than is customary in other classroom activities, drama might present the teacher with more opportunities with which to enact a motivated self-regulation in children. However, there is also more scope for disruption, and if there is too much disruption, the product of the excitement provided by the situation, then the adventure of the drama also has the potential to comply in its own counter-productivity. Amy's response to this danger was to try and make something sacred from drama, to use the children's existing motivation for it to convince them that only through a 'tempered' subjectivity (T. Miller, 1993) towards the drama would they extract the most from it. Amy also came armed with a 'technology of regulation' through which she attempted to achieve her aims. The first requirement was an internalisation of the objectives and rationale of 'the drama'; it constituted the social order of the situation, and it was one in which Amy wanted to get everyone invested. Through an assumption that the majority would want such an order to be delivered, Amy was able to justify the use of sometimes exclusionary techniques of regulation for the maintenance of an order in which, compared to the typical classroom situations discussed here, the children had some relative ownership of the means of production.

This example is relatively clear in offering children the chance to regulate themselves according to something that they were motivated to be involved in, and yet, as the discussion suggests, even within such attempts there might be elements of exclusion, persuasion and coercion (Amy's disciplinary apparatus and her whispering tactic designed to produce 'docility'). The *clearness* of this as an example of self-regulation can be seen in comparison to the French group, which shared the divide and rule of PPA time. The French teacher's willingness to take on the bigger group resulting from this redistribution was to ensure that every child would have a chair, that dominant groups would be split, that all children wear name badges, and that there would be silence unless otherwise stated. There is a sense, therefore, in which Amy's tactics are exonerated principally in comparison to those of the French teacher.

What makes self-regulation of this kind so difficult to distinguish is that the boundary between 'motivation' and 'coercion' is necessarily difficult to draw, because of the essential investment of both in social relations. This difficulty is made more acute in the context of the school and the everyday, sanctioned coercion of adult–child power relations (Cannella and Viruru, 2004). The possible distinction is, therefore, contingent on further contextual variables such as the extent to which the children have been informed of and participated in the conditions by which the social order has been fashioned. Motivation of the kind exemplified here needs to be distinguished from 'carrot and stick' type reward and response sequences, where the child only internalises a self-referential desire for the reward offered, rather than a motivational rationale towards the task. Such external systems are present in the gold stars and gongs, the cloud faces and sad chairs of Amy's disciplinary apparatus. These are available should the motivational rationale of 'the drama' fail.

## Authorisation

Authorisation is used here to describe the attempt made by those in authority to confer legitimate authority on others. Once again this category has in part emerged here due to the reflexive position of researcher-object; a consistent component of Simon's work was attempting to produce himself as 'authoritative'. However, there are several commonplace examples of this category: the use of pupil 'monitors', responsible for the protection of a particular task – library monitor, dinner monitor, book monitor, milk monitor and so on, and 'mentors', responsible for the protection of a particular body, a new pupil for example. Here segregation is used in combination with authorisation to promote the 'norms' of good behaviour to which others must aspire, via their embodiment in a trusted role model. The 'protection' inherent in the attempt to legitimate another's authority is the social order of the classroom and school: the routine.

Awareness of authorising as a category arose from the unfamiliar role that Simon adopted in the classroom. The teaching assistant lacks the authority of the teacher, yet within class their presence and their authority must be seen as legitimate if they are to usefully participate in protecting order:

> Margaret … had sent the kids out early, only to realise that there was no TA out there – so I was asked. As soon as I got outside I encountered an argument – Kilcott has a new set of tyres attached to the ground which the children play on. It is obviously highly popular as (unbeknown to me) only one group can use it at a time – so I initially worsened things by saying 'Can't you all share it?'.
>
> *(fn 14–9)*

Only one group was authorised to use the equipment but the attempt to authorise Simon to cover a threat to routine functioning assumed knowledge he did not possess – the strategy was thus counterproductive.

Sometimes the children's perception of Simon as 'non-authority' was a barrier to maintaining order, as in the example of the segregating library task, where he fell back on the legitimate authority of Sarah. In the example of 'the examination' he found the only way to project himself as 'authoritative' or even 'adequate' was through coercion of the children.

The 'special person' on whom teachers confer particular responsibilities, awards or privileges is an example of an 'authorised' child, and stands in contrast to the *abnormal* child who has *special needs*. Both are singled out and differentiated in relation to routines. Children who are *delayed* or inappropriately behaved are authorised to undertake routine tasks in order to help them learn what is required. In this latter case, routine is assumed to have an integrative, even therapeutic function. We suggest that in order to achieve this integrative aim the routine must first separate and differentiate.

## Docility

Docility has been dealt with last of all, because more than any of the other categories docility is the desired product to which the generative energy of all the other mechanisms is directed. Proverbial assumptions regarding categories such as surveillance ('seen but not heard', 'out of sight out of mind') or distribution/segregation ('divide and rule'), reflect the rationale of the field of continuous visibility. The school day abounds with instances of the docile directive: 'shhh', 'be quiet', 'sit still', 'legs crossed arms folded', 'hands up before speaking', 'form an orderly queue', 'silence, I'm speaking'. The song which was cited at the beginning of this chapter illustrates this admirably:

> Only one can talk at a time; So what shall I do?
> Listen while you talk to me; And then talk back to you.
>
> *(fn 21–9)*

This drill not only contains abstract directives to make oneself docile, but also, repeated by the children around 20 times in this instance, provides a concrete strategy by which docility can be produced: connecting the noun and verb of discipline. If a child fails to internalise these directives then they are made visible, once visible they are *recognisable* (Butler, 1997) according to particular knowledge epistemes. Currently fashionable epistemes in early years schooling are those of child psychology and psychiatry (Bailey, 2010).

## Time/space routinisation

We have described the function of routine as bringing together bodies in space, where it determines and polices *appropriate* conduct. Within this order maintenance, consistency over time is key; for the routine to appear rational and legitimate it must be enacted in the same way every day. Routine has an acknowledged place as a therapeutic device in the schooling of EBDs (Bailey, 2007; Hjorne, 2006), where both equity and efficiency depend on the enactment of routine in a consistent, unchanging manner (Sellman, 2009). Through this temporal and situated rhythm (Lefebvre, 2004), the routine constructs a social order according to what ought to be happening in a given place at a given time and in a given way. In so doing, routine prescribes what becomes the classroom's naturalised ontology; transforming the conditional nature of reality into a predictable and knowable order; arrhythmia can be exciting, but it is inevitably abnormal.

At Kilcott days generally had a regular and reoccurring pattern. Using our routine functions as interpretive frames, we present below a timetable (Table 4.2), typical of a morning at Kilcott. Next to each activity's description is our interpretation of the strategic function it fulfils.

The activities in Table 4.2 illustrate the interaction between the categories and the contribution this makes to the docile functioning of the classroom.

The frequent appearance of 'distribution' suggests that it plays an important role. Perhaps the reasons why it appears so often is because it acts on/for/with a number of other functions, such as surveillance and docility. By creating legitimate and illegitimate spaces, distributing allows the entry of another frequently appearing function; differentiation. Differentiating ability to follow one's distributed order would frequently seem to be directly related to protecting the routine itself; if one is sitting well, then one's reward for sitting well is often to be the 'leader' of the

**TABLE 4.2**  Kilcott Infants: routine timetable

| Time/Activity | Description | Function |
|---|---|---|
| 8.45–9.00 'Arrival' | Hang up coat and store activity book | Surveillance |
| | Write name on board | Differentiation |
| | Sit on carpet with a book | Self-regulation |
| 9.00–9.30 'Registration' | 'Silent' register | Docility |
| | Line up for 'Omega 3' and toast | Distribution |
| | Take water bottle and own seat | Segregation |
| 9.30–10.15 'Morning work' | Receive instructions as a group | Distribution |
| | Individual work with teacher help | Segregation |
| | Re-group for progress report | Examination |
| 10.15–10.45 'Break time' | Change shoes and take biscuit | Docility |
| | Outdoor play – tyres and trees | Differentiation |
| | Line up in playground | Distribution |
| | Door monitor for re-entry | Authorising |
| | Change shoes, sit with water bottle | Surveillance |
| 10.45–11.45 'Morning work' | Complete individual tasks | Distribution |
| | Those finished help others | Differentiation |
| | Individual portfolio work with TA | Segregation |
| | Discuss/present/perform/display | Examination |
| 11.45–1.15 'Lunch' | Group-at-a-time wash hands | Distribution |
| | Rest of group singing activity | Segregation |
| | 'Sandwiches' and 'School meals' | Distribution |
| | line up for dinner monitor | Authorising |
| | Eating, no noise or movement | Docility |
| | Let out based on lunch 'performance' | Differentiation |

next routinised stage; the first in line, the door monitor, the new child's mentor, the 'special person'.

There certainly seems to be nothing inherently productive about the ability to sit still, it might seem an odd skill for teachers to reward *for itself*. Perhaps what the teacher seeks is the child's ability and inclination to accept the classroom order and its rationale. Taking on this self-referential character would seem to detract from the routine's ability to foster self-regulation, for the only rationale for 'appropriate' behaviour is tied to the immediate ends of the routine itself.

In such instances the governance of routine hides behind the responsibility of the mentor or the accolade of the 'special person'. In its self-referential form routine acts to separate and mark as *risky* those who, for whatever reason, do not *fit* the prescribed order. Routine thus acts to include and exclude and becomes the basis for some children coming to be noticed – and/or 'identified' early:

> The individual child, it would appear, emerges via the disciplined, spatial implementation of the timetable which instills a regularity and a rhythm in all the activities and tasks of children, including control of the material body through the performance of duty and style of life.
>
> *(James* et al., *1998, p. 55)*

## Producing the classroom subject 'ADHD'

This chapter has questioned the assumptions implicit in education policies, that it is children possessed of behavioural conditions who are the problem, suggesting that at least some of the behaviour in question is produced by the regimes of the school itself through the material workings of its taken for granted discourses and epistemes.

The purpose of encouraging children to *do school* through routinisation can be seen as encouraging the production of the docile self-managing subject, to promote what Miller (1993) calls 'a sense of oneness among increasingly heterogeneous populations' (p. xii). Inevitably this is about marking some diverse forms as illegitimate and in need of change. However, as often as not, the self-referential nature of routine and reward produces a subject, to paraphrase Foucault (2004), who has little or no motivation to *defend* the social order of the classroom. This lack of motivation is read as an apparent failure to self-manage, a deficit lurking in the individual child and in need of *treatment* according to an array of available techniques: from IEPs to nurture groups, Omega 3 to Ritalin. Yet what warrants interrogation are the systems by which children, teachers and schools alike are bound, and the conditions of possibility, in terms of choice/coercion, motivation/self-regulation, and instrumentality/getting the job done, which they might afford any party.

The diagnostic criteria for ADHD lean heavily on the context of the school to give its descriptions referent and meaning, and to gauge the *severity* within the afflicted child (Bailey, 2010). The child with ADHD emerges through the analysis here as the very antithesis of the routinised, orderly school child. The inattentive child who 'often does not seem to listen when spoken to directly ... often loses things needed for activities ... is often forgetful in daily activities' (APA, 2000) is made visible by the routine order just as readily as the hyperactive child, who 'often gets up from seat when remaining in seat is expected' and the impulsive child who 'often has trouble waiting one's turn' (APA, 2000). The images created by these criteria point to children who are incapable of regulating themselves in the manner demanded by and of the performing school. In mapping the production and maintenance of routine and describing its exclusive effects, the attempt has been to highlight the conflation of social with organic pathology, as individuals only become known and knowable as *deficient* according to a set of spatial and temporal norms the production and protection of which they might very well have neither investment nor involvement.

The maintenance and protection of social order is essential for the requirements of mass schooling, and implicit in this is the notion that some children will not accept the order as it is offered to them. The beginning of school might represent the first time a child is expected to internalise the needs of others in their own decision making and one might expect there to be variation in the ability to accept and adapt to the other. However, one might not expect such a rigid and medicalised policing of such variance, nor concrete dispositions to be so easily created through the temporary and transient embodiment of such self-referential positions.

Therefore, the questions posed here do not concern complete abandonment of routine from every child's schooling; routines are productive and essential. What is questioned here is the extent to which authorities who enact routine within school are aware of the divisions being made in the name of order and the individualised conclusions which are reached for one who rejects it.

In moving now to the work undertaken at Alderley Primary, I carry with me this position on the routine conduct of schooling. Through this analysis I have come to see routine as a metaphor for the discursive ordering of the school and classroom, a material embodiment of Foucault's notion of *discipline*, it has become *routine logic*. This chapter serves this embodiment well at a relatively broad structural level. The next chapter attempts to get inside the broad notion of routine to analyse some of the power relations at work in the ability to routinise different bodies in different ways through an analysis of gendered positioning at Alderley Primary.

# 5

# BOYS WILL BE BOYS

Estimates suggest that males are between five and ten times more likely than females to be diagnosed with ADHD, however, critical gender analyses within this area are few (though see: Singh, 2002, 2003; Bennett, 2004; Carpenter and Austin, 2008). Within education one might seek a formula whereby *failing boys* (BBC, 2008) plus *feminised primary schools* (Parkin, 2007) equals an oppressed residue of young males whose particular brand of masculinity is deemed unacceptable, pathologised and drugged. This chapter seeks to understand some of the reasons why so many more young males than females are pathologised in this way. Yet while the formula above might be seen as a point of departure, it is based on various gender assumptions which will be contested here. Placed within a gender equity framework several alternative conceptions of *failing boys* and *feminised schools* will be discussed. The data presented from Alderley Primary constructs an argument on gendered positioning in three stages: (1) The normalised dominance of boys in the classroom; (2) The gendered allocation of risk and resources; (3) Pathologisation and the new normalisation of deviance. Between them, these three stages produce a *constitutive circularity* (Jones *et al.*, 2008) of masculine dominance in the classroom. This dominance is naturalised through buried assumptions of gender, made essential through institutional responses, and re-established through the *special* treatment derived from a psychiatric label.

Lloyd (2005) sates that; 'the literature of "EBD" is dominated by concern with disruptive boys and by male writers' (p. 130). Though I have tried to ground the following argument according to a gender equity discourse, my data does not contain the experiences of girls. I can partially account for this in methodological terms; I was *exploring* the script of the school and classroom, therefore I became aware of the *problem* of boys, who dominate everyday discourses of classroom disruption. Perhaps, as Lloyd (2005) implies, my own gendered positioning meant that I was not sufficiently aware in the moment to make the leap to the other side of this perception in questioning the invisibility of girls. However, while I present the argument from the boys' side, my point of departure is also that expressed by Lloyd (2005): 'girls are less likely to be excluded or diagnosed with EBD *because they are not boys*' (p. 130, emphasis in original).

I will begin this account by situating ADHD and gender, before relating this to assumptions about gender and education.

## ADHD and gender

It has for some time been accepted within medical perspectives that approximately five times as many boys as girls will be diagnosed with behavioural disorders such as ADHD (e.g. Jenkins, 1973). More often than not, this has been accepted unproblematically or simply assumed to be so; a *natural*, though unexplained, consequence of pathology. Paediatrician Geoff Kewley (1999), for example, introduces his widely read guide to ADHD with a set of nine patient vignettes, eight of whom are males. In an equally popular guide by another doctor, Paul Wender (2000), the opening case exhumes 'fidgety Phil', the subject of an 1863 poem written by a German physician. Wender credits Phil as the first recognition of ADHD before embarking on an account of the disorder littered almost exclusively with male pronouns.

The most common medical explanations for ADHD seek the abnormal workings of brain chemistry, yet, as Singh (2002) notes, 'if ADHD is presented as a neurochemical problem, neurochemistry must explain the gender skew' (p. 589). Currently no such explanation exists. When medical researchers have taken up this line of investigation it has usually been to identify gender or sex differences in the aetiology, presentation and treatment of the disorder (Anderson and Teicher, 2000; Hartung *et al.*, 2002), which has the effect of further naturalising rather than problematising the terms of the debate.

Outside psychological and medical perspectives, there are many accounts which seek alternative *inclusive* or *holistic* understandings of ADHD (Hartmann, 1997; Southall, 2007), yet these also tend to reproduce naturalised conceptions of sex and gender roles. The focus with these works is with 'healing the emotional "scars" of boyhood' (Frank *et al.*, 2003, p. 119). Similar attempts can be read in many accounts which in other places present radical criticism of ADHD (e.g. Armstrong, 1997; Walker, 1998). In *The Hyperactivity Hoax*, Walker (1998) states that:

> little boys tend to be more active, aggressive, and annoying than little girls, and in the current pro-Ritalin culture, any little boy who squirms in his seat, gets into scuffles in the playground, or clowns around in class is a target for a hyperactivity label and a pill.
>
> *(Walker, 1998, p. 27)*

Here, Walker achieves his critique only by re-inscribing existing gendered assumptions. One exception to this pattern is critical psychiatrist Sami Timimi (2005a), who draws attention to the effects of narcissistic Western cultural ideals in distributing limiting models of masculinity, creating systems of winners and losers, where 'concern for social harmony contradicts the basic goal of the value system' (p. 102). Here, psychiatry becomes a 'cultural defense mechanism' (p. 107) for the outcasts of disharmony.

A collection of papers edited by two mental health professionals (Quinn and Nadeau, 2002), offers some evidence of a deeper interest in gender issues from within medical perspectives. Although the primary concern is with more efficient diagnostic targeting of females, this collection also generates some interesting questions. The observation in one chapter that 'almost everything that researchers, clinicians, and parents know about AD/HD is based on studies that exclusively studied boys' (Gershon, 2002, p. 23) presents a very obvious problematisation of the assumed skew in highlighting the fact that such figures are socially constructed. In applying this view to the classroom, both psychological and psychiatric literatures suggest that teachers tend to perceive a greater number and greater severity of ADHD symptoms in boys (Condry and Ross, 1985; Nolan *et al.*, 2001). However, having found the terms on which contestation could legitimately be based, these accounts choose not to delve into the constitutive interplay of the classroom, leaving many questions unanswered. The most obvious of which is: *Why?* Through their conflation of sex and gender, Condry and Ross (1985) apparently suggest that there really are some natural phenomena within the bodies of males which make them of primary concern to teachers, researchers and clinicians. An alternative would be to suggest that the definition and identification of *concerns* is the product of further social construction.

In considering this suggestion, the work of George Still (1902) could be cited. Still is commonly credited with the *discovery* of what is now called ADHD, through his 1902 description of a *morbid passionateness* in young boys lacking *moral discipline*. As Laurence (2008) notes, patients only arrived in Still's clinic because their disobedience in school had deemed them 'backward' and in need of separation (p. 102).

Equally influential for contemporary ADHD practices were Charles Bradley's (1937) experiments with amphetamines, again conducted upon young boys and recording 'striking' effects on school performance. Singh (2002) argues that these experiments were part of a vast movement at this time concerned with what was then called young boys' 'emotional disturbance'. At the centre of this problematic was 'the relationship between mothers and sons' (p. 599). Bradley's experiments aided the construction of an organic aetiology for this *disturbance*, a cause that was furthered through the mass experimentation the electroencephalogram (EEG) received through the Second World War. Again, all subjects were male (Laurence and McCallum, 1998).

Therefore, each advance in medical perspectives has been based on the availability of a male problem population upon which to drive the science, through the imposition of a 'microscopic of conduct' (Foucault, 1977). In the case of the experiments and observations on young children, primary concern was 'backward' and ill-disciplined performance in school. Though the precise terms have changed, this concern with boys' performance in school has remained. The next section will discuss contemporary fears around boys' schooling and their relation to the medicalised understanding of *problems*.

## Bad, sad, stupid and mad

Contemporary moral panics concerning the education of young males bear a striking resemblance to the descriptions of backwardness, disobedience and moral indiscipline that Still (1902) described over a century ago. The 'failing boys' rhetoric claims that boys are being disadvantaged by contemporary schooling as illustrated by their apparent underachievement, misbehaviour, exclusion and pathologisation. These concerns are all represented by ADHD.

### Bad

Boys are understood to be *naturally* more boisterous, disruptive, aggressive and badly behaved than girls, with an 'instinctive need for activity and risk' (Palmer, 2007). Boys dominate data on school violence and vandalism, and the question of school discipline is seen almost exclusively as a 'male issue' (Slee, 1995, p. 107). Males also make up the large majority excluded from school (Osler and Vincent, 2003), from where potential pathways include further violence and criminality.

Bad behaviour is one of the key features of ADHD, which is one of the APA's 'disruptive behaviour disorders of childhood' (APA, 2000). The 'hyperactive' and 'impulsive' components of the symptom profile best represent the *bad ADHD child*, who leaves their seat, runs, climbs, shouts, interrupts and often acts 'as if driven by a motor' (APA, 2000). Of the many co-occurring psychiatric diseases that exist for ADHD, the strongest correlations are with Conduct Disorder and Oppositional Defiant Disorder, which are found in over 50 per cent of children with ADHD (Biederman, 2005).

### Sad

The image of the *hyper* child – the Tiggers and Bart Simpsons of this world – is the one which dominates popular perceptions of ADHD, and *sad* doesn't immediately match this image. The 'inattentive' component is perhaps the place to look for the more withdrawn, disengaged and harder to spot *sad ADHD child*, and clinicians bemoan what they see as the under-recognition of this category, with conduct problems much more likely to elicit intervention (Sayal *et al.*, 2002). In terms of what are described as some of the 'outcomes' of ADHD, it is commonly associated with higher than average rates of depression (Able *et al.*, 2007; Torgersen *et al.*, 2006), drug abuse (Greene *et al.*, 1997; Klein and Mannuzza, 1991) and suicide (Brook and Boaz, 2005; Singer, 2006). While exclusion might lead down the 'bad' route described above, equally it could lead to the disaffection and withdrawal that these outcomes describe.

## Stupid

'Failing boys' have been given a great deal of attention in the mass media (BBC, 2008; Clark, 2006; Henry, 2006; Parkin, 2007). The fall of boys' achievement at Key Stages 1–4 as compared with girls, even in *traditionally male* subjects, such as science and maths, has been widely publicised (Raphael Reed, 1999). Boys also make up the majority of school's remedial and special needs programmes, with around the same 5:1 ratio as ADHD (Raphael Reed, 1999).

ADHD leads many children into special needs education, though outside the US it is rarely associated with any specific source of educational funding (Graham, 2007c). In the past ADHD was considered to be primarily a learning disorder (Laurence and McCallum, 2009), and there is a debate for considering it a category of educational disability (Reid *et al.*, 1993; Taylor, 1994). Children with ADHD score poorly on an array of task-oriented cognitive functions, known collectively by some neuroscientists as *executive functions* (Barkley, 1997). ADHD also frequently co-occurs with learning difficulties such as dyslexia.

## Mad

The UK Mental Health Foundation suggests that as many as 20 per cent of school-aged children experience some form of 'mental disturbance' with an estimated 10 per cent in need of professional help (BBC, 1999). ADHD is the single most common diagnosis, however similar increases in diagnosis of a range of other psycho-pathologies have been recorded, such as Autism and Bipolar Disorder (Hershel and Kaye, 2003; Moreno *et al.*, 2007). Most of these pathologies are thought to be related to one another (APA, 2000), together representing a profusion of multiple and inter-related forms of neurocentric othering (S. Rose, 2005), yet lacking a cohesive underlying conception of what *mental disorder* actually is (Bailey, 2010).

What supposedly separates ADHD and other pathological forms from *normal bad*, *sad* and *stupid* behaviour is the *significant clinical impairment* (APA, 2000) that must present in addition to symptoms in order to demarcate mental illness. The view of ADHD as a brain-based disease is perceived by some to be robustly backed by correlations with petrochemical agents and genetic paths, and this set of theories is commonly used to justify the use of psychoactive medication (Barkley, 2002; Kutcher *et al.*, 2004).

To foreground the argument to come in the terms offered by the psychiatric and psychological literatures, there is evidence of the interaction between these four categories: bad, sad, stupid, mad. Abikoff *et al.* (2002), for example, conducted classroom observations, finding that 'boys and girls with ADHD display similar inattentiveness' (p. 351). Combined with the evidence already cited of gender bias in teachers' perceptions of symptom count and severity (Condry and Ross, 1985; Nolan *et al.*, 2001) comes the suggestion that ADHD is most readily imagined in terms of hyperactive, impulsive, disruptive behaviour. Aditionally, psychologists suggest that behaviour has a significant impact on teachers' judgements of academic skill (Bennett *et al.*, 1993; Cole *et al.*, 1998), thus the *bad* and the *stupid* talk each other into pedagogical concerns, leaving the *sad* in silence.

The next section moves on to look at some of the popular sociological explanations for so many boys being identified as *bad, sad, stupid* and *mad,* primarily focusing on the idea of the *feminisation* of primary schooling. That schools can be described as *feminised* is illustrative of a natural and essential concept of gender. Alongside this assumption lies the notion that if boys are receiving attention, intervention and resources for their poor conduct, then these signify *their* oppression.

## The feminisation rhetoric

Claims of the *bad, sad, stupid,* and *mad* suggest that schools are contributing to some kind of *crisis of masculinity* (Lingard, 2003) at the centre of which sits (or squirms) *fidgety Phil:*[1]

> But fidgety Phil, He won't sit still;
> He wriggles and giggles, And then, I declare,
> Swings backwards and forwards, And tilts up his chair.

The spectre of the failing, disruptive, dropout male has driven theories concerning the feminisation of primary school (Miller, 1993). The substance of these theories lies primarily in the recent emphasis on literacy, which is seen as a more *feminine* domain, and on the fact that the majority of primary school teachers are women. Yet when contextualised within a gender equity framework, both crisis and reaction can be turned on their heads.

The widely publicised figures concerning failing boys as compared to girls tell an incomplete story. Further stratification by class and ethnicity tells of more complexity, where white middle-class girls are narrowly ahead of white middle-class boys, at the top of the pile across all subjects (Raphael Reed, 1999). Conceiving of the debate only in terms of gender eclipses the class dimension, rendering the relative struggles of working-class boys and girls invisible, as well as those of some ethnic groups (Gillborn and Gipps, 1996; Davis, 2001). A narrow focus primarily on GCSE results also conceals the continued dominance of males in further and higher education (Elwood, 1995), which feeds into the substantial inequities of the division of labour, illustrated by 'female low pay, part-time work and continuing correlations of motherhood with childcare' (Arnot and Mac an Ghaill, 2006, p. 8).

While it might be the case that males and females are 'differently literate' (Millard, 1997, p. 31), it is also argued contrary to the feminisation rhetoric that recent directions in school have favoured males, returning to teaching in 'more didactic and structured ways (phonics-based approaches to literacy; whole-class inculcation of mathematical rules etc.)' (Raphael Reed, 1999, p. 100). Further, Millard's (1997) research on literacy practices at home and in peer group settings suggests that statements about male or female propensities for a given subject are constructed via self/other perceptions and expectations, and mediated by helpful or hindering environments. In other words, gender differences in literacy are discursively constructed. This point could be transposed and repeated for any statement predicated upon the *natural differences, characteristics,* or *propensities* of males and females.

Claims about the feminisation of primary teaching, based on crude figures concerning the number of male vs. female teachers, tell nothing new as females have always made up the majority of this workforce (Skelton, 2002). Women might outnumber men in the classroom, but men are allowed to climb the ranks faster, and are proportionately over three times as likely to become a head teacher (Skelton, 2001). Attempts to *re-masculinise* the workforce through the employment of male teachers disregard the fact that it is the behavioural agenda faced by the female classroom assistants that sustains *normal* classroom functions (Arnot and Miles, 2005). Nor does the crude statistic say anything about specific forms of femininity or masculinity available to and employed by individual teachers. Skelton (2002) draws attention to this simplistic concept with the question: 'can only females "do" femininity and males "display" masculinity?' (p. 88), and in a similar vein, Francis (2008), in asking what it means to 'teach manfully' (p. 109). While conduct might not be wholly determined by gender, the argument that gender differences are discursively constructed implies that there are heuristic, socially desirable and dominant forms of masculinity and femininity which shape perceptions, actions and interpretations of behaviour, contributing to the construction of *gendered matrices* of schooling (Butler, 1993); an interpretive mesh through which the world is perceived according to objectifying understandings of gender. What the *feminisation* rhetoric masks is the fact that in early years schooling such matrices favour masculinities. The next section re-casts this debate in terms of the continued masculine dominance of schooling.

## The masculinised reality

Connell (1995) has offered the term *hegemonic masculinities* to describe heuristic, desirable and dominant forms of masculinity that tend to get reproduced through everyday social settings. Hegemonic masculinities operate through the deployment of:

> physical strength, adventurousness, emotional neutrality, certainty, control, assertiveness, self-reliance, individuality, competitiveness, instrumental skills, public knowledge, discipline, reason, objectivity and rationality.
>
> *(Kenway and Fitzclarence, 1997, p. 121)*

Several authors have noted the extent to which these positions are reflected in neo-liberal discourses, which have distributed the masculinising forces of 'commercialization, commodification and rationalization' (Mac an Ghaill, 1994, p. 7) through schools over the last three decades. Examples cited include the gender blind Education Reform Act (Mac an Ghaill, 1994), hierarchical and autocratic management structures (Skelton, 2002) and child-centred, psychologised and individualised pedagogies (Walkerdine, 1984), which feed into de-politicised 'standards' agendas (Raphael Reed, 1999), and classroom management 'predicated on control' (Meyenn and Parker, 2001, p. 174).

Perhaps the largest amount of research exists in relation to masculine violence and the heterosexual identity of schools. Dominating the cultural descriptions made of masculinities that are available in schools are assumptions that 'maleness equals aggressiveness, competence with females, misogyny' (Haywood and Mac an Ghaill, 2006, p. 55). Everyday gender oppressions and heterosexual abuse are normalised within both secondary and primary school between male teachers and female pupils (Skelton, 1997), between male pupils and both female and male teachers (Epstein, 1997; Skelton, 1997) and within male peer groups (Mac an Ghaill, 1994; Nayak and Kehily, 2001; Renold, 2007; Skelton, 1996).

Viewed from a masculinities perspective, connections between the *bad, sad, stupid* and *mad* begin to emerge. A young male who ascribes to an exaggerated hegemonic masculinity might well find himself on the *bad* list, however, such a position might well have been predicated upon a rejection of the learning values of the school (Mac and Ghaill, 1994; Willis, 1977), in which case he could be branded *stupid* in addition. Equally, a young male could reject certain aspects of hegemonic masculinity. The policing of masculinities in school suggest that he will have to keep this rejection well hidden and will likely face rejection by his peers (Mac and Ghaill, 1994; Nayak and Kehily, 2001). From here, withdrawal, disaffection and rejection of the learning culture are all potential pathways.

## Gendered positioning in action

There is a growing research literature on hegemonic masculine, violent and sexualised performances in the primary school (Epstein, 1997; Renold, 2007; Skelton, 1997). Yet studies of this nature within Years One and Two are rare (though see Skelton, 1997, 2001). This chapter contributes to this field with observational data exploring the masculine and heteronormative *relations of ruling* (D. Smith, 1987) that can be read in the everyday work of the Year One and Year Two classroom. A particular focus here will be on disciplinary practices and the implications that pathological forms such as ADHD bring to these practices. This focus will be pursued through three problematics: (1) The normalised dominance of boys; (2) The gendered allocation of risk and resources; (3) Pathologisation and the new normalisation of deviance.

The research presented in this chapter was carried out at Alderley Primary, where I encountered several children with ADHD, and a Year One class with what I described in Chapter 3 as a 'dominant group of boys'. When I started work at Alderley it was commencing its third year since amalgamation with another school. The head teacher, Sue, was employed at the same time as the two schools joined:

Sue:  In terms of revelatory experiences, this has been the one to end them all because actually on the surface it looks like a really sort of well-balanced community; it looks like a school with wonderful facilities; a lovely setting; has plenty of staff but actually the story is not like that at all.

*(Int 21–3)*[2]

Sue's two priorities on joining Alderley were to build a team out of the huge mistrust that she found between the two schools, and to tackle the behaviour issue in a school where she described the children as very *emotionally brittle*:

> Sue:  They have very complex and various emotional needs. They have very little in terms of life experiences.
>
> *(Int 21–3)*

However, Sue also stated that:

> Sue:  What we can't do is use the children as the excuse for having low levels of achievement and that's traditionally what's been done.
>
> *(Int 21–3)*

The setting and recent history of Alderley Primary and Sue's discourse tell us that anything here said in relation to gender must also be considered in light of both social class, local politics and school-home expectations. These expectations have a tendency to govern interactions with parents as well as perceptions of children's behaviour as a natural consequence of a *difficult* or *disruptive* home environment (Vincent, 2000; Swadener and Lubeck, 1995). In the above excerpt, Sue is firm in her rejection of such *derisive* discourse (Kenway, 1990) and keen to re-emphasise the achievement that should lie at the centre of teaching objectives, nevertheless this derision was part of the everyday discourse of many of the teaching staff at Alderley.

I will now move to the main argument, which is organised, first, around the everyday, normalised dominance of the group of boys in the Year One classroom.

### The normalised dominance of boys

The Year One class teacher, Tina/Miss Chapel, had particular concerns about a group of boys who not only demanded a lot of attention in class, but also displayed a level of violence which she found quite disturbing in children this young:

> Tina:  In Year Six, I've had chairs thrown at me, I've been told to 'F-off', but I've never seen this amount of getting at each other.
>
> *(fn 4–10)*

This disruptive group was made up of a core set of around six members, however, most of the rest of the males in the class were included, or drawn in peripherally and the dominance of the group and its values within the classroom did not leave any young male with a consistently positive *learner identity* (Renold, 2001).

The excerpt below is taken from a morning class where the activity is jewellery making. In addition to this activity, Tina has a spelling test to administer, for which she splits off small groups at a time while the rest are split into various stages of the jewellery-making process: drawing designs, cutting out materials, writing descriptions and stringing or painting beads. The following scene is an excerpt from one of these splitting processes. All the boys mentioned are regular members of the core group:

11.34     The shaker is brought out to try and reduce noise levels a bit. Greg continues to shout out and is reminded of the shaker's purpose. However there is still too much noise especially from the writing table.

Tina:     'Umm boys? I was going to choose one of you, but now I'm not sure. It won't be you Joe.'

    Tina starts to choose people, but has to remind everyone that she won't choose anyone shouting 'me me me', and reprimanding the boys in the writing area for continuing rudeness.

11.35     Four children, including Andy and Ed, are chosen. Tina chooses some more, but some don't want to do it. She turns to me to comment on this when Joe pipes up 'I do'. Despite having just told him that he wouldn't be, Tina capitulates with a weary sounding 'Ok, you go paint beads.'

*(fn 19–10)*

Here the boys' behaviour has been marked as *bad* according to routine logic. The group of boys at the writing table has successfully manipulated the situation to produce a new and favourable group in a different activity. They disrupted sufficiently to make Tina's task of selecting groups more difficult. At first Tina admonished this disruption, but eventually gave in. The group painting beads ended up being made up almost entirely of boys. From here the group were able to dominate the attention of the female classroom assistant, Haley, and disrupt Tina's attempts at administering a spelling test to another group.

11.54     Tina and Haley both have to ask Lewis to forget about what the spelling table are doing and return to his own chair. Alex is shouting and Tina reprimands. Then Haley has to 'Shh' the whole group of boys on the painting table.

11.57     Lewis persists in coming over to the spelling table to see what they're doing, much to Tina and Haley's annoyance.

Haley:     'James! Put your bottom on a chair and leave Ben alone . . . Lewis!!'

    Haley is now repeatedly 'Shh-ing' what is being called Ben's table although my impression is that Ben himself is working quite well.

11.59     Greg now decides he's had enough painting, takes off his apron and leaves the table. Haley admonishes him, telling him he hasn't finished yet.

> Greg:   'No, I'm done.'
>
> Tina:   'Greg if you're finished then go and glue.

*(fn 19–10)*

In the above excerpt the dominance of the boys was sufficient to allow Greg to manipulate the ordinary rules of the classroom in his favour. For Tina, this special treatment appeared preferable to continued disruption from the group. However, as this scene drew to a close, Tina was forced to make further dispensations, when the boys made the transition to break time problematic:

> 12.25   Haley is trying to make sure that once the children have left the carpet that they do actually get their coat and make it to the line by the door. Lewis is the first person she picks up not doing this. He says that he cannot find his coat. Tina enjoins those on the carpet to watch and listen and those lining up to be quiet.
>
> Lewis:  'Miss Chapel! I can't find my coat!'
>
> Haley:  'You're not looking!'
>
>     Haley finds the coat almost straightaway and gives it to Lewis.
>
> 12.27   Three more children are chosen to line up. Ben is waiting by the door which he now opens and announces that he can see people already outside. He shouts this to Tina before running off.
>
> 12.28   Tina doesn't notice this at first but then asks Haley where he is. 'He just ran out', comes the answer. Tina raises her eyebrows but does nothing and tells the rest on the carpet to line up.

*(fn 19–10)*

Once again, disruption from one of the boys, Lewis, allowed Ben to disrupt the routine norms by running out to break without first lining up. Tina was then faced with the choice of either deserting the rest of the class to chase up Ben, or to sanction his rule breaking. In a no-win situation, she chose the latter, and reinforced the norm by making sure everyone else lined up. The other thing worth noting from this scenario is that Haley was on a voluntary work placement at the school. This might have meant that she was not authorised in disciplinary terms (see Chapter 4) in the same way as permanent staff, allowing the boys extra leeway. However, had she not been there then Tina would have had the same demands to negotiate on her own.

In the above examples the dominant group of boys have been able to undermine the female authorities in the classroom, marginalise the needs of the rest of the group and threaten the integrity of the routine. According to naturalised notions of gender, males are understood to be boisterous and females are understood to be passive. In the above examples, such a conception has determined the subject positions taken, with the result that the dominant males are made visible in their ascendancy while the needs or wants of the females are ignored. These examples are just that – single, situated fragments of masculine dominance. However, the extent to which these instances become mechanised is determined by the manner in which the disciplinary structures respond to this dominance, which is the subject of the next section.

## The allocation of risk and resources

One of the responsibilities of the *performing school* (Gleeson and Husbands, 2001) is to enable children and young people to achieve academically in the form of results and qualifications. In order to try to maximise this output, schools are encouraged to survey and differentiate their populations; finite resources making the early identification of potential problems a priority. The collective nature of schooling demands social order; those made visible by routine logic are perceived to threaten this and, therefore, to be in need of intervention. By its very nature, the routine provides a patterned response to conduct, and that which it makes the most visible is not necessarily that which is most in need. These ideas will be examined through the responses made to the conduct of two Year One boys, Kyle and Ben.

The normalised dominance of the group of boys created spaces into which greater levels of disruption could feed, and this was clearly seen in two core members of the group, Ben and Kyle. Both boys were regularly disruptive, both boys had an acknowledged *difficult* situation at home. Kyle attended the nurture group four mornings per week and had been seen by both an educational psychologist and paediatrician. It was 'suspected' that he had ADHD, but according to SENCO, Heather, the paediatrician did not wish to diagnose someone so young.

The first excerpt comes from a morning just before assembly, where Tina was having some difficulty controlling disruption:

8.53  Sue came into the room about a minute ago and now sits at the front of the carpet and goes through some counting games with the children.

Sue:  'Kyle, look at me, I want to see your eyes!'

8.56  Sue uses some breathing exercises to try to regain some calm after the excitement of the number games.

8.58  All are attentive to Sue as she takes them through the need for oxygen to feed their brains and make them work better. Kyle occasionally shouts something out.

9.00  Sue moves on to talking about water but is interrupted by Kyle.

Sue:  'No shouting out Kyle!'

9.01

Sue:  'Kyle, put your hand up if you want to say something.'
        Sue is asking children whether they have a plastic bottle of water in the classroom. Kyle is laughing about something and is given a firm 'No thank you!' by Sue.

9.02  Sue is now asking questions about the reasons why we need to eat vegetables.

> 9.03   Kyle is shouting out again
>
> Sue:   'Practice something for me Kyle, put your hand up first.'
>
> Kyle does so then says 'you get big and strong on veg' and is commended for both his answer and putting his hand up to say it.
>
> *(fn 19–10)*

During a previous conversation in which Tina and I had been discussing mornings such as these, which were frequently overtaken with disruption, Tina said one of the worst things for her was on the occasions when Sue came in and had the class 'eating out of her hand'. Tina obviously felt scrutinised when Sue was in the class, and her frustration at Sue's ability to calm the children implies she would seek some tactics from Sue's example.

However, in the above excerpt, although there was no serious admonishment, Kyle still managed to dominate Sue's attention and create his own normative space. Sue chose to try and uphold the classroom norms by not sanctioning his disruption. However, this meant that she was required to attend to Kyle on five occasions in only ten minutes in the classroom. Kyle was then given a commendation at the end, despite having been disruptive all the way through.

This is a routine tactic in interactions with *difficult* children, whereby they receive an abnormal amount of praise for completing tasks in a manner ordinarily expected of most. Though the intention is to encourage more of the same appropriate behaviour, there are also *incidental effects* (Graham, 2006). First, though it is a routine means of management, and underscored by the self-referential reinforcement of routine logic, it contradicts routine norms, which are usually constructed via a philosophy of treating everybody the same. Second, for the child to whom it is directed, it implies a sanctioning of the inappropriate behaviour that went before it, conferring or reinforcing a *special* status.

Though the above example is relatively low-level disruption, instances of Kyle or Ben's disruption were not always so. Frequently the whole class would be disrupted and several different adults' attention would be required. The following excerpt concerns an incident involving Ben:

> 11.02   Ben has had a bit of a tantrum and is now hiding beneath the table, much to the amusement of the others on the table, and distress of Hayley. Tina has now gone over and is crouching next to him.
>
> (...)
>
> 11.08   Sub-table tantrum is still going on. 'Just ignore him', says James. Ben now starts kicking the chairs and tables, Tina gives him a sharp 'Stop!', he doesn't.
>
> (...)
>
> 11.14   Mary [deputy head] comes in to aid the cause: 'Maybe I'll come back in a minute and the room will be straight again, what do you think Ben?' Tina is trying to concentrate on the rest of the class but is obviously distracted by what's going on.
>
> (...)

11.22 Ben has now emerged from the table and is sitting with Mary. Now she tries to get him to move the furniture back, he doesn't want to so she does it and then returns to him. I can't hear what is being said, but Ben is now verbally responding.

11.28 Ben and Mary leave the room together.

(. . .)

11.42 Ben is back in but heads straight for the corner where he stands facing the wall and refusing to move, so Mary takes him out again.

(. . .)

11.51 Ben is now back in the room but has missed the entire lesson.

*(fn 11–10)*

In contrast to Kyle, I often observed Ben to be relatively shy and quiet, and this matched the perception of many of the staff. This incident was one of the several examples where this wasn't the case, and even through this 'tantrum' it seemed that rather than disrupt Ben was seeking to avoid and hide. Tina asked me at the time whether I had noticed any immediate pre-cursor to the incident, but I could offer nothing. There is whole class disruption, an abnormal amount of female adult attention given to one male child, with the male directing the interactions. However, in addition to these, Ben's incident brings a slightly different set of concerns with it. For the day or two following such an incident there may be more conversations about Ben amongst staff, and Tina would usually go out of her way to be positive and encouraging with him in class. Once Ben had gone back to his usual quiet, shy and non-participatory role, the concerned conversations and special treatment would stop until the next 'incident'.

Unlike Kyle, Ben did not have a consistent *problem* discourse attached to him, and this appeared to be because on a day-to-day basis he did not threaten the social order to the extent that Kyle did. Both boys were towards the bottom of the class in terms of literacy and numeracy standards, yet, with the exception of what were seen as isolated incidents such as these, Ben slipped beneath the radar which Kyle repeatedly forced himself on to. The result was that while Kyle received all the attention, resources and interventions, IEPs, nurture group, psychologists, paediatricians, Ben received nothing.

Out of the naturalised domination which the males were able to impose on the classroom, comes the focus on two *problem* boys: Kyle and Ben. Through routine logic Kyle has been identified as the most immediately in need of intervention. This is because on a day-to-day basis, he threatens the social order to the greatest extent. Resources are targeted within schools in the interests of creating more successful outcomes. According to a finite budget, the allocation of resources to Kyle denies them being allocated elsewhere. Therefore, implicit in the institutional response to the domination of boys is that it will be responded to with resources in the interests of improving the outcomes of those who are most visible in risking their educational future.

The gendered allocation of resources produces circularity; Kyle will be represented in the ever-increasing figures on problem boys, the larger this figure gets the more the male population are seen as failing, or failed by, the system, and the more energy and resources are devoted to better integrating them in the future. As the next section argues, pathologisation provides a heuristic for this circularity, in demarcating distinct financial and normative spaces for *problem* children within school.

## Pathology and the reproduction of dominance

One can take several critical perspectives towards special needs interventions, which might be exclusive, stigmatising, individualistic, medicalising, deficit ridden and primarily interested in the *needs* of the social order. Kyle and Ben's contrasting stories reinforce this last notion, with the *benefits* of attention, resources and professional energies directed towards those who persistently disrupt the docile directive.

As noted at the beginning of this chapter, the ratio of boys to girls receiving special needs provision is estimated to be 5:1 (Raphael Reed, 1999). In light of the benefits of time and money, as well as any positive psychosocial change the intervention might promote, this ratio represents a significant dividend for the children in question, as well as a bolster for the statistics on male problem populations. The fact that some males are able to manipulate this extra provision on the basis of the masculinised script of the classroom means that, following Connell (1995), this can be called a *patriarchal dividend*.

Within special needs provision, pathologisation might be seen as a kind of gold standard dividend for both the school and child. For the child, a diagnosis might signify extra funding, more personal attention, fewer academic demands and above all, a new normative space affording greater freedom in their conduct. The school also benefits from any extra funding, and can be seen to be responding constructively to the challenges of disruptive behaviour.

For better or worse, a diagnosis and label intervenes in self-other perceptions. Alongside negative implications such as stigma and self-fulfilling prophecies, lies the greater support, understanding, patience and sympathy that might attend the child who is not simply *bad*, *sad*, or *stupid*, but pathologically so: the *label of forgiveness* (Reid and Maag, 1997). This has significant implications for the everyday maintenance of norms in the classroom, where teachers may now be required to make one rule for some and not for others on the basis that the pathologised child requires understanding and support rather than external discipline. Pathology thus takes an important place in the circularity of male dominance. Through naturalised conceptions of gender, males are allowed to disrupt classroom scenes and marginalise the teacher's ability to maintain control. The routine classroom functions to make those who threaten the social order the most visible, and the case is stated for intervention. Intervention essentialises the gender relation by providing resources and new subject positions for disruptive males to inhabit, thereby in part sanctioning the disruption. Pathologisation brings with it material changes in the division of labour in the form of resources and access to specialist discourses, it also effects a discursive change by offering exoneration to the child, who is freed of responsibility for their actions. This represents a unique subject position within the routine classroom, which separates in order to integrate; to *responsibilise* (N. Rose, 1989). This conditions the future response to disruptive males, while also progressively weakening the integrity of routine logic, which teachers then have to invest more resources into protecting. Rather than signalling a gendered oppression against males, increasing numbers of them described in *bad*, *sad*, *stupid* and *mad* terms might add up to a significant dividend.

This argument will be examined through observations of a Year One boy, Chris, and a Year Two boy, Ali. Chris had been diagnosed with ADHD at the age of five. He was prescribed Ritalin and he attended the nurture group four mornings per week. At other times he would join the mainstream group, if possible with an assistant (though no specific funding was available for this). Ali had a diagnosis of ADHD and Autism, but was not on any medication. His diagnoses gave the school sufficient funding to supply him with a teaching assistant in the morning, at other times he joined the rest of the class.

When I first started observing the Year One classroom I was not aware that Chris had a diagnosis of ADHD. He had his own rug to sit on when the group was altogether on the carpet, and he rarely participated any more than minimally in either whole class or individual activities. His free movement and occupation within the class was quite normalised, as long as he was not disruptive then he did not usually threaten social order and would often be left to his own devices. His communication skills were very poor, with speech little more than a quiet mumble. Chris was the second youngest of five children in his family all of whom were being or had been schooled at Alderley. The derisive discourse that the family had accumulated drew not only from the school, but also from social services, which had carried out several home inspections unannounced. Chris's behaviour was seen as an unsurprising, even inevitable consequence of these circumstances.

This view of the inevitable tended to govern Chris's schooling regardless of his actual behaviour. If he 'kicked off', as some staff described it, then three or four staff might have been called on to control him and his medication would be used liberally. If Chris was not disruptive then he would be untalkative and non-participatory and there would likely be no great concern about his almost non-existent academic output.

The following excerpts are taken from an afternoon where Chris was to be *included* in the mainstream classroom:

| | |
|---|---|
| 1.24 | Chris is crawling around on the floor and refusing all attention. |
| Tina: | [To Haley] 'If he's crawling around leave him, but I need someone to keep an eye on him.' |
| 1.26 | Chris has made it back to the carpet but is shuffling around on a chair and still not participating, and now is back to crawling under tables. |
| 1.30 | Chris is still under a table but playing quite contentedly by himself. |

*(fn 4/10)*

From this restless and non-participatory but not disruptive role, Tina, Haley and another assistant, Andrea, attempted to draw Chris into some activities:

1.37    Haley has come over to the carpet with an eye on Chris. He emerges from under the table and then fetches his ball and starts chasing it round. This is confiscated and Chris sulks off ... he is soon up looking for something to do and now lurks around the work tables. Haley can't interest him in drawing though. He wants a jigsaw now but they are on a shelf he cannot reach. He sits beneath the shelf and now seems occupied with something he's found on the floor. He seems quite content for now and Haley leaves him to it.

1.39    Andrea is now trying to get Chris to come and do some designing in her department but he is being unresponsive.

1.40    Tina now tries to engage Chris, but he disappears angrily under a table again and is now throwing his shoes at Tina.

1.41    Chris has now been coaxed out from under the table and persuaded to play with some beads.

*(fn 4/10)*

The pattern that can be observed here involved Chris attracting the attention of the female adults in the room through his non-participation. His disruption then appeared to increase relative to the attempts made to bring him back toward something productive. The task then became an attempt to minimise harm; as long as this objective was met then the nature of the activity that Chris pursued seemed by comparison unimportant.

My observation whereby Chris's levels of disruption seemed to increase with the amount of attention given him was most clearly evident in the nurture group. Nurture groups are an increasingly popular means through which schools attempt to manage certain problem populations. Based on the assumption of emotional deficit within the child, the combined result of 'biological factors' (Cooper, 2001, p. 18) and 'developmental impoverishment' (Boxall, 2002, p. 3), they are small groups with increased individual attention and an emphasis on pastoral care. The groups aim to provide a positive, relaxed and encouraging environment in which children might learn to express themselves better and build their sense of *emotional literacy* (Sharp, 2001; also see Chapter 7).

The Years One and Two nurture group at Alderley was usually overseen by two classroom assistants, Andrea and Clare, and regularly attended by six children, four boys and two girls, with other members joining the group sporadically.

The smaller group had some observably positive effects on Chris, particularly in the improvement in his communication skills. However, the increased confidence he might have felt resulting from this, combined with the group's relative freedom from the constraints of the classroom, and lack of academic agenda permitted more disruptive and violent behaviour from Chris:

Everyone is encouraged to set their own targets for the following week … Clare suggests that Chris tries not to hit any staff. Apparently in the last week he has hit both Tina and Andrea.

*(fn 23–11)*

Later that day, in conversation with Heather and Tina:

Tina is finding Chris's behaviour particularly upsetting. Yesterday he gave her a whack in the stomach which almost knocked her over.

*(fn 23–11)*

The following week in the nurture group:

Chris is about as talkative as I think I've ever heard. When it's audible then his speech is basic but otherwise there's not much wrong with it. He is also pretty active today and the consensus amongst Andrea and Clare is that he hasn't had his medication.

(…)

When the work activity is set, Chris refused to join in and instead went and sat on the cushions with a book … Clare tried to get Chris involved, he refused repeatedly, becoming increasingly angry at Clare's attempts which culminated in him hitting her and running into the corner … Clare continues to try and bring him back, he hits her again and storms out of the room.

*(fn 27–11)*

Afterwards I was discussing this incident with Heather:

Just then someone else came into the staffroom announcing that Chris and Kyle had been in a fight and now Chris was on the rampage, lashing out freely. Heather went off to investigate this, returning back a few minutes later to say that he was up a tree and wouldn't come down.

*(fn 27–11)*

When Chris was eventually coaxed down he was swiftly given more medication and then while everyone else went to Nativity rehearsal he stayed in the Year One classroom playing on the computer and colonising the attention of the classroom assistant, who was attempting to take several other children through some extra literacy.

In the above excerpts, as Chris's behaviour became more violent the nurture group assumptions were not disrupted and attempts were made, in this case by Clare, to try to encourage him back. This was met with further violence. After this, while he was the topic of conversation in the staffroom, the violent behaviour worsened. At this point he had colonised the attention of a large proportion of the staff.

Damage limitation was then sought in the further administration of medication and exclusion from the afternoon's activities.

From the 'developmentally impoverished' (Boxall, 2002, p. 3) assumption of the nurture group came the assumption that when something went wrong with Chris's behaviour it was due to disregard at home:

> In the staff room this morning there was a great deal of congress going on about Chris. Apparently he had a bad day yesterday and again a lack of medication was blamed. More aspersions were cast as to the parents' ability to administer the medication correctly with someone claiming that they had heard that some parents kept back the dose intended for school to help them manage at home.
>
> *(fn 23–11)*

In Chris's case the dividend his diagnosis provided was a complex question, mediated by several externalities. If he chose not to disrupt, then he was free to behave in almost any other way he chose, free from the academic agenda of the school, and free to choose whether or not to follow the directions and encouragement of the staff around him. Perhaps Chris experienced the increased attention he was given in the nurture group as compromising this masculine privilege, and he reacted in hegemonic manner with violence. This violence attracted more attention until the resource of medication was sought.

So, freedom, attention, resources were all on Chris's side. However, educationally he received no dividend regardless of his behaviour. If he did not disrupt then he was left to his own non-participatory and unproductive devices. If he did disrupt then he was made docile with medication and excluded from ordinary proceedings. The externalities of ADHD and the background which was presumed to have caused it were held as the inevitable and inescapable assumptions by which his schooling was governed according to a fatalised, *laissez-faire* approach, leaving alternative explanations and solutions unexplored.

Ali's case contrasted to Chris's in several immediately obvious ways: first, his combined diagnoses came with a statement of funding, through which the school could provide him with a classroom assistant, Anna, every morning, and this allowed him to be kept in the mainstream classroom without recourse to either nurture group or medication. Second, Ali's mother was on good terms with both Anna and the Year Two class teacher, Rachel, and I heard of no associations made between Ali's home situation and his behaviour.

Chris and Ali were also very different physically; where Chris was a small, shy and usually very quiet child, Ali was bigger and taller than most of the class, and he was frequently very loud. Though he went about it in different ways, Ali also had a tendency to control interactions with the female adults around him, and held his own very visible normative space within the classroom:

> 11.26   Group activities have been back on for about 4–5 minutes now, when Rachel has to stop them for noise levels. She says she

knows Ali shouts out during work time, but that doesn't mean everyone can.

*(fn 02–11)*

This normative dispensation could often be observed physically:

9.50   Rachel starts to call out addition sums … Ali is wandering around with what looks like a plane made out of plastic cubes. Anna currently seems content to let him as he does a lap of the classroom.

9.52   Ali does another lap of the room and gets a cheery hello on the way through from the rest of the children who are sitting on the carpet. He then starts to go on what looks like another lap, but Anna stops him to suggest a more constructive activity. Ali is now clambering over one of the desks and Anna prizes him away from this and leads him back to his work table.

*(fn 06–11)*

As well as his freedom of movement, Ali was relatively free with the amount of noise he could acceptably create. At times he and Anna had what seemed a good natured and productive relationship, however, Anna was often directed by Ali's whim. He was the dominant force and frequently violent in his interactions:

10.12   Ali wants to use a crayon to write with but Anna would rather he used a pencil, he throws his pencil away and takes a green crayon. Anna takes the box of crayons away to a loud scream of 'NO!!' from Ali. She manages to get him holding a pencil again by threatening to put a sad face in his book for his mother to see. Ali obviously doesn't like this idea but still won't write down the work given, he keeps swinging little plastic letters around and refusing to write anything. Now he has scribbled all over his paper. 'The end', he says, 'No', says Anna, 'it's not the end'. 'The end! The end! The end!' screams Ali. He stands up, upending his chair and oblivious to Anna's gentle admonishment goes over to the group on the carpet.

*(fn 06–11)*

As with Chris, it seemed that Anna's 'gentle' approach was based on damage limitation. For Chris, this approach continually sanctioned his lack of academic output, for Ali, it was his rude, violent and anti-social means of asserting himself that was sanctioned.

Nevertheless, there were considerable benefits to Anna's patient approach in what with time she could sometimes get Ali to do. The following excerpts are taken from a quite lengthy scene between the two of them (the demands of notation did not allow me to also record the time):

> Ali is still banging around and shouting 'Shut up!' at regular intervals . . .
>
> . . . Ali continues shouting various things at Anna . . .
>
> . . . It sounds like he wants to do some patterns, Anna asks him to do something and gets told to 'Shut up!' and again when she asks him to pick up his book, now he has left the table . . .
>
> . . . Ali has now scribbled on and ripped his book, Anna threatens to tell his mum. This causes even more consternation from Ali, but with no reasoning, he just responded with more 'Shut up!' . . .
>
> . . . Anna now takes the crayons to put them away which is greeted with another scream and he runs over to stop her . . .
>
> . . . Anna introduces the idea of a lunchtime sanction but at the last minute he throws the book down again with a scream that he wants to do numbers not patterns. Finally Anna capitulates and agrees to let him do numbers, but Ali is still not happy . . .
>
> . . . it sounds like he doesn't want to do numbers in the number book so Anna offers him the pattern book, 'No patterns!' is the shouted response . . .
>
> . . . Ali has thrown all his pencils away so now has nothing to write with, he tries to grab his book back but Anna persists and eventually she has Ali sitting on a seat and looking at the sums, which once he gets into he performs very competently.
>
> *(fn 06–11)*

Here Ali was being about as persistently difficult as I ever witnessed, and yet Anna kept attempting to bring him back to the task in hand. She allowed him to shout and throw things without sanction, but in so doing managed to eventually re-capture Ali's attention and get him doing some work. As I observed at the end of this excerpt, he performed this competently. In fact Ali's literacy and numeracy levels were around average for the class. Ali, therefore, was not limited in the same way that Chris was by his social externalities. His problems were supported financially and were not seen as the inevitable product of a *disordered* upbringing.

However, in the afternoons when Anna was no longer in class, Rachel had to manage the class often without any help. In the following example one of the part-time classroom assistants, Sheila, attempts to reason with Ali:

> 2.14   Sheila is back in the room and trying to get Ali to read a book. 'Just go away' is his response. Now he throws some pictures on the floor, tells Sheila to shut up, walks out of the room and slams the door. Sheila pursues him, though she is now back in the room without him, I think he may be using one of the computers outside.
>
> *(fn 06–11)*

Here, the pattern followed is much more similar to the approach taken with Chris. Ali no longer had Anna with whom he might have been expected to be relatively cooperative. As soon as he started showing any aggression or opposition the primary objective became attaining peace and quiet. This acted both to sanction the aggression through inaction and also to place social order ahead of trying to provide a constructive activity for Ali.

A distinction thus emerged between Chris and Ali's schooling and between the times when Ali had the full-time attention of Anna and when he did not. First, and most obviously, Ali was much more academically productive than Chris. The vast majority of this production took place when he was with Anna, and so she represents the clearest indication of the additional dividend that he received compared to Chris. When Anna was taken away, then interactions with Ali tended to take on a similar pattern to those with Chris, with the emphasis on *docility* (Foucault, 1977).

However, for over half the time Ali was in school, he had resources and attention directed at him not only to try and control and normalise his behaviour and protect the immediate social order, but also to regulate his attention towards the needs of his schooling, from which he will likely draw future dividend. With his dual diagnosis, perhaps the message sent by the institutional response is that a child's best chance of success is not simply with one label, but with a matrix of them. The distinction between Chris and Ali also illustrates Foucault's (1981b) distinction between a power that seeks to *discipline* through 'an *anatamo-politics of the human body*' (p. 139; emphasis in original); which is the *docility* approach taken with Chris; and, a power that seeks *regulatory control* through 'a *bio-politics of the population* … a power whose highest function was … to invest life through and through' (p. 139; emphasis in original). One is a power that seeks to *control* by *domination*, the other seeks to *regulate* through *optimisation*.

## Dominance and dividend?

The perceived need to alleviate the struggles of boys in schools is inscribed through discourses of the *bad*, *sad*, *stupid* and *mad*. Yet these narratives mask the continued dominance of boys in school, which has been demonstrated here both through some of the existing research on school and gender and through observational data.

This initial dominance opens up normative and resource driven spaces within schools. From the increased attention of teachers in class, to special needs interventions such as nurture groups and in some cases the resources of the psychiatric profession. The medical intervention distributes a new set of normative positions that encourage adults to further sanction hegemonic masculine behaviours. This feeds a circular motion whereby male dominance breaches the routine order, creating spaces into which psychopathology can intervene to open up new normative space to allow for further dominance. The contrasted cases of Kyle and Ben imply that the mechanism by which the circular motion initially takes hold is the need for social order. Thus overtly hegemonic behaviour is required to attract resources and interventions.

Within an overall situation of dominance, some finer distinctions can be drawn out as to the extent to which psychopathology may represent a dividend. In Ali's case the dividend appeared relatively clear cut. He had his own normative and physical space in the classroom; his violent and dominating behaviour was sanctioned through this space and through the assignment of a teaching assistant to him; because of the sensitive and productive nature of this relationship Ali was often successfully integrated into the academic demands of his schooling.

In contrast to this was Chris, whose label conspired with naturalised assumptions regarding his family background to produce a bind which in some ways limited his available subject positions. Chris had been offered both the resources of the nurture group and Ritalin. However, he often seemed to enact a dichotomised ontology within school whereby he would either take up a non-disruptive and non-participative role and be left to his own unproductive devices, or he would take up an active, over-exuberant role in which case he would likely be dosed. Once again it could be argued that the presentation of violent masculine behaviours attracted resources and attention for Chris. But this was only in the questionable dividend represented by medicalisation and Ritalin.

The case of the children largely missing from my data; the inattentive, the sad and the girls, is illustrative of a more generalised problematic. Through his absence, Ross (see Chapter 3) represents an extension of the problematic whereby masculine dominance will only be sanctioned and resourced if it threatens social order. Like Chris, Ross's diagnosis has not forced a confrontation with his academic difficulties. Equally, if Ross did not disrupt then he remained invisible. For Chris and Ross the diagnosis has had something of the reverse dividend effect where the naturalised assumptions it produced guided a laissez-faire approach to their schooling.

The complexities of individual statements about the precise nature of dividend do not detract from being able to speak of a generalised dominance of males in the classrooms presented here, and this is testified to by the distinct lack of female children in the analysis. The valorisation of social order seems to hold primary dominance, however, and this implies that individual males will be differently served or limited through their actions.

There seems little sense in which, on its own, psychiatric diagnosis generates significant dividend unless it is backed up by practical resources at the classroom level. Additionally, though I have posited the new normative space which it opens up for some children, and the overall sense in which this serves male domination, at the individual level this is to some extent an exclusionary space, predicated on the assumption of an internal, naturalised or developmental deficit in the child.

Through the next two chapters the issue of naturalisation and development will be probed further with gender remaining one of the primary frameworks for analysis. Chapter 6 moves away from the school and classroom to look at the conditioning of diagnostic possibilities through the narratives of two families. Within these two narratives, my focus also shifts from looking primarily at the child in question to look at the work required of parents of children with ADHD.

# 6

# INVISIBLE PARENTWORK

Retaining the focus on issues of gender and family from the previous chapter, the analysis in this chapter moves away from *problem children* to explore individual accounts of what it means to be a parent of a child with ADHD. In the two cases presented here, the *condition* of parenting a child with ADHD (Carpenter and Austin, 2008) produced feelings of guilt and responsibility, which led to positions of advocacy being taken up by each parent on behalf of their children. Parents adopted this position in order to regain some agency in decision-making processes regarding their children, however, the reverse effect was frequently experienced, with each parent facing repeated subversion of their identity, leading them further into a *project* of parenting according to medically conceived truths of behavioural disorder. I will begin by introducing the different perspectives on the relation between the family and ADHD, before moving to the analysis of the interview data.

## Situating the family

ADHD and the mass medication of young children is an area of some considerable contestation within professional, academic and popular media, which makes up 'an intellectual territoriality characterised by struggles over whose knowledge is of most worth' (Graham, 2007c, p. 12). Within this struggle, one of the most hotly debated topics is the question of aetiology: who or what is to blame for this disorder?

Among medical and popular scientific perspectives on ADHD, social critique is often seen as unsupportive for those in families, schools and health services grappling with the *reality* of ADHD in their everyday work. By comparison, medical professionals are able to project a *value-neutral* self-image; blame is reframed as pathological inheritance. This contestation is important as it has bred a politically charged discourse, implying a particular ordering of legitimate, and illegitimate, actors and actions, and this has repercussions for the everyday experience of ADHD for families.

It has been argued that women are more vulnerable to discourses of responsibility and blame and to the belief that any problem with their children is their fault (Carpenter and Austin, 1999). In relation to ADHD mothers have told of the feelings of guilt, shame, responsibility and blame which become attached to the experience of parenting (Bennett, 2004; Singh, 2004). Singh (2003) describes conflicts created when parents hold different perspectives on notions of behaviour disorder, in which fathers might adopt the fatalised *boys will be boys* perspective, which brings many of the implications for circularity introduced in the previous chapter.

In the account below, while the insinuation of guilt did seem to be experienced more keenly by the mothers, parental conflict was not in evidence. Different perceptions existed between parents as to their place in the disorder discourse and the responsibilities this implied, and these are separated out within the analysis. The high degree of involvement of one of the fathers in this account, has allowed a move to be sketched from invisible *motherwork* to *parentwork* (D. Smith, 2005). No assumptions have been cast regarding the applicability of this move outside this particular context. I begin with a discussion of medical and psychological perspectives on ADHD and the family.

## Psycho-medical perspectives

Within some of the more prevalent medical opinions on ADHD, it is suggested that the parental role in the production of behavioural problems should be played down in favour of neuropsychiatric and genetic discourses. As an 'international consensus statement' puts it:

> To publish stories that ADHD is a fictitious disorder or merely a conflict between today's Huckleberry Finns and their caregivers is tantamount to declaring the earth flat, the laws of gravity debatable, and the periodic table in chemistry a fraud.
>
> *(Barkley, 2002, p. 90)*

Things are not always quite as clear cut as this suggests, however, as can be read on the same page of this same document:

> This is not to say that the home environment, parental management abilities, stressful life events, or deviant peer relationships are unimportant or have no influence on individuals having this disorder, as they certainly do.
>
> *(Barkley, 2002, p. 90)*

Unless it could be shown that 'stressful life events' have some impact on the 'laws of gravity' then it seems that these two statements both employ a certain reductionism. National health guidance for effective treatment of ADHD doesn't only promote stimulant medication, but also various psychosocial interventions such as family therapy and parent training (NICE, 2006; NIMH, 2006). As suggested between the two *consensus statements* above, this suggests that parents hold an ambiguous place within this field, with the desire to denigrate those who lay blame in the immediate society of the family tempered by the admission that this environment must mean *something*.

Further complicating this picture is what has been called the 'awkward alliance' (Graham, 2007c, p. 13) between several different medical and mental health discourses within prevalent understandings of ADHD. The description of the disorder originated with the American Psychiatric Association, yet in addition to psychiatrists, paediatricians, general practitioners and clinical and educational psychologists all use this definition, and it is recognised by professionals across the spectrum of education and social care services (SCIE, 2004). While professional boundaries are blurred and many individuals will not fit a neat discursive position, it can be argued that psychiatric and paediatric responses to behaviour disorder reflect more of a biological developmental approach, while the discourse of psychology, while still developmental, might emphasise alternative, *cognitive*, or *psychosocial*, or *environmental* factors in their approach. This does not mean that attention to variables associated with the family are the sole province of one or other perspective, merely that the family is differently implicated in both the presumed cause and projected response to the child's problems.

In terms of response this difference could be read in a doctor's recommendation that the child should be put on medication, while a psychological response might recommend a more behavioural therapeutic approach. The psychological response carries the most obvious responsibilities for parents in terms of behaviour modification techniques and family therapy, which in turn carries a fairly obvious indictment of their current and past behaviour in relation to their children. However, one should not ignore the somewhat more invisible work of parenthood with regards medication (Singh, 2004, 2005), which will be returned to in the analysis below.

From the more biological developmental perspective, various aspects of pre- and post-natal physical development implicate the actions of the mother in the presentation of the behaviour. Frequently cited, though inconclusively evidenced, is the effect of gestational exposure to cigarettes or alcohol (Bhatara *et al.*, 2006; Rodriguez and Bohlin, 2005).

Within the psychosocial developmental perspective the importance of mother–child *attachment* (Halasz *et al.*, 2002), maternal *attributions* (Collett and Gimpel, 2004), maternal *psychopathology* (Banks *et al.*, 2008; Harvey *et al.*, 2003) and maternal *obesity* (Rodriguez *et al.*, 2008) are all implicated in the production of the child's behavioural anomalies: 'Fat mums link to hyper kids', reads a headline from the *Daily Mirror* (Cook, 2007).

These approaches are epitomised in the desire of one group of psychologists to re-brand ADHD as 'attachment-deficit-hyper-reactivity disorder'

(Halasz *et al.*, 2002). This alternative translation of ADHD is predicated upon the hypothesised impact of post–natal depression on children's behaviour:

> In those earliest interactions, the infant of a depressed mother will mirror the difficulties both with facial expressions as well as with measurable changes in brain activity.
>
> *(Halasz et al., 2002, p. 4)*

This leads to the 'conceptually creative hypothesis' that:

> the traumatic experience for the infant who is not held in his mother's mind due to his mother's depression displays symptoms of early trauma characterized by hyper-vigilance and difficulty focusing on anything other than the threatening situation. Over time, the picture that emerges resembles ADHD.
>
> *(Halasz et al., 2002, p. 4)*

This theory first takes what could be judged a *natural* response to the accumulation of work and emotion associated with the post-natal lifeworld and labels it 'depression'. It then assumes that this depression will not only represent the child as having no place in 'his' mother's mind, but that this fact will be read consistently by the child and reacted to in a consistent manner. The formula is complete with the convenient 'resemblance' to ADHD.

These excerpts illustrate a somewhat more complex picture of professional perspectives on ADHD than is evidenced in Barkley's (2002) claim that the indictment of the family in the account of ADHD is solely the province of 'the wholly unscientific views of some social critics in periodic media accounts' (p. 89). For here is an account, in the 'scientific language' that neuropsychiatrist Barkley might recognise as allied with his own, which places mother and son at the very centre of a reductive and judgemental hypothesis.

Far from being *conceptually creative* the attachment hypothesis of Halasz *et al.* (2002) appears practically unchanged from past psychoanalytic theories of pathology, such as the idea that schizophrenia was caused by the 'frigid mother'. Singh (2002) traces the 'schizophrenogenic mother' to the immediate post-war period and the moral panic over boys' *emotional disturbance*. Here, Singh (2002) quotes a psychoanalyst from this period; Frieda Fromm Reichman:

> The schizophrenic is painfully distrustful and resentful of other people due to the severe early warp and rejection he encountered in important people in his infancy and childhood, as a rule mainly the schizophrenogenic mother.
>
> *(Singh, 2002, p. 583)*

Almost every element of this argument, right up to the two way gender indictment of mother and son, is reproduced over 50 years later in the attachment hypothesis of Halasz *et al.* (2002). Singh (2002) argues that texts such as these, along with more populist writing such as Dr Spock's *Baby and childcare*, created the detachment of which they spoke in the relation between mothers and sons. For Singh (2002), the shared assumptions over a child's *adjustment* or *pre-delinquent* states, 'combining psychoanalytic premises with biomedical understandings of disease prevention' (p. 589), could be read from specialist discourses such as the mental hygiene movement, through Spock's manual, down to the articles in popular women's magazines of the same period.

Dr Spock produced an early and well-known example of parental guidance, today the market is littered with parental guidance regarding ADHD, which invoke the same detachment and vulnerability. As one such book opens:

> Do you feel that you can no longer cope with your child's behaviour, that you and his school have done everything possible for him and that he is beyond redemption?
>
> *(Train, 2005, p. 11)*

Concerning images abound: the gendering of his, him, and he, the quasi-religious tone of the aberrant child in need of 'redemption' for *his* sin, and the manipulative condescension of the personalised style of address; this is an account about 'you and your ADD child' to borrow the title of another such text (Wallace, 1999). Train's (2005) account continues:

> You may deeply resent him because his behaviour has turned you into a physical and nervous wreck, destroyed your career or your marriage, caused friends to desert you and neighbours to shun you. In your eyes he may have become the embodiment of everything you hate in yourself and others. In essence, you may feel that he has made your life a misery and that you have had enough.
>
> *(Train, 2005, p. 11)*

Having melodramatically opened up this essence of exclusion, helplessness, and loathing, the account moves in for the reassuring kill, 'you should not feel guilty about this' (p. 11), before launching into its miracle cure for the helpless mother and demonic child.

The deployment of this personalised and emotive language marks passages such as these in using 'words that perform in that they evoke images that increase the effect of the statement' (Graham, 2007d, p. 11). This *performance* only serves to draw attention to the attempt which this genre repeatedly invokes; to manipulate individuals into a pedagogical relationship with their own bodies, and their own *bodily efficiency* (N. Rose, 1989).

The representations of parents, children and families that can be found in these texts can be read as what Donzelot (1979) referred to as 'the regulation of images' (p. 169), through which he describes the diffusion of the methods of psychoanalysis throughout the social body. Fragments of this *medico-psycho-pedagogical centre* (hereafter; *med-psy-ped*) can be traced across social institutions and discursive planes: 'in a discrete room of the divorce courts, in the services for the protection of mothers and children, in the birth-planning centers, and in the sex-education organizations' (p. 169). To this list one could add, 'in the *support* literature for parents of children with ADHD'.

## Cultures of blame

Through her analysis of the mental-hygiene movement, cited above, as well as through empirical work with parents and children, Ilina Singh has critiqued what she calls a *culture of mother blame* within ADHD discourse. The proliferation of images of inadequacy, based on naturalised conceptions of maternal relations, produces cultures within which 'mothering with Ritalin' (Singh, 2004, p. 1193) becomes a similarly natural response to the work of parenting the behaviourally disordered child. Due to their positions of mediation between the public worlds of medical and educational discourse and the private sphere of the family, parents 'occupy space in most positions around the web of blame', consequently: 'parent blame is both specific and scattered, both highly visible and diffuse' (p. 1194).

For Singh (2004), parents seek absolution from their self-images of blame and inadequacy through psycho-medical discourses, in which neuro-genetics and Ritalin become panaceas; currencies with which to make the exchange: 'mother-blame-brain-blame' (p. 1194). As Donzelot's (1979) *med-psy-ped* relation reminds us, however, this is also a pedagogical discourse, one by which parents are expected to regulate themselves, *learn* about themselves and conceptualise parenting as a *project*, or to borrow Foucault's (1988) term, a *technology*.

The social relations established here, blame and absolution constituted through attachment theory and the popular representations of parental *support* literature, provide the conditions limiting the possibilities of parentwork. Parenting through a diagnostic process becomes technical; the steps ascribed by external, therapeutic narratives. I argue here that re-imagining parenting on this basis involves the effacement of a personally meaningful narrative of responsibility in favour of therapeutic 'mechanisms of obligation' (Dermott, 2005, p. 93).

## Active parenting

The data to be presented here is drawn from my interviews with the two families introduced in Chapter 3: Louse and Mike Bartlett, and Sian Hyland. The sense in which both Louise and Mike and Sian all saw their place in the world of ADHD as one of continuous struggle perhaps has something to do with the way I sought access for the interviews via a parent support group. Membership of such a group implies a certain position regarding collective activism and one would perhaps not join such a group if there were not a prior perception of struggle or mis-representation. These positions of struggle and advocacy have fed into the *active parenting* that I describe below.

Membership of support networks implies an active role in the everyday work of parenting a child with ADHD. The experiences detailed below explore what this advocacy role meant for each parent in the implications it had for the way they were viewed, and viewed themselves, as parents. In terms of self-image, I offer *active* as a rejection by Louise and Sian of the image of the *inadequate* mother: 'characterized by her lack of sufficient care, positive emotion, knowledge, insight and action' (Singh, 2004, p. 1196).

For each family, the active work of parenting started with the attention to and identification of behaviours in their children which they deemed problematic or abnormal. For Louise (L) and Mike (M) the initial basis for abnormality was in Liam's divergence from both his brother's behavioural patterns and an external standard of expected young-child behaviour:

L:   About three years ago I started looking into it [ADHD] because I knew my child was different to my older child then. From three months old we knew that he was completely different; even just sitting in the bouncer. He was sat in the bouncer but he was just constantly on the go ... He wouldn't sit and watch the telly. He has never ever played with a toy. I'm not saying that if there was a baby sat here now with a car he would get the car and push it up the room but then that's it. You know, he's never done something and it's lasted for an hour.

M:   And the concentration level has been no more than seconds.

From this basis of over-activity and inattention Louise recalls typing 'hyperactivity' into an online search engine, which is where she first learned about ADHD. Once this conclusion over the nature of Liam's problems had been reached the work of parenting became one of actively seeking support:

L:   From about eighteen months I was taking him down the Health Clinic asking the health visitors, doctors, to sort him out and they just said that he was coming up to the 'terrible twos' and when he was two it was the same and when he was past two it was – no he's still got the 'terrible twos'. Well he had the 'terrible twos' for about two or three years. So, like we said, two years ago we went down to the doctors and said that we were not happy with this – this child is different to other children and we pushed and pushed and pushed to see a paediatrician first.

What ADHD offered to Louise was the chance to think of her son's problems as something *other*, something that was separable from *him*, an internal 'evil agent' (Hacking, 1999, p. 113), which acted *upon* him and which could be *treated* as such. In the above comment, the institutional response that she received, which was one of *ordinary* deviance described as the 'terrible twos' was unhelpful for Louise as it offered no means to re-normalise the family environment according to an external abnormality over which they had no control. What this frustration led to was the active role of 'pushing' in order to try to objectify Liam's difference as outside *ordinary boy-ness*.

A similar story was told by Sian (S) in relation to Charlie, who at three years old was:

> S:   Very physically aggressive; he would attack me and thump, kick, bite; trash the house; pull curtains off the walls; broke toys; ripped clothes. We'd have huge tantrums that would last for two or three hours at a time where he would be inconsolable. You couldn't reason with him at all.

As Sian did not have other children of her own to compare Charlie to, it was not until he reached school that she was able to start thinking of his behaviour as something *other*:

> S:   Being the oldest child you always think that it is you being a bad parent who can't cope with the way they are and that sort of thing. It's only when you start talking to other parents and all the things you've tried have worked on other children but they don't on your own. Like taking toys away and stopping them watching telly and that sort of thing. Whatever you've tried to control his behaviour has not worked whereas on their children it worked.

From this perception of abnormality, in comparison to other children, for whom *normal* behavioural controls were sufficient, Sian encountered various media through which she came to the conclusion of ADHD:

> S:   I'd actually seen a programme on telly about a young girl and I thought: 'That's what he does!' So I rang up the NHS help line and they sent an inset pack out that came from MIND and they suggested a book in there to read and I went and bought this book and virtually every page I turned over was about him.
> Res: What book was that?
> S:   Dr Green: *Understanding ADHD*. And I could highlight virtually on every page and it was him.

Like Louise and Mike, Sian also received what she perceived to be unhelpful responses from outside agencies:

> S:   I was referred to [local mental health services] and they came back and they said that they couldn't see him because he wasn't suicidal. So I was

referred to another clinic and they said that perhaps I should go on a behaviour management course and that it was a parent issue and not a child issue.

With the same frustration for this as an explanation, Sian took on a more 'active' role in gaining the responses she sought:

>S:     So I spoke to [a parental support agent] and she suggested that there was a [specialist clinic] and perhaps we could go down there. So I spoke to the GP and he said that he would refer us and that the local authority would fund him to go down and he said that it would take about a week to get through and six weeks later we still hadn't heard so I rang him up and asked him what was going on and he said that he hadn't heard but he'd ring again and I said: 'No, I'll ring. Give me the number'. So I rang up the Health Authority and they agreed to fund him to go down for an initial assessment and they've been paying ever since.

Though details differ, both accounts so far have followed a similar pattern whereby a perception of abnormality led parents into contact with professional discourses that did not always provide the responses each parent required in order to initiate the blame exchange that they sought. What this meant is that in order to help their children, parenting had to become active *self-help* (Giddens, 1991), through which parents attempted to re-appropriate specialist information according to their own knowledge and experience of their children. The next section will go on to discuss what some of the consequences of making oneself such an active agent might be.

## Struggling for agency

The struggle has started with the everyday work of ADHD for each of these parents, in the active role taken in terms of gaining some recognition and support for their children. Now, I explore how this attempt brought parents up against institutional knowledge by which their agency was frequently undermined and their knowledge subjugated.

This relation was frequently enacted through dealings with the school, as Louise says in relation to trying to get Liam assessed for learning difficulties:

>L:     Yes, he's going for a test for dyslexia now. Again I've been telling the school that he's dyslexic. Alright I'm no professional but I am a mother and I know when he is struggling. So I've talked to the SENCO for over a year to try and get an assessment for dyslexia but they said: 'No, no, no, there's nothing wrong with him.'

This assertion of the legitimacy of her knowledge as a mother is testament to the agency that Louise felt she needed in decisions being made about Liam, which she was being denied, she continued:

> L: With a statement we wrote the letter ourselves and sent it off to them ourselves. The school was going to do it but we got in there first so I wanted to refer Liam myself but she said that I couldn't do it.

For Louise, the institutional ideology of the school has denied her the agency to influence decisions both regarding the specialist assessments Liam receives in school and his statement. The frustration both Louise and Mike felt in terms of the unresponsiveness of the school was well illustrated by Mike's comment that:

> M: Up to now we've had two years of education where nothing has happened at all. Basically we've had enough, haven't we? Come August we said that we can't cope with this anymore. We've had two years of going back and forth between the school trying to solve this; trying to solve that; going to the psychiatrist once a month and nothing was getting done. So really we took it in our own hands and said that we weren't having it anymore. We're not going to allow it to happen.

Mike's statement makes clear reference to the difficult position of mediation in which these parents found themselves, 'at the junction between the private world of the family and the public world outside' (Vincent, 2000, p. 27). The 'public worlds' that they encounter are those of education and psychiatry, yet what they perceive as their duty, what they will not 'allow to happen' in terms of Liam's future, has been introduced to them through discursive means, which to some extent undermine the public/private dualism.

Where once it might have been useful to consider the *particularistic* family feeding into the *universal* values of school (Parsons, 1961), what can be read through these accounts is that new universalisms proliferated through *med-psy-ped* centres (Donzelot, 1979) have re-formed the social body according to much more diffuse distinctions. Ready-formed norms of behavioural development, accounts of being, which are conceived as acting 'regardless of culture' (Barkley, 2002, p. 89), and complete with a set of 'outcomes' by which the future can be known and subverted, provide one example of this invasion. This is part of the process by which families become *technologies*, in which: 'parenting has shifted imperceptibly away from something that is "natural" towards something that has to be learned and that can be perfected, or at least improved' (Vincent, 2000, pp. 22–3). Nevertheless, *naturalisation* is the means by which pedagogies address individuals.

The *natural* parenting role within this account was predicated according to the Western *cultural* model of child psychiatry. This was an active role through which parents encouraged others to become literate in the same behavioural discourses they had: from pupil to teacher. That biological inference is deemed *genuine causality* testifies to the status of truth that medical perspectives attain in the contestation of ADHD, as does the seeming ease with which Barkley (2002) can brush 'culture' aside. That Barkley's quote, above, was taken from an 'international consensus statement' and counter-signed by around 90 other mental health professionals only serves to reinforce the point.

Such buried assumptions give biology a claim to the *rhetoric of naturalness*, in service of which parents are expected to undertake *repair work* (Murphy, 1999), producing and sustaining the image of the self-improving *good parent*. Re-inserting culture into the equation would require *natural* to be re-termed *normal* according to whichever social knowledge is most desired. *Normal* requires emphasis; scare quoting, 'What is normal?', the now clichéd response. Using *normal* therefore is a statement, it draws greater attention to the arbitrariness of the apparently self-evident: the political production of scientific knowledge, the socio-economic production of the family, and the cultural regulation of parental imagery.

Sian experienced a similar regulation to Louise, first, through the loss of personal agency in an exchange with her GP:

> S:     So I had to go back to the GP and explain it to him that we needed the pure Ritalin but he said that he wasn't prepared to give me that prescription and he asked why I needed the pure Ritalin. You almost feel like ... I actually said to them: 'Well I'll tell you what I'll do. I'll bring my son in when he's off medication and you can keep him here for a week if you like.'

Through further investigation Sian found out that this refusal by the GP was the product of a correspondence between the school and the GP about Charlie's medication, which had been conducted without Sian ever being contacted; she had been physically *effaced*:

> S:     But I thought: hang on a minute! You have nothing to do with him. You've never seen him and you can't judge from the outside. And it was only because I went to the GP that I found out about this letter and it had been openly discussed at a teacher's meeting with outside teaching advisors there and everything and nobody had asked permission. So I sent a copy of the letter to [Charlie's paediatric specialist] and he got very stroppy and wrote straight back saying that this child has been under our care since he was eight and that the school weren't qualified to comment on medical conditions.

In both these excerpts from Sian's interview a similar mechanism can be seen at work, in which her knowledge and agency regarding Charlie was undermined and each time she responded with a reinforcement of Charlie's problems. In the first excerpt this came in the form of asserting her own everyday work in managing these problems, in the second it was to the greater expertise of Charlie's specialist that she turned. In each case Sian experienced a threat to her legitimacy as a claimant in her son's affairs, and to each threat she responded by reinforcing his deficits.

This raises the question of why it might be that either Sian or Louise was required to assert the legitimacy of their claim to a stake in decisions regarding their children. Each parent's perception of their responsibility for their child was reinforced through the subversion of their identity by the ideology of the school. This introduced a 'mechanism of obligation' (Dermott, 2005, p. 93) whereby they advocated for their children in order to gain the *correct* recognition and support, and escape images of inadequacy. As detailed above, this responsibility was, first, felt in relation to the initial presentation of disorder. Insinuated by professional and popular discourses of guilt and blame, this fed a responsibility to fight for whatever support and recognition was available.

The spectres of *aberrant child* and *bad parent* were sufficiently influential for both parents to be motivated to find an alternative set of descriptions for their children's behaviour, however, they did not always find comfort in these 'enclosures of expertise' (Rose and Miller, 1992, p. 188), and were forced to take on progressively more active roles. Each time this resulted in a reinforcement of the child's deficit and the family's dependence on specialist knowledge. Against insinuations of the inadequate, an active role was taken, which required parents to conceptualise parenting as a project: a normatively structured process of learning and improvement.

A relation has emerged here between the technologising of individuals and the formation of psychiatric objects. One of the ways this formation might take place is through what Hacking (1995) calls the *looping effect of human kinds*, in which a subject becomes conscious of a description about them and by which they must modify their action. Whether or not the description is seen as fitting, consciousness of it demands the subject to be positioned in relation to it. However, the description is not always as dynamic as subjectivity, so 'what was known about people of a kind may become false because people of that kind have changed in virtue of what they believe about themselves' (Hacking, 1999, p. 34).

The story told here began with parents becoming conscious of their position in a discourse, making themselves active in relation to that discourse and in relation to what they believed about themselves. An attempt was made to falsify that discourse about them, encouraging the means by which their action might loop back 'to force changes in the classifications and knowledge about them' (p. 105). However, what this story so far tells is that this is a dangerous position to adopt, and that 'the current mode of being' (p. 121) a parent of a child with ADHD is a severely limiting subject position.

I argued above that the relations articulated through psycho-medical and popular representations constitute a discourse of blame and absolution, which limits the possibilities of parentwork in relation to behavioural problems. In seeking absolution through falsification of the blame rhetoric, parents in this account were themselves made progressively more dependent on specialist knowledge, creating a loop through which 'blame is reconstituted rather than abolished' (Singh, 2004, p. 1194). The child, therefore, becomes governed according to the *pedagogicalisation* of the parent (Popkewitz, 2003).

This governance can, first, be read in each parent's attempted self-improvement, through the acquisition of specialist discourses of behavioural development. Here, Sian's frustration at the 'common sense' explanations she received from early referrals illustrate this:

> S:   We tried everything: star charts; money in a jar; taking toys away; stop him watching the telly. But none of it worked. He just shrugged his shoulders . . . we found it wasn't a good idea to send him up to his room because he would trash it. So we sat him down on the bottom step of the front door because that was the only place where he couldn't do any damage but then he went through a period of banging his head on the wall.

This comment echoed similar experiences in Louise's story:

> L:   You know, we've done all the positive parenting classes even before we had the diagnosis . . . even those really you can push out of the window – the positive parenting classes – because with ADHD, you know, a lot of it doesn't really work.
>
> Res: Where did you do that?
>
> L:   I did one in the crèche and I did one up in the nursery when he was in state nursery.
>
> Res: And they were telling you the fairly generic . . .
>
> L:   Yeah, pick a chart . . . praise the good when they are being good and ignore the bad. You just can't do it, you know. Like I said when Liam is being bad he can be bad for five hours if we don't stop him. You tell me where he gets the strength to pick up things and throw it and I've got to ignore that and say: 'Don't do that Liam.' You know . . . when he is off on one, as we call it, he don't care who he hits. Whoever is in his path will get it.

Again, what can be seen in both mother's responses was a battle for legitimacy, citing examples of the failure of *normal* approaches to parenting, a kind of defence: *I'm a good parent, but it doesn't work.* This outsider status was reinforced with every perceived lack of support, again this reinforcement happened through a re-assertion of the child's difference.

Sian, unhappy with the 'problem parent' explanation sought advice from a support group through which she was able to contact the specialist who would become both the means to Charlie's treatment and to Sian's ability to make the *blame exchange* (Singh, 2004). Louise went a stage further and after consulting a parental support group, set up her own. For Sian it was the medical discourse that offered her the opportunity to reject this culture, but it is not always so clear cut, as Mike's response to his *responsibilities* will now illustrate.

## Enacting blame

While Louise and Sian both enacted their responsibilities through advocacy, Mike seemed to conceive of his responsibilities in terms of a personal project. Both share an implicit acceptance of responsibility, however, for Louise and Sian the means to blame exchange was in changing the perceptions and practices of others. This was not necessarily so for Mike, who seemed to enact a more personalised responsibilisation of *the good parent*.

In response to a question about his and Louise's use of the term 'anxiety' to describe Liam's state of mind, Mike stated:

> M:     It probably comes through the way we've looked at it and the way that we've been taught ourselves because with this [specialist] assessment it's as much about parents as it is about children, you know. The whole assessment about Liam is also about us as parents and it's for us to be able to understand each stage that Liam is going through.

So, for Mike, part of receiving specialist intervention has been to take on board certain responsibilities in relation to his own assumptions and practices as a parent. Modifying one's behaviour in terms of a professional discourse has implications for thinking about one's position in relation to that discourse:

> M:     But, again, it's about us being positive as parents. Because we are now positive and we know what's happening with the hospital and so on and that has an impact on how we deal with Liam. Ultimately if you are feeling negative about it then that negativity will come through you into Liam.

The job of parenting a child with ADHD is understood here by Mike as a project of self-improvement, whereby, it is them as parents who have to acquire specialist discourses not only to describe their children's abnormality, but also to interrogate themselves, an embodiment of *reflexive modernisation* (Giddens, 1991) in which individuals react to feelings of powerlessness through an attempted appropriation of specialist discourses. Yet actors may become *engulfed* within these discourses. Searching, whether for certainty or absolution, takes them into choices whereby they must either abandon the search for support or submit entirely to the authority of specialism and relinquish the agency they sought in the first place. As Mike states in relation to the decision whether or not to medicate Liam:

> M:     Because [the specialist assessment] have said that he needs medication but, of course, it's us as parents who have to ultimately make that

decision and it's a difficult one to make. He's a child of six coming on
seven and to commit him to long term stimulants is a big ask of parents.

What Mike struck with this comment is central to the paradox that operated
through these attempts at empowerment via specialist knowledge, in which it was
this specialism that required parents to constantly check their own agency, their
own actions and behaviour: 'it's us being positive as parents', 'it's us as parents who
ultimately have to make that decision', 'it's as much about us as parents as it is about
children'. The notion that Mike's narrative repeatedly draws near is that one cannot
appropriate specialist knowledge without becoming an object of it.

Both parents have sought a responsibilisation according to naturalised expectations of *the good parent*; yet the meaning of *good parenting* is socially constituted. In
distancing themselves from images of blame and inadequacy, these parents found
themselves obliged to accept responsibility in a different manner, which effaced their
own agency entirely. Thus, reflected in the loss of autonomy the child experiences
according to their *internal agent* is the loss of agency experienced by the *responsible*
parent.

## Taking responsibility for their children

From the image of the bad parent in relation to their child's behaviour, parents sought
an active and supportive role; a 'good parenting' role, in establishing support and
recognition. Within this role they were regulated according to further derogatory
images: from 'bad' parents to 'pushy' parents. In this struggle for recognition parents
faced a double bind, which is encapsulated in the phrase *taking responsibility for* their
children. Either they must accept a perspective, which holds them responsible for
the production of the disorder in the first place, or, in rejecting this perspective,
they must take responsibility for the 'correct' recognition of their child, which
will involve the submission of the active subjectivity they sought and the implicit
acceptance of the illegitimacy of their own knowledge and experience. Either way,
the deficit resides in the child and the responsibility lies with the parents.

The image of naturalness is held against parents of children with ADHD,
defining their responsibility for their children's aberrance, however, once parents
make themselves vulnerable to the social knowledge of therapeutics, they sacrifice
personal agency and autonomy and face threats to their knowledge as parents.

Louise's narrative illustrated notions of subjugated mother-knowledge: 'I'm no
professional, but I am a mother and I know when he is struggling.' Linked through
the popular representations discussed above, this subjugation creates 'an imaginary
line of what is unacceptable and acceptable in motherhood by having a child whose
behaviour does not conform' (Carpenter and Austin, 2008, p. 38).

Once this obligating mechanism had been introduced the task for each parent
was in becoming responsible themselves in relation to it. However, the therapeutic
discourse which fashioned the image of the *natural, caring, good parent* also made
it unattainable, therefore, parents faced the permanent frustration of the very

*naturalness* they strove for in the first place. Additionally, what this story tells us is that it is not the repressive therapeutic state forcing its labels through institutions such as the school upon the powerless parent. Therapeutic discourse supplies the descriptions and makes the insinuations, but it is each parent that must take up these descriptions and then fight to have them accepted. Rather than make a re-appropriation of expertise through this advocacy, each parent was complicit in constructing the means by which they themselves faced appropriation.

Parents in this account were held responsible for the behaviour of their children, and according to this they sacrificed control over some of the means by which their children were encouraged to develop: psycho stimulants being one example. Yet, their parenting retained legitimacy; they were still responsible for the everyday work of parenting, they were not *held irresponsible*. The next chapter will connect these images of mothering and responsibility back to the classroom, to discuss the further substitution that parents may face in relation to their children's development implied by the rise of 'the nurturing school' (Doyle, 2003, p. 252).

# 7

# THE NURTURING FORMULA

Nurture groups have proliferated in early years education in response to what is seen as the equivalent proliferation of EBDs in young children. They were consistently supported by the New Labour government as central to a school's inclusion policy and Behaviour Support Teams were established around the country offering in-service training and good practice guides. The 'emotional literacy' (Rudd, 1998, p. 5) which they aim to foster meshes with cognitive psychology as well as policies such as *Every Child Matters* (DFES, 2004) and the social and emotional developmental components of the *Birth to Eight* curriculum. Beyond the confines of individual groups, some authors suggest that good early years schools are 'nurturing schools' (Doyle, 2003, p. 252).

Nurture groups can also be placed at the centre of many of the aspects of schooling so far discussed in this book. They made no appearance in my original research designs and my work in them was opportunistically schematised around emergent themes. Yet here they have become a vehicle upon which I shall discuss many of the problematics of early years schooling and care that I have raised so far. After contextualising the groups within project and policy, the implications of this particular style of intervention will be discussed.

Nurture groups join a set of languages and practices in schools aimed at fostering emotional *growth* (Colwell and O'Connor, 2003) and contributing to what has been termed the *therapeutic turn* in education (Hyland, 2006). Questioning this rhetoric of *growth*, Ecclestone and Hayes (2008) attack therapeutic ideals as contributing to the 'diminished self' through the creation of 'fragile identities' (p. xi), which *demoralise* the *actualisation* which should lie at the heart of educational ideals (Ecclestone, 2004). Ian Hunter (1994) provides a challenge to this rhetoric of actualisation, and through his work one can see the regulative, administrative, and governmental ideals to which nurture groups can be understood as a contribution.

The nature binds of the previous chapter will be pursued further here through a discussion of the paradox implicated by the notion that emotional and behavioural disorder, the product of deficiency in *natural* maternal relations require the supplement of *nurture* groups in school. At issue here is the entrenchment of naturalist assumptions for particular marginalised groups and the governmental aims that can be accomplished through a discourse of *nature*.

## The formula

Nurture groups were first seen in UK schools in the Inner London Education Authority of the early 1970s, where it is claimed they were 'ahead of their time' (Cline, 2002). The dissolution of this organisation some years later brought an end to the groups as well. Recently, educational practice has seen a return of the nurture group and they are now an integral part of many infant and primary schools. The original model of the nurture group is known as the Boxall nurture group, reflecting the wisdom of Marjorie Boxall, whose original project in the East End of London in the late 1960s spawned this intervention, and whose related publications (Bennathan and Boxall, 1998, 2000; Boxall, 2002) provide a blueprint for the groups and their pupils.

Beginning with what are seen as the problematic actions and enunciations of the child with EBDs in school, Boxall's (2002) theory moves to the *dysfunctions* of family and community:

> Nurture Groups had their origin in the 1960s in an area of East London that was in a state of massive social upheaval. Families had been resettled there following slum clearance, migrants from other parts of the UK had moved in, and there was a large recently arrived multicultural immigrant population.
>
> *(Boxall, 2002, p. x)*

Boxall claims that where social conditions such as these exist, what also exists is a deficit of the natural nurture normally associated with the formation of the child, in other words: *poor parenting*. Therefore, what is needed is a school-based restorative in the form of the nurture group. The social conditions that were understood to be creating this deficit in the East London of the 1960s were relative deprivation and social exclusion. These broad and generalisable conditions have also been connected with several other social phenomena, for example: the inequitable distribution of labour through the de-industrialisation of national economies and resurgence of free market capitalism (Fraser, 1997), the shifting ethics of the cultural move towards consumerism (Bauman, 2005), and the assimilative force of the increasingly global territoriality of individualism (Giddens, 1990). If these conditions are thought to feed the need for nurture then the resurgence of the nurture group in schools is perhaps unsurprising: 'systems and policymakers are troubled by these things and want to find ways to end the troubles' (Thomson, 2002, p. 42). Indeed, it is arguable that broader socio-cultural processes and the apparent need for nurture in schools are mutually constitutive. In drawing these particular conditions out here, my aim is to foreground the argument that socio-economic imperatives may underlie the new *will* to nurture.

Therefore, we have a *nurturing formula*, whereby social change creates *troubled communities* producing *dysfunctional families* who feed *maladjusted children* into *stressed schools*. Into these *troubled places*, nurture groups express their formula to substitute the naturalised deficits of community and family, through therapeutic intervention on the overt behaviour of the individual child. The assumptions of this formula, that social change produces dysfunctions of nature in community and family, that these can be read in the overt behaviour of children, and that therapeutic individualism is required to mould these children into the new order of school and society, are some of the contentions against which the practices of nurture groups must be held.

The increasing popularity of the language of *emotional intelligence* (Goleman, 1996) has also aided the re-insertion of nurture groups into the educational agenda. Couched in the thinking of cognitive psychology, this language aspires to supplant older means of psychological administration, such as IQ, with a new emotional differentiation. Similar to Boxall's (2002) 'social upheaval', Goleman's imagination of the need to administer the emotions is grounded in contemporary images of youth violence, crime and disorder. Through the fostering of emotional intelligence, Goleman aims to replace internal and external states of disorder with self-motivation, delayed gratification, empathy and hope. Pedagogical narratives that seek to translate these ideals into a schooling agenda have coined the term *emotional literacy* (Sharp, 2001), defined as: 'the ability to recognise, understand, handle, and appropriately express emotions' (p. 1).

## The nurture group at Alderley

The data I present here are drawn from my time spent participating in the nurture group at Alderley, including observational and interview material. In addition to this I attended three good practice meetings for nurture groups, which were held at Alderley and which included speakers from other schools as well as from regional Behaviour Support Teams.

I first heard of nurture groups during an interview with an infant school teacher in the Summer of 2005. Then, they were referred to as one of the key ways in which the school approached the inclusion of children with variously described EBDs; a notion consistently supported in the literature (Bennathan and Boxall, 1998, 2000; Boxall, 2002; Cooper and Tiknaz, 2005; O'Connor and Colwell, 2002). In the two groups I worked with there were several children with diagnoses of ADHD, Conduct Disorder and Autism. Those that hadn't yet embarked on this discursive journey were almost without exception considered by staff in the school to be suitable for it; if not already diagnosed as *disorderly* these children were considered *at risk* of being so (Harwood, 2006). The groups had not been part of my original research strategy, however, they had established a central role at Alderley in the management of such risky populations, and the *normal* functioning of the mainstream classroom was heavily reliant on them.

The emphasis on communication in the group was very helpful to me. I was able to talk to children on a much more open basis than in the classroom. Through this experience I learned that Chris (see Chapters 3 and 5) had much better communicative ability than my mainstream experience had suggested. In this respect I could see that this particular group successfully accessed skills and characteristics that might have remained unseen in the mainstream class; hopefully building the individual child's confidence as a result. However, the group sometimes seemed to suffer by its own openness and could frequently fall into disorder (see Chapter 5).

Implicit in this success is an acknowledgement of one of the functions of nurture groups in school: social order. In the sense that children were removed from the mainstream class and had a special status attached to them, the groups could be seen as partially resting on a logic of deficit (Valencia, 1997). However, the point was made in Chapter 4 that the routine works to separate and divide certain bodies, marking them as inappropriate. If these same bodies were then removed from that routine and placed in a different one, then this could be read as the school remaining sensitive to the needs of those who do not appear to *fit* the mainstream; though this move characterises the child, rather than the routine, as abnormal. However, if the routine works as I have suggested, then remaining in the mainstream classroom might in some cases be a more exclusive and alienating experience than being removed from it. Additionally, nurture groups are seen by many to be a positive advance from the more vacuous and punitive disciplinary action that one might conventionally associate with the term *exclusion* (Colwell and O'Connor, 2003; Cooper *et al.*, 2000; Doyle, 2003).

The Years One and Two nurture group at Alderley was located between the communal areas of the dining room and assembly room. The room was rather small; its other function was a store cupboard. This meant that one side of the wall was full of boxes of tambourines, shakers, maracas and wood blocks, which the occasional teacher or assistant or pupil would interrupt the group to locate. I never observed any of the equipment being used by the group. This wall of shelves and boxes was on the opposite room to the door, which opened into a narrow area with coat pegs just before entering the main room. The main area was roughly square with a low set of tables and chairs in the centre and floor cushions in one corner with a large display called a 'feelings tree' to the right of the entrance. To the left was a wall-sized window onto the senior playground. All the walls were lined with tables, sets of drawers and cupboards, all containing materials for the group; on one of these was a fish tank with four goldfish in it. The different areas of the room all had names according to the activities to be pursued there: 'breakfast bar', 'tree house' and 'brain box'. A timetable of events for the nurture group is given in Table 7.1.

**TABLE 7.1** Alderley Primary: nurture group timetable

| Time | Activity | Location |
|------|----------|----------|
| 9.30–9.45 | Feelings Tree | Tree House |
| 9.45–10.15 | Breakfast | Breakfast Bar |
| 10.15–10.30 | Jobs/Choosing time | Breakfast Bar |
| 10.30–10.45 | Show and tell | Tree House |
| 10.45–11.15 | Numeracy/Literacy | Brain Box |
| 11.15–11.30 | Playtime | Outside |
| 11.30–11.45 | Choosing time | All |
| 11.45–12.00 | Tidy-up | All |
| 12.00–12.15 | Nominations/Targets | Tree House |

The activities on offer were a mixture of more flexible, choice-led equivalents to mainstream work. Where work was expected (numeracy/literacy, show and tell), expectations were set low and encouragement set high. There was space for relatively unstructured activity time (choosing time, playtime), often used as an incentive to finish work, and some 'managed' interactive time (feelings tree, breakfast), where children were encouraged to talk about their thoughts and feelings, out-of-school activities and home life. The guiding rationale for these activities could be characterised as 'learning to learn' (Sanders, 2007, p. 56). The assumptions were: first, that these children did not fit into the early years mainstream because they were not yet ready for it; second, that what they lacked was not academic ability but social skills in large group environments; third, that these skills could be acquired, if they were not currently held by the children, then they could be *nurtured*.

## The nurturing school

The suggestion by one author that good schools are 'nurturing schools' (Doyle, 2003, p. 252) implies that some essence of the nurturing formula is seen as beneficial, not only to the aforementioned risky populations, but to the young school child in general. The first way in which I would like to interrogate this idea is through a look at the way in which many of the aspects of schooling so far discussed in this project are centrally manifest in the nurturing formula.

The analysis looks first at the ordering of nurture groups according to routine logic (see Chapter 4). In this regard the nurturing formula shares one of the assumptions of the penal system; that those seemingly incapable of integrating themselves into the routines of ordinary society require an intensification of routine. As in Chapter 4, the ideal of the routine is to generate docility via surveillance. The second part of the analysis moves from the structure of the routine to the subjectivisation which lies beneath it in the everyday work of the group.

## *Routine*

The chief objective of the nurture group is to provide a structured experience of *attachment and support*, which it does, as Boxall (2002) suggests, through the application of a consistent and unbending routine:

> Procedures vary from school to school, but whatever the variant the same routine is followed in the same way, every day, in the school concerned and, except for unavoidable events, the same familiar people are in the same expected place, every day.
>
> *(Boxall, 2002, p. 24)*

The rationale for this is that it counters the effects of the poor organisation, inattentiveness and high anxiety, which it is claimed these children have inherited from their *disturbed* upbringings. At the level of everyday action the routine can be seen to operate in both overt and normative ways.

Overtly, in the structural and temporal guide of the timetable (see Table 7.1). Short demarcations of time seek security for all, leaving no period of time ungoverned and open to disorder. For each one of the activities on this timetable exists a sub-level of routinisation, in the norms and expectations; the correct procedure, by which each task should be carried out, each piece of interaction performed, and by which each person should conduct themselves (see Table 7.2).

This is routine regulation in the mainstream classroom, the presumed tacit knowledge of the ordinary pupil, however, 'for pupils with special educational needs the gaze reaches further' (Allan, 1996, p. 222); there is an intensification of routine logic and it is the perceived deficit in these skills, and what this might imply within the individual, that is under particular scrutiny.

**TABLE 7.2** Some nurturing norms

---

- **Saying you're sorry:**
  Look at the person
  Use a nice voice
  Say why you are sorry

- **Ways to calm down:**
  Tell yourself to stop
  Give your thinking brain time
  Count backwards from 10, 20, 100
  Walk away

- **Traffic lights:**
  **Green** – A good level, everyone is able to work: **KEEP IT UP!**
  **Amber** – Noise levels are rising: **ACT NOW TO RETURN TO GREEN!**
  **Red** – The noise level is too high: **ARE YOU ABOUT TO GET A WARNING?**

---

### Enunciation and confession

Leading out of the routine norms, there are specific ways of speaking and specific forms of speech that are considered appropriate by the nurturing formula. In order to develop appropriate enunciation, nurturing practice must first draw out confessions of all considered damaging. The *feelings tree* provides an illustration: each child in turn will choose from a given list of physical/emotional states to describe how they are feeling today and then describe why. There is something worthy in the attempt to encourage young children to reflect on and express their experiences and feelings in this way, for participation and empowerment might be read in it. However, through the interpretation that the adults around them are empowered to impose on the content of their speech, this attempt is one which ultimately casts the child as more vulnerable. The following excerpt is from an interview with Andrea (A) and Clare (C), the main two nurture group assistants at Alderley:

> A:    It's like Paul isn't it, with Uncle Pete, except that he's not Uncle Pete, he's his dad. And now Uncle Pete is in prison. But unless you do some digging we don't find out.
>
> *(Int 28–2)*

In this excerpt, Andrea used the family circumstances of a Year Two boy, Paul, to illustrate the task of 'digging' which her and Clare felt they were required to do in the group. The groups were built around encouraging children to open up and share their thoughts and feelings, and numerous opportunities for participation of this sort were integral to many of the daily activities. In the following excerpt, Clare details the response of a Year Two girl, Lola, to a task involving descriptions of after-school activities:

> C:    She wrote, 'I go home from school and I go to bed' and we were saying, 'oh no, we don't do that – we have our tea when we get home from school' – but not Lola. She goes to bed. That's her day. Now that's awful. So what she does now is she will copy off the person next to her so if they had sausages then so will she or if they had pizza she'll have pizza.
>
> *(Int 28–2)*

Here, the activity requiring children to give descriptions of their lives outside school, has given the opportunity of some more digging. The effects of the surveilling routine can be seen here in Lola's desire to *hide* certain details of her home life, in order to be *seen* as *normal*. In line with the task, Lola has confessed to going straight to bed after school, however this confession cannot be made *intelligible* (Britzman, 2000) within the institutional order. The result of this is that Lola is cast into a position of vulnerability sufficient to make her want to lie in her responses to subsequent tasks. The excerpt continues:

C: And she will sleep on the settee. If we ask her where she has slept last night we will get all sorts of stories: on the settee; in the playpen ...

R: And we've had 'on the floor' before now. But mostly it's on the settee. I mean you shouldn't let your child of seven sleep on the settee. It's just basic parenting skills that are needed.

*(Int 28–2)*

The conclusion that is reached here reflects one of the central assumptions of nurture; that it is the perceived dysfunctions of the home situation that causes the overt disorder at school. That Lola has felt forced into lying in her subsequent confessions challenges the notion of emotional *growth* that is desired through this intervention, though perhaps Lola has gained some *resilience* through the experience.

This example partially fits N. Rose's (1989) description of the therapeutic confessional as a technology of autonomy. Rose claims that an overt shift has occurred from technologies which yield security of state to those that are seen to secure the self. The confessional, cast in displaced images of Christian rituals, becomes one of the principle means through which the self is contracted to a notion of actualisation. In seeking to downplay an emphasis on top–down repression, Rose emphasised the voluntary and cathartic action of the confessional encounter. Yet such an encounter cast Lola into a position of greater vulnerability, perhaps due to her relative powerlessness within the legitimate relations in school between adults and children (Cannella and Viruru, 2004).

The question of what is culturally appropriate within adult–child interaction brings power relations into play. I was able to make use of the confessional voice (see Chapter 1), on the basis of a conceptual tactic; using a personal exemplification of some of the ideas I wanted to introduce in this project. I was aware of the dangers involved and I made an informed choice, fully aware that I was regulating myself according to a governmental ideal; it was an active, voluntary and participatory move based on my awareness, and at least partial control, over *the conditions of my actions* (Young, 1990, p. 38).

Lola, however, is not free in the extent to which she participates in these conditions; they are hidden from her by the legitimate dominance of the surveilling institution; she confesses unknowingly, unsighted to the drives and consequences of her expression. Because of this, Lola's actualisation through therapeutic technologies recasts and reinforces the vulnerability it was designed to alleviate (Ecclestone and Hayes, 2008; Furedi, 2003). While I could partially enact Rose's (1989) anti-repressive position in holding on to the voluntary and cathartic elements of my confession, Lola's position seems to lack even this partial autonomy, appearing by comparison oppressive and *neuroticising* (N. Rose, 1989, p. 244).

Lola's experience also draws out distinction within the rhetoric of emotional literacy, undercutting its ability to be transformative, instead appearing to restrict

Lola's possible expression according to what is deemed appropriate. This echoes Burman's (2009) critique of emotional literacy as: 'the suppression of variation (in emotional response) which endorses conformity and consensus and denies the actual struggles/conflicts of interest' (p. 142).

## Family and gender

Routine and confession are both linked here to the internal *ordering* (Foucault, 1981a) of the discourse of nurture groups; the mechanisms by which they operate. Now analysis examines what might be generated by these ways of working; the truths told about particular groups through the nurturing formula. The family comes under persistent interrogation here according to Boxall's (2002) indictment of the 'developmental impoverishment' (p. 3) of the child's home situation. The task of 'digging' that the nurture assistant pursues is therefore given this specific focus. For Boxall (2002) these are families in need of substitution: 'typically such children have grown up in circumstances of stress and adversity sufficiently severe to limit or disturb the nurturing process of the earliest years' (p. 1). From this heuristic, comes good nurturing practice in school:

> Res: And was there anything about the specific nurturing principle that attracted you?
>
> A: I think a lot of children that come here aren't cared for. They don't have the basic care that others have. They're not fed; they're not clean; they're tired ...
>
> C: The ethos behind the nurture group makes sense to us.
>
> A: They can't function, can they? You sit them on the carpet to do, say, their times table and they don't really know how to put two words together. Everything goes over their heads.
>
> *(Int 28–2)*

This excerpt draws out the relation between emotional literacy and responsibility. Though the literacy of children in school has come under attack here it is the lack of responsibility at home that is thought to be the cause. Burman (2009) criticises this emphasis on responsibilising the emotions with the implication that 'emotional literacy begins at home' (p. 145). This is made explicit in the above excerpt in which emotional literacy is perceived to have failed at home, and requires a school-based restorative. Once inside the home, further means of gender regulation are readily available (Walkerdine and Lucey, 1989).

Nurture groups share gendered relations with the infant classroom, where the majority of the time disruptive males are attended to by female teaching assistants (Arnot and Miles, 2005; also see Chapter 5). These conventions find their immediate derivative in the assumptions of the nurturing formula and the supposed deficits in early childhood experiences at home on 'mother's lap' and 'mother's knee' (Boxall, 2002, p. 6). Boxall's (2002) account includes an author's note, which explains the almost exclusive equation of nurture staff with female pronouns and nurture children with male ones, first, by saying that this reflects reality, second, by claiming that it aids the ease of reading. Any reading that sustains and reproduces existing stereotypes might be easy but is certainly also *dangerous* (Foucault, 1984); here Boxall betrays naïve assumptions, disregarding the relations of power through which *reflection* becomes *constitution*. The equally persistent equation of mothers and sons is not addressed. Therefore Boxall's (2002) nurturing formula enacts the historical equation of *emotional work* and *female work* (Walkerdine and Lucey, 1989). Embedding this relation in the masculine oriented school extends the institutional *use value* of emotion (Skeggs, 2003), resulting in a culturally approved relation: *troubled boys* being *mothered* by female teaching assistants. Therefore the nurturing formula contributes to the more generalised feminisation rhetoric in early years schooling (see Chapter 5).

The first illustration I will present of this concerns the question of which children should enter and leave the nurture group, which at Alderley was not governed by any set policy or procedure. The first excerpt concerns a brother and sister, James and Emma, six and five years old respectively. James has diagnoses of ADHD and Oppositional Defiant Disorder and only attends school in the morning, most of which he spends in the nurture group.

> I was also chatting to Andrea and Clare about James and Emma, who are brother and sister – they don't like the two of them being together in nurture group as all the problems which Emma encounters being a younger sister to James at home are repeated at school – he bullies her, answers for her and gives mum a full report of any misbehaviour – which A and C feel is largely a reaction to his dominating behaviour. However, him and Ross together is too much for the already difficult year two group. Both A and C feel that Emma would benefit from the nurture group but that she is not really at the moment – however they don't have any input on who ends up in there.
>
> *(fn 27–11)*

In this example, there are two significant gendered effects. It is claimed that the potential effectiveness of the nurture group is at stake with Emma because of James's dominance of her. Andrea and Clare do not feel that the group is the right place for James to be. However, despite the everyday work of the groups being theirs, their voice is not heard. Their work and their agency are effaced and Emma is left in the dominating presence of her brother.

There is also a local politics which is seen as relevant here. James was from what was perceived throughout the school to be a very problematic Year Two group, a group of three boys with diagnoses of ADHD (see Chapters 3 and 5). James and the other boy mentioned in the excerpt, Ross, are a particular inter-personal concern, and this governs James's placement in the nurture group. Thus the behavioural discourse that surrounds this group of boys, and particularly James, is given primacy over the lived experience of the people in the group which is felt in Andrea and Clare's sense of powerlessness.

The most obvious manifestation of Andrea and Clare's truncated sense of ownership could be seen whenever one of the children started behaving particularly aggressively or violently. In the following excerpt a Year One boy, Chris, has hit Andrea twice and stormed out of the group into the unoccupied assembly room next door:

> Chris is now in the assembly hall again and the group door is open so if he comes back through they will see him. So Clare suggests leaving him to it, but after a couple of minutes another teacher comes along to say that he is messing around on the stage and she is worried he'll hurt himself. There are some problematic complications here as well – neither Andrea nor Clare are trained to physically intervene with Chris – even though they are responsible for him four mornings a week ... so for now Chris is left cavorting around in the hall and Andrea and Clare feel a little helpless because of their lack of training. Clare also commented to the effect that they feel a negative implication when teachers alert their attention to what Chris is doing, as though when he is in nurture he stops being so hard to deal with.
>
> *(fn 27–11)*

There is a paradox at work here: the behavioural discourse surrounding the children placed in the group holds a great deal of influence within the school, determining their placement outside the mainstream. I have noted above how with the three boys with ADHD in Year Two, this behavioural discourse subsumes the needs of the group as a whole beneath the need for order in the mainstream. Therefore, Andrea and Clare were expected to take on the care of several children whose *disorderly subjectivity* (Harwood, 2006) was believed to carry the likelihood of aggressive and violent behaviour, yet they were not sufficiently trained to deal with this likelihood. Thus, apparently, the rationale for outside placement evaporates and Andrea and Clare are left powerless to the behavioural discourse of the school, the violent actions of the male children and the aspersions of other teachers.

This instance illustrates the contradictory assumptions around nature/nurture which the philosophy and practice of nurture groups generate. The nurture group is deemed necessary to assuage the *natural* deficits of Chris's EBDs. This implies that nature is to some extent *nurturable*. Andrea and Clare became frustrated by the negative implications they felt from other teachers who assumed that Chris would be better behaved while in the nurture group. Yet this is precisely what the group is supposed to do. Thus, while Andrea and Clare stated above that they subscribe to the 'ethos' of the groups, this illustrates a limit to this subscription, whereby *nurture* might not be able to make up for certain *natural* deficits. This testifies to the entrenchment of a fatalised view of Chris's *pathology* as well as bearing witness to the inconsistencies of the school's behavioural discourse and the ambiguities produced by the contradictory assumptions of the group.

## Risk and class

Extending the *emotion equation* that nurture enacts with regards gender can allow social class to become visible as well. Class could be conceived as lying *prior* to gendering within the nurture formula, for the model describes a process whereby inappropriate, working-class, mothering can be neutralised by the appropriate, middle-class values of the school.

Enacting class on the basis of a formula of 'cultural deficiency' (Fairclough, 2000, p. 61) allows one to frame political discourse according to dichotomous understandings of *outcomes*: order/disorder, which can be managed through the language of risk (Bailey, 2010). What this produces in the nurturing formula is the *at-risk EBD child*, the *at-risk adverse upbringing* and the *at risk conditions of class and community*. To draw once again on Boxall's (2002) heuristic: 'from the beginning the work that developed [into the nurture group] was an attempt to ameliorate a desperate situation in schools and to help the large number of children who were facing a disastrous future' (p. viii). Placing the nurturing formula within the future-bound language of risk allows it to be easily transposed on to *safeguarding* policies in school, such as *Every Child Matters* (DFES, 2004) and related policies aimed at building *Brighter Futures* (DCSF, 2008) through *Community Cohesion* (DCSF, 2007).

*Every Child Matters* is built around what it refers to as five 'outcomes': 'be healthy', 'stay safe', 'enjoy and achieve', 'make a positive contribution' and 'achieve economic well-being' (DFES, 2006). While these are all labelled 'outcomes' there is an implicit linear temporal assumption whereby achieving one will lead into the fulfilment of the next. Such that 'being healthy' and 'staying safe' become fundamental building blocks in determining future states of 'achievement' and 'economic well-being'. Listed with these outcomes are the 'responsibilities' that are considered important for the attainment of each one, conceptualised in terms of the duties of 'children and young people's parents, carers and families' (DFES, 2006). The *Every Child Matters* framework, therefore, sets up a system in which there are understood to be risky ('unhealthy and unsafe') children whose family duty it is to promote their better well-being in order to successfully integrate them into economic society. In this document a political naturalisation occurs where the school, the classroom and the structures, systems and practices therein are conceived as neutral vessels in which this individual *responsibilisation* (N. Rose, 1989) can take place.

The nurturing formula therefore meshes with this policy, seeming to offer amelioration to the *Every Child Matters* dropout: the working-class child and family who are considered irresponsible, incapable of attaining these outcomes without supplement.

This discussion has focused so far on the limiting relations required and reinforced by the nurturing formula. A spatial/temporal means of surveillance is provided by routinised norms. Confession is similarly routinised, drawing out inappropriate enunciation and attempting to stabilise emotional responses. Existing gender relations in school and at home allow children, parents and teaching assistants little room for autonomous thought or action, rather they become instrumental, yet lacking participatory rights; a narrowly defined political rhetoric is able to flow through their action with little possible resistance. Thus, in contradiction to the rhetoric of growth, in both the nurturing formula and the wider discourse of emotional literacy, the groups appear through this analysis instead as limiting and levelling. Emotions are acknowledged, interrogated and transformed, and this has emancipatory potential. However, actualisation is restricted according to an individualised neutralisation: children are to be taught to 'understand, handle and appropriately express emotions' (Sharp, 2001, p. 1), according to the needs of economic integration. This depoliticises emotions, denying the existence of social conflict from which a valid and angry emotional response might have arisen, replacing it with a therapeutic discourse of detachment and containment, where 'no leakage from the personal to the impersonal is permitted' (D. Smith, 1975, p. 9).

Through this routine commitment to therapeutic orthodoxies, the nurturing formula appears to offer limited means to actualisation (Ecclestone and Hayes, 2008), offering only actualisation according to a prescribed and assimilative ideal, presumed by *Every Child Matters* to be an economic one. This ideal will now be discussed with reference to Ian Hunter's (1994) analysis of school's pastoral power, of which nurture groups are one enactment.

## From routine to ritual

Hunter's (1994) description of school as 'an improvised technology for living' (p. xvii) can help make sense of schooling as a means to economic and state security. Where Ecclestone and Hayes (2008) suggest that therapeutics offers no means to actualisation, Hunter (1994) suggests that actualisation plays only a rhetorical role in educational values. Instead, as a system established through Christian doctrines of ascetic self-governance, Hunter (1994) suggests that education's primary role is in the production of the self-responsible subject.

Hunter's (1994) description of pastoral discipline and its 'articulation of surveillance and self examination, obedience and self-regulation' (p. xxi) would seem to align it to the analysis of nurture groups provided here. Drawing on Weber (1930) and the *elective affinity* he described between pastoral discipline and the rise of capitalism, Hunter (1994) suggests that educational ideals, shaped around the productive economic subject, have become part of the state's means of enhancing collective wealth and security, 'and *thereby* the well being of its citizens' (p. 39). Within this model, the supposed educational ideals of actualisation, empowerment and autonomy are secondary to the 'survival and security of state' (p. 40), which is the primary function. This is the model Foucault (1991) termed *governmentality:* 'a plurality of forms of government and their immanence to the state' (p. 91). One of the tasks of this 'art of government' was the establishment of a 'downwards continuity ... which transmits to individual behaviour and the running of the family the same principles as the good government of the state' (p. 32).

The assumptions and practices of the nurturing formula reproduce this downward continuity, with the future image of the economically productive subject tied to the present responsibilities of family and child. Yet the effect of the distanced governance that Foucault's model implies, is to produce continuities which break a linear 'downward' movement and circulate on the back of the naturalised discourses discussed here. The school takes up a governmental position within the valorised notion of social order. Government is diffused further within school according to the interaction of inequitably distributed social forms: gender and family, mother and teaching assistant. This diffusion is only made possible by the burying of the contradictory nature–nurture–normal assumption, which is managed on an individual level through techniques such as risk. Risk is re-inserted into the political order through the threat of future economic dependence; perpetual motion is thus produced where this feeds back into the reinforcement of ideals such as free market liberalism, which distributes new inequitable positions producing the new perceived *need* for nurture.

The consistent replication of the routine on a day-to-day and week-to-week basis offers the means to achieving naturalisation (see Chapter 4). Here, routine norms combine with confession and various other subjectivising relations (gender, class and family) to make up a ritualised approach to schooling.

In Chapter 4, a progressive distinction was introduced whereby the routine could be judged according to its ability to autonomise the self through a motivated contraction to the immediate value of social order. Having established a certain relation between the nurture discourse and Christian doctrines here, an allied distinction drawn by Mary Douglas is enacted:

> ritual conformity is not a valid form of personal commitment and is not compatible with the full development of the personality . . . the replacement of ritual conformity with rational commitment will give greater meaning to the lives of Christians.
>
> *(Douglas, 1970, p. 4)*

The subjectivisation that the nurture formula enacts now becomes of some significance for its potential to either progress into the fostering of 'rational commitment' or fall back into 'ritual conformity'. On the one hand the nurture formula seems predicated upon at least a rhetorical commitment to alternative approaches to the external disciplinary structures of schooling. It allies itself with the emotional content that is at the heart of many progressive models of education: the *social pedagogue* (Cameron, 2007), or the *pedagogy of the emotions* (Kenway *et al.*, 1997), which seek active and participatory routes to growth and inclusion. Yet, while these approaches channel a certain *feminism* in the interests of making structures more inclusive, the nurturing formula falls back on *feminisation*, and the truths it has told within this analysis implies that this restricts ability to foster growth. The heart of this distinction lies in the formula's enaction of a masculinised therapeutic rhetoric of 'emotional neutrality, certainty, control, assertiveness, self-reliance' (Kenway and Fitzclarence, 1997, p. 121). This represents only a 'superficial convergence with a feminist commitment to acknowledge and interrogate emotions'

(Burman, 2009, p. 138), instead seeking to order appropriate emotions and regulate those which sit outside; the adversarial and angry, defiant and oppositional, which are defined as *threats* and *toxins* to be drawn out and neutralised with *poisonous pedagogies* (Kenway *et al.*, 1997). Blind to the subjectivisation it obliquely creates, the nurturing ritual can continue to hold fast to the notion that it produces safe passage into psychological adjustment, and thus its *functions* become the stuff of school-wide recommendations. Through this *mainstreaming* of the formula, it loses any ability to actively re-interpret the dominant discourses of the school, instead re-inscribing them, turning children, teaching assistants and mothers into 'cause and effect metaphors for educational change' (Kenway *et al.*, 1997, p. xii).

In contracting itself to the discursive relations governing schools and in turn to the governmental aspirations of bureaucratic administration, the nurturing ritual at once reinforces and destabilises Foucault's (1991) arts of government. The capacity to distribute limiting subject positions along accepted boundaries leads to the nurture formula's own objectification as a government artifice. Yet through the same subjectivisation the ritual complies in its own failure to live up to its objectification. That is to say that if the subject produced through therapeutic individualism is vulnerable, dependent, anxious and neurotic (Ecclestone and Hayes, 2008), then this would appear unbecoming of the steely image of the upright and dependable *self-managing citizen*.

Therefore, in discursive terms, rather than working together, the nurturing ritual might not best serve the social governance of categories such as EBD and ADHD. Jenny Laurence (2008) argues an allied position through the *executive functions* that are believed to be the neuro-cognitive deficits of ADHD: 'self-directed covert actions that assist with self-regulation' (Barkley, 2003, p. 79).

Laurence's (2008) argument identifies the contemporary valorisation of *information processing* and its production of desirable social forms interacting with the dominant understanding of individuals in terms of bio-pathology: 'the figure of the "business woman" acts to translate a particular kind of workspace onto psycho-biological space' (p. 108). The contrast between the upright and dependable image of the executive and the emotional deficiency described here implies for Laurence that:

> both 'attention' and 'hyperactivity' may be approaching redundancy, given that they no longer seem to describe 'the primary problem'. A science of 'executive function disorder' may much better translate onto an enterprising administration's need to know.
>
> *(Laurence, 2008, p. 109)*

Such a change would be empowering in the relative sense in which the new nomenclature would draw near the means by which governance is deployed and the meaning of the actions which are being encouraged in the name of self-responsibility. Viewed through the lens of governmentality, *relative liberation* might be the most that can be hoped for, with distinction required as to the extent to which governmental relations are entered into in a knowing and participatory manner.

## Where to for inclusion?

The nurture formula is centrally placed within school and governmental inclusion policies and practice. Yet what can more readily be observed is at best integration, at worst assimilation, according to the thought and practice of deficit, pathology and regulation.

The central tenet of nurture groups, it is claimed, is their focus on 'growth, not pathology' (Boxall, 2002, p. 10). However, this 'growth' is conceptualised according to *normal development, normal parenting, normal learning experiences* and a *normal educational continuum*, and the role that each can play in averting the 'disastrous future' which these children would otherwise face. Therefore, despite the claims of non-pathology, this conception of the need for nurture in the face of dysfunctional families and future disaster is illustrative of nurture's adoption of the naturalised language of risk and governmentality, and a therapeutic dualism of the normal/pathological.

Hunter (1994) encourages us to look beyond daily practices to some of the mundane and administrative ideals the education system might be aspiring to. Yet neither his ideas, nor Ecclestone and Hayes's (2008) critique, nor the writing of Boxall (2002) leave us in any kind of comfortable position as to notions of inclusion. If inclusion means the efficiency of a system in bringing an individual back within a pre-ordained notion of citizenship, then such schooling might be described as inclusive, yet integration or, with further restriction of expressive space, assimilation, would seem to fit this description more closely. According to this argument inclusion can perhaps only be glimpsed in momentary fashion, in a child's participation in the means of their integration, for example, or temporary re-negotiation of some structure to better fit their character, ideal, or action.

# 8

# ANOTHER ORDER IS POSSIBLE

Using the overarching theme of 'conditions of possibility' (Foucault, 1974, p. 89), I have offered an account of some of the institutional and individual coordinates that make the ascription of a diagnosis possible. In general terms, I have argued for the need for alternative conceptions of childhood that move away from the binaries and internal deficiencies represented by ADHD. I have pursued this argument through the complexities encountered in my research sites, which contrasts to the cookbooks of psychiatric discourse. I have presented the main argument according to four empirical chapters which each do different but related work in achieving the de-naturalisation of ADHD and all its associated social coordinates.

In terms of the stated objectives of plotting some of the conditions which make the ascription of a diagnosis possible then each chapter can be seen as contributing a set of clues. Informed by each of the previous chapters here, I argue that the application of a diagnosis rests on the ability to:

- Group people and represent them holistically according to a set of essential characteristics.
- Make 'truth' statements based upon binary separations between 'real' and 'non-real'.
- Examine and differentiate individuals according to an institutional order.
- Enact naturalised conceptions of social groups to reinforce existing inequalities.
- Cast obligations based upon notions of blame and responsibility.
- Situate naturalised essentialisms within a cultural context and make them articulable.

The most consistent themes across these points are naturalisation and binary and de-historicised thinking. These styles of thinking link together in various ways: naturalisation links with binary thinking to produce categories such as male/female.

Naturalisation acts paradigmatically, in that once the assumption of naturalness is in place then further assumptions become logical imperatives. Perhaps the most recurrent example of this process in action here is in the naturalisation of the social order, which distributes governmental ideals upon which individual subject positions should proceed. Therefore, routine, gender, family, class and risk all become naturalised categories according to which the *good-citizen-in-the-making* (Graham, 2007b) will align themselves. Further binaries are distributed to adjudicate such a performance: order/disorder, male/female, functional/dysfunctional, working/middle, safe/dangerous. Each binary in turn implies domains of knowledge through which one can interpret the action of the individual so placed and new categories are spawned: EBD, pushy parent, developmentally impoverished, hard to shift, ADHD.

To de-naturalise the social order requires bringing subjects into close contact with the means by which their everyday action is known and governed. To de-naturalise a category such as ADHD first requires the de-naturalisation of all the conditioning categories around it – those related to individuals (choice, risk) and groups (gender, class), those related to institutions (school, family) and those related to knowledge epistemes (pedagogy, psychiatry).

For each of these the process of de-naturalisation requires subjects to interrogate the reason why they might be performing a certain action or pursuing a certain goal in a certain way as well as the implications of doing so.

In arguing for the need for ways of seeing which seek to get inside the conditional nature of existence, the very first thing it is necessary to say is that nothing can be said 'regardless of culture':

> Various approaches have been used to establish whether a condition rises to the level of a valid medical or psychiatric disorder. A very useful one stipulates that there must be scientifically established evidence that those suffering the condition have a serious deficiency in or failure of a physical or psychological process that is universal to humans. That is, all humans normally would be expected, regardless of culture, to have developed that mental ability.
>
> *(Barkley, 2002, p. 89)*

The mis-representation of culture within this passage is first attested to by the notion that one can 'normally' be expected to do something 'regardless of culture'. Culture and norm imply one another; without cultural notions of order and society and what is acceptable to each there would be no norm.

The contradictions continue: 'psychiatric and medical conditions' are derived here from the Western cultural discourse of child and adolescent psychiatry, part of the Western cultural discourse of medicine. Even within the so called 'West' this discourse attains nothing like universal status, with its differential treatment of ethnicities, genders, classes and ages, as well as the different moral orders which become attached to different conditions; from the unlucky to the preventable to the negligent.

The idea that there is a 'valid' condition draws on more culturally derived notions of what 'validity' is. Once again these derive from Western scientific and philosophical discourses which concern the ways in which we come to know something as an object of knowledge, in the case of Western medical thought, the meaning of validity is governed by an overarching positivist epistemology, which sees one true object and one rational means of describing it (Tait, 2010). Another of the guiding assumptions of Western philosophical thought that has particular relevance within the Western cultural discourse of medicine is the ontological separation of body and mind (S. Rose, 2005).

Lastly, the notion of the 'universal'. I wonder if Barkley and his 88 counter-signatories can provide any examples of a 'condition' or 'deficiency' or 'physical or psychological process' that is 'universal to all humans'. I can think of only one such category, culture, and within this 'universal' category is to be found infinite variety, particularity and pluralism.

'Culture' is perhaps the ultimate 'discourse' when it comes to human beings. It is what defines the limits of knowledge and the means with which to extend those limits. It is our daily practice, the means by which we might make meaning of those practices and the means by which we might seek something else. It cannot be disassociated from anything we do, say, think, feel or experience:

> culture is not a power, something to which social events, behaviors, institutions, or processes can be causally attributed; it is a context, something within which they can be intelligibly – that is, thickly – described . . . [the exotic is] a device for displacing the dulling sense of familiarity with which the mysteriousness of our own ability to relate perceptively to one another is concealed from us . . . understanding a people's culture exposes their normalness without reducing their particularity.
>
> *(Geertz, 1973, p. 14)*

Therefore, when something is said 'regardless of culture' is it said *regardless of everything that made it meaningful*. Yet, in Barkley's (2002) 'consensus statement' culture seems to be implicated as something which may threaten or falsify the *truths* of biological doctrines. This misrepresentation of culture polarises debate, it makes those who talk of the importance of culture guilty of denying the existence of a set of problems. The statement makes one party the bearer of truth and friend to the sufferer, and the other the subversive and politically motivated.

When Foucault critiqued truth he was saying neither that there was no truth, nor that there was no need for truth. Instead he said that what is considered true in any given space and time is contingent upon who is being addressed and the means and resources by which the address is made. Thus what is considered true does not have to be so and the task of re-ordering and making a *new politics of truth* (Foucault, 2000) should be the ultimate task of the critic.

What Harwood (2006) calls the *truth of the disorderly child* has been told within this account through the ready availability of *enunciations* and *technologies*

(Graham, 2007c) both holding some status in the *play of the true and the false* (Foucault, 1996a) in schools. The orderly school child, the responsible parent, the nurturing school, are all examples of things held against subject positions with the status of truth. So too 'boys will be boys', yet the wistful fatalism should by now strike a discord as the truth subsides and infinite others are left, where what 'boys' (or any other such category) *might* be is only dependent on the economic, cultural and linguistic means available to them (Fraser and Honneth, 2003). Therefore, to say that ADHD plays no necessary part in constructions of self and society is not to throw out all means of recognition or all the needs of social order, it is merely to try to re-define them on more transparent, participatory and socially just terms.

The system that I have explored is not one which necessarily produces the effects I have posited. Human agency decrees that nothing is necessarily so, and in this there is promise. However, diagnostic rates are rising and more such categories are appearing. Therefore I hope that the arguments I have brought to bear on this object of study might prompt pause for reflection and resistance. The need for an orderly society is not in dispute, merely the means by which one might attain this. This all rings high and lofty and doesn't really seem to mean much at the level of everyday action, yet an interrogation of one's own everyday positions in terms of what seemed an abstract critique brings it down to the level of the concrete.

Resistance requires both opportunity and motivation in order to carry any effect. Expectations reside around children, teachers, parents and medical practitioners, thus it takes something *out of the ordinary* to think and do something contrary to what has become acceptable, competent, recommended, 'good' practice. Yet this statement is true in a double sense, if we add *from* just before *out of the ordinary*, then the role of culture is brought back into play and the conclusion may be reached that the extraordinary, the radical, the different, the challenging and the resistant is borne out of that which is most familiar; it is in the recognition of it as familiar, habitual, default, automatic that may derive the conscious and constant effort to make it strange again so that the assumptions upon which a situation, event, utterance or description attained the status of *truth* may be better known.

In Chapter 4, it was argued that conduct in school is organised and maintained according to the routine. Within this argument, *the routine* acted partly as a situated construct for the action Foucault (1977) described as *discipline*. Through this enaction the routine argument took a constitutive place in the progression of the argument into subsequent chapters; in Chapter 5 some of the effects of routine divisions between males and females in school were posited in terms of their constitutive effects on the ascription of labels such as ADHD, as well as the effect of diagnosis on future routine thinking. In Chapter 6, routine understandings of gender, motherhood and parenthood, interacted with notions of responsibility to create a set of precepts by which *good parents* would find themselves bound. In Chapter 7 routine logic is expressed and intensified through the nurture group, the *nurturing school* then becoming a metaphor for the ritualised hierarchies of gender and class and the reification of risk and choice enacted in the everyday of early years schooling. The routine enters again now for its material status within the culture of early years classrooms, and for the promise within it for instituting change.

The routine offers a very straightforward critique of mass schooling in making visible the notion that one size does not necessarily fit all. This notion is fundamental to the critique presented here, for implied by the diagnosis of ADHD and the very notion of pathology is a size into which everyone *should* fit. A routine is designed to govern a body towards a particular function; if contemporary schooling is marked by the prescription of routine then one of its primary functions appears to be governance. The more intense the prescription the more legitimately this can be described as a form of oppression (Young, 1990). This is emotive language, yet in this statement is both the extent and limit of routine logic. The culture of schooling works to routines; the culture of routine might be more or less prescriptively enacted, in the relative degree of dominance therefore lies the relative degree of freedom. Therefore, routines, like everything else, are *dangerous* (Foucault, 1984), yet distinction is required in the precise enaction of routine logic within the means by which the work of the classroom is accomplished.

At a discursive level, if routine logic works to efficiently draw a group of bodies towards a function, then it is worth spending some prior time considering *the function*. I have used Foucault's (1991) term *governmentality* in order to describe schools in terms of a partially sighted internalisation of self- (and therefore social) governance. Putting aside relative questions over whether or not this function is desirable, at an absolute level, the governing function of schools can be critiqued according to the manner in which it is *not* presented. That is to say that if school is to contribute to social governance then it should do so in an open and participatory manner. To do otherwise is to admit irrationality somewhere; either the cause of governance is irrational and needs hiding from people on this basis, or the cause of governance is a rational one and people are too irrational to be shown it.

Part of the routine argument of Chapter 4 was a sketched example of the enaction of self-regulation through a weekly drama class. This was still governed by a routine which distributed a set of norms. Indeed for the first few weeks I observed the group I was critical of the amount of time the teacher spent explaining the rules and the need for them. After about six weeks the rules were internalised and I concluded that the children were now 'integrated' into the regime of the drama. What I have only come to acknowledge subsequently, is that this internalisation happened according to the approach taken by the drama teacher, whereby she explained the means by which she wanted to govern the class. At no point did she pretend that she was not in authority, or that she did not expect orderly behaviour. However, in making clear the rules and the need for them in keeping 'the drama' alive, Amy had exposed the rationale of the system to those who were to be systematised. In order to keep the rationale as it had been explained, Amy did have recourse to disciplinary technologies, which in the moment struck me as divisive, exclusionary, visible; all the things I critiqued according to routine logic. Yet, working on the assumption that 'the drama' was a good motivational rationale and making the workings of the system visible to its subjects, Amy was able to restrict the construction of 'others', for those who had transgressed were only othered in the immediate sense that they had apparently chosen not to follow the rationale. In this they were not necessarily bad, sad, stupid or mad, they were just those who had chosen in the moment not to follow the rationale, and routine logic was then enacted to try and persuade them back in. Additionally, judging by the fact that most if not all were 'integrated' after about six weeks, Amy achieved a motivated *responsibilisation* (N. Rose, 1989). Therefore, in this example, a participatory *ethics of the self* (Foucault, 1990) became something achievable within the early years classroom.

Drama is not a typical subject, and this is not meant to be a blueprint for participatory schooling. It was nothing more than the occasional instance, which in retrospect appears to have enacted the routine in a more participatory manner. It is the mechanism by which this was enacted that is more important to me than the potential for re-enactment of the precise situation. The notion of there not being a size to fit all means that there are no blueprints. Yet, while the attempt may have to some extent been afforded by the activity, the relations that Amy enacted were not only bound to the potential fun-ness of the drama, they were also bound to the more generalisable ideals of participation, motivation and openness in the pursuit of a *rational* self-governance.

Offering this kind of recommendation, to get inside, to know and understand and be aware of the limits to action, on the basis of ethnographic work into the 'conditioning of possibility' (Foucault, 1974, p. 89) involves a degree of *constitutive circularity* (Jones *et al.*, 2008). The same objection has been levelled at Foucault's critique of modernity (Habermas, 1981). Yet, all of these critics share in the notion that the manner in which we look at something shapes the conclusions we can draw from it. The particular ethnographic method employed here and the frame of the infant classroom are the things which lend this argument distinction. My *contribution* to the ADHD narrative has been to describe the complexity, the individual, social, discursive, complexities, that attend a so-called *behavioural* phenomenon. I do not believe it is possible to make sense of behaviour with ADHD: it is efficient, it might 'work' in the immediate context of the family and classroom, but it holds no explanatory power. It offers no understanding of self and other and, therefore, cannot enrich the means by which we might come to knowledge of ourselves; it offers no understanding of the conditional nature of choice and accountability, and, therefore, offers no means to emancipation; and, it plays far too transparently into the dominant discourses of differentiation, development and the dichotomised fear of order/disorder that clouds the future bound pessimism of the classroom performance. To this performance it offers its alleviation, its exoneration, and it is in the acceptance of the *label of forgiveness* that the cycle of blame and responsibilisation is set, the *alleviation* of the label appears more to me as a world weary fatalism, a conclusion, a resignation.

Unsurprisingly, therefore, I argue the need to become more aware of the structural conditions which have shaped this disciplinary specification. In using the term *structural* I do not wish to cast people as transparently reflecting institutional dogma. However, I find myself caught between two positions, whereby all good intentions are leading towards more and more diagnoses, thus I consider intentions to be too easily subverted according to disciplinary specification. This is because, though I talk of 'structural' conditions, the rationale that emerges on an individual level for the embodiment of institutional discourse lays waste to all but analytic distinction between structure and action. Additionally, I talk about *structural* conditions in reference to the undeniably *always already there* (Foucault, 1980) of existing means of interpretation, existing institutional objectives, and existing means of inter-relation; subjects are *inaugurated* into speech, not the other way round (Butler, 1997).

Of most immediate relevance to this account and to this indistinction is the notion of *blame*. Young (1990) states that blame is a 'backward looking concept' (p. 151), it does not allow one to progress towards change, only to hold back to account; and in so doing forces certain relations between people, based on subjectivising assumptions about individual responsibility; the pushy mother, the performing teacher, the pathological child. I have critiqued the notion that choice and responsibility is individualised, yet this critique holds only according to the present structural conditioning of possibility:

> The 'well-behaved pupil', boy or girl, does not simply behave because of a visible system of rewards and sanctions; they choose to be 'well behaved' and they participate in processes that define and redefine acceptable actions.
>
> *(Lloyd, 2005, p. 130)*

This statement is positive, optimistic and potentially empowering. Yet, for it to hold true, for it to not instead be co-opted into further subjectivisation, requires there to be a prior re-imagination of the conditioning of choice and the interpretations made of choices. Under present conditions, I would feel extremely nervous about stating that the individual child with ADHD *chooses* to behave badly, not because I believe them to have no agented control, but because those present conditions imply that following such a conclusion, the individual child will become more tightly regulated according to a failure at the individual and structural level to understand the complexities, the plural meanings, of that choice.

I remember very clearly what became the familiar experience for me of being questioned upon my rationale for disturbing the norms of the classroom in the manner I repeatedly did as a child. When called to explain my behaviours I remember never offering any more than a shrug. In the past these very distinctly felt memories have made me disconsolate about the opportunities that might exist for drawing children into a more active participation in their schooling, they have made me despondent about the idea that any professional, no matter how committed, caring and supportive, will be able to offer alternative opportunities to some children, because what I wanted more than anything was just to not have to answer any more of these questions.

Yet, I am able to see that though I could not rationalise my own choices, I was aware, most of the time, of having made a choice. I was also aware, most of the time, of the immediate consequences of that choice; the disciplinary sanction. On one occasion I even sought the institutional backlash in actively trying to get myself expelled. This was because the regime I was offered through the school at that point in time was not one that was personally meaningful to me. I did not wish to internalise the norms of obedience and community, so I chose not to. More often than not, in certain subjects, I did not wish to acquire the knowledge they offered and, therefore, saw no reason to apply the considerable energy it would have taken to do so. What I chose instead was to resist, to challenge the authority around me; to transgress. The immediate sensory experiences of resistance and transgression appear to me poorly represented by a set of disciplinary mechanisms that merely seek to govern them. There is a great deal of danger in taking a transgressive action and creating a transgressor out of it; it is an unequal play of knowledge and power that allows such slippage between subject and object. Transgression should be understood as an act, with a purpose in itself:

> transgression does not transcend limits, since that would be to end being, nor transform individuals, rather it provides an unstable space where limits are forced . . . transgression allows individuals to peer over the edge of their limits, but also confirms the impossibility of removing them . . . it allows individuals to shape their own identities, by subverting the norms which compel them to repeatedly perform, for example, as gendered or disabled subjects.
>
> *(Allan, 1999, p. 48)*

If one was made more aware of the conditioning of possibility, then perhaps one could read another's transgression as a rejection of those immediate conditions. Perhaps one could reach the conclusion that if a child is misbehaving, and they are doing so because they have chosen to, then perhaps, rather than recourse to a discourse of irrational internal deficiency that renders the child powerless, one could consider their transgression a rational opposition to the immediate limitations of their existence.

The existence of a range of responses to apparent deviance implies that some of this thinking already goes on, yet, the proliferation of internalised explanations for socially derived phenomena implies that this thought is not being taken far enough. The response to transgression should not, for example, involve blame, but it should perhaps involve responsibility. Foucault's (1991) *governmentality* offers a distinctive account of responsibility, which provides specification to the notions of a *social contract* (Rousseau, 1762) or an *invisible hand* (Smith, 1776), by drawing out the individually meaningful, but structurally obscured, manner in which people make themselves governable. It is in this obscurity that responsibility, as a collective notion, is lost; for what rationale exists for someone who does not perceive purpose in his or her own action? Yet this is the assumption of the diagnosis of ADHD; it represents a child denied a purpose, their action is not made meaningful by the diagnosis, their purposes for misbehaviour are denied, buried beneath a language of biological determinism.

# APPENDIX I

## Information for participants and parents – Kilcott Infant School

### Investigating inclusion in an infant classroom

#### Information for participants and parents

This research focuses on inclusive school practice, particularly: the contribution that language use and classroom social practice makes to experiences of inclusion; the strategies that different teachers employ to accommodate all pupils; and the way the whole school organises itself in relation to the implementation of government policies on inclusion. I hope that from this study I may learn valuable practical and methodological lessons, which will aid my planned doctoral research in this area.

I will observe one infant class, for a period of one week. In addition to my observations I will place a tape recorder in the class while I am there, which I will subsequently use for language analysis. I will also carry out supplementary interviews with the class teacher and the head of the school.

The research has the potential to provide valuable insight for anyone who works with the reality of inclusion in schools – teachers and pupils alike. Given this school's strong inclusive ethic, I hope that my research will also provide those involved with a chance to reflect on and enrich their own practice, and allow me to learn valuable lessons concerning the practical challenges associated with inclusion which I could take forward to the benefit of others.

The research is both teacher and child focused, and the children, therefore, have a significant role. However, the study will be based wholly on observations and recordings of classroom practice, and I will not be asking them to do anything outside their usual routine. I will make notes from my observations concerning: the spatial and temporal layout and organisation of the classroom; children's interactions with each other and with the teacher; and the ways in which the teacher organises and manages the class. These notes will be developed to create a holistic picture of classroom practices. I will also have a tape recorder running the whole time I am in the classroom, from which I will subsequently develop an analysis in terms of language use and speech acts in the classroom.

To supplement my classroom observation, I will also interview the head of the school and the class teacher involved; both to gain insight into their own views on inclusion and to provide me with an opportunity to reflect on what I have observed.

I learnt of the school through a personal communication with one of the teachers, who described the school as a mainstream infant school with a strong inclusive ethos and high intake of children presenting challenging behaviour. I subsequently spoke to the head of the school and briefly described my research interests. I have permission from the head to conduct research in the school. Anything I learn from my research will be fed back through the head or class teacher. I am also happy to provide written feedback on any aspect of the research.

Confidentiality and anonymity will be protected for all participants throughout; by changing the name of the school, the head and the class teacher, by not using any child's name, nor providing personal description of any individual sufficient for them to be identified. Initially the findings of this research will be reported as part of a post-graduate dissertation, and as such will not be seen by anyone beyond my supervisor and examiner. If in future I publish any work containing findings from this study, I shall ensure confidentiality and anonymity as described above.

Participation in this research is entirely voluntary and participants are at liberty to withdraw for any or no reason, at any time, without prejudice or negative consequences. If you do not wish your child to participate in this research please fill out and return the attached consent withdrawal form.

All research will adhere strictly to the British Educational Research Association's and the British Sociological Association's ethical guidelines for educational and social research. This includes strict observation of Articles 3 and 12 of the United Nations Convention on the Rights of the Child and compliance in relation to the storage and use of personal data as set down by the Data Protection Act (1998). Copies of both these sets of guidelines, along with any other information concerning the research are available on request.

# APPENDIX II

## Information for participants and parents – Alderley Primary School

### Investigating inclusion in an infant classroom

#### Information for participants and parents

I am a research student in the School of Education at the University of Nottingham. As part of my doctoral studies I would like to spend a term in Alderley Primary School and would like to take this opportunity to inform all those affected of my objectives, and give each person the chance to withdraw if they so wish.

This research focuses on inclusive school practice, particularly: the contributions that the use of classroom space and time makes to experiences of inclusion; the strategies that different teachers employ to accommodate all pupils; and the way the whole school organises itself in relation to the implementation of government policies on inclusion. In combination with work in other schools, this research will provide the empirical basis for my doctorate, which is due to be completed in 2008.

For the main part of the research I would like to observe two classes from Nursery to Year Two. In addition to my observations I may sometimes find it useful to make audio recordings, though I would seek permission for use of this from any individuals concerned at the time.

As the chief participants in my research, the children have a vital role to play and representation of their point of view is a major objective of the research. I will make notes based on observations and conversations concerning: the spatial and temporal layout and organisation of the classroom; children's interactions with each other and with the teacher; and the ways in which the teacher organises and manages the class. My presence in the classroom is likely to cause some distraction to children and I will do my best to minimise this impact, and try and always stay sensitive to the needs and perspectives of both children and teachers.

Ideally I would like to be able to do some pictorial work around the school with some of the children – this would involve me asking children to show, describe and take pictures of places and spaces around the school which have some significance for them. I realise of course that this may well not be possible, and along with any other work I wish to do in the classroom I shall always take the direction of the relevant authority.

Anything I learn from my research will be fed back through the head or class teacher. I am also happy to provide written feedback on any aspect of the research. Confidentiality and anonymity will be protected for all participants throughout: by changing the name of the school, the head and the class teacher and by not using any child's name, nor providing personal description of any individual sufficient for them to be identified. As well as being included in my doctoral dissertation, I may use data in publications for academic journals or conferences; I shall ensure confidentiality and anonymity in any such work as described above.

Participation in this research is entirely voluntary and participants are at liberty to withdraw for any or no reason, at any time, without prejudice or negative consequences. If you do not wish your child to participate in this research please fill out and return the attached consent withdrawal form.

All research will adhere strictly to the British Educational Research Association's and the British Sociological Association's ethical guidelines for educational and social research. This includes strict observation of Articles 3 and 12 of the United Nations Convention on the Rights of the Child and compliance in relation to the storage and use of personal data as set down by the Data Protection Act (1998). Copies of both these sets of guidelines, along with any other information concerning the research are available on request. I provide below contact details for myself and my supervisor, if you have any questions, concerns or interests concerning this work please feel free to contact either of us at any time.

# APPENDIX III

## Information for participants – parental interviews

### Investigating families of children with ADHD

#### Information for participating families

This letter contains information concerning an intended research project. You have been sent this letter by your support group in response to my request for any family who has a child with ADHD to be given the opportunity to participate. As such, no personal details or other confidential information has been divulged to me.

I am a research student in the School of Education at the University of Nottingham, and as part of my doctorate I would like to investigate different families' experiences with ADHD. I would like to conduct the study over a period of three to four months, in which time I would conduct three interviews and also ask you to keep a research diary. One of my main concerns is to represent the everyday experience of ADHD in the words of those most immediately affected by the diagnosis, and as such I would hope that this research would be a positive and empowering experience for all concerned.

My interest in ADHD has both personal and academic roots; I found myself referred to educational specialists several times throughout my early childhood and I eventually received a diagnosis of ADHD in 1990, aged 12. After dropping out of school four years later I returned five years ago, and through my studies I have developed an understanding of the disorder grounded in both social theory and this personal experience.

I have several interests which I would like to pursue through your experience of the disorder. I would like to trace back with you the path which eventually led to the diagnosis, I would like to know about the everyday work associated with ADHD, the routines and strategies developed to manage it and the role that others play and have played in your experiences, and the relations that exist between you and your child's school.

Much of this work will lead us into private and possibly sensitive aspects of your life and I ask you to consider this carefully before making a decision. However, I am keen to be directed as far as possible in our interviews by you, and you would be free to decide the nature and extent of the experiences that you share. It would also be extremely useful to me to have access to medical notes and reports, but of course this would only be with the permission of all concerned.

All research will be conducted in accordance with the ethical guidance provided by the British Sociological Association, British Educational Research Association and the Social Care Institute of Excellence, copies of which are available to you should you wish to consult them. Anonymity and confidentiality will be strictly maintained in any publication arising from the research. You will have the opportunity to review and remove personal data before any publication, and you are free to withdraw from the research at any time for any or no reason.

Below is a consent form, which I would ask you to complete and return to me as soon as possible. I have also included below both my own contact details and those of my supervisor. Should you wish to contact either of us at any time for any reason, please do not hesitate. I hope that you will consider my proposal carefully and I look forward to hearing from you.

# APPENDIX IV

## Sample of fieldnotes from Kilcott Infants

### 14 September 2006

Chatting to Sarah this morning, who was talking about the PPA time which they are introducing this term. This is going to involve all the teachers being in the staff room for most of the afternoon, so two cover staff are being brought in and the TAs are to make up the rest. In order to organise this better the Year One and Year Two classes are being split into groups – badgers and rabbits, which is their class animal. Sarah said she wanted to pursue this theme with some classroom decoration and name badges. This meant that much of the rest of my morning was spent searching the net for info on badgers, Sally sent in two children for me to show what I'd found and I think she's going to do this for the rest of the class from next week.

Once I had some info and pictures, Sarah gave me a box of metal discs, and lots of circular pieces of paper with each child's names on them. She pointed me through to the room next to the library where there was a badge press on the table. The machine was straightforward, but this took most of the rest of the lesson. By the time I came back to the classroom the class were getting together for assembly.

Sarah led the class into assembly and I followed at the back of the line. Other classes appeared in similar fashion.

I alone stayed in assembly with Margaret. I soon inherited Cameron from Susan's class who requires pretty much non-stop attention and pays little notice to what's going on. Margaret also brought another disruptive influence to sit by me.

I had expected Margaret to command some respect from the children, because she's the head, but they were very fidgety and restless, kept looking round the room, out of the window, talking to each other and not paying any attention to the moral story that Margaret was telling them. I don't think it helped that one side of the room had double doors leading out on to the large outdoor area, where the sun was shining and where after a while some younger looking children could be seen playing. I think assembly had started a bit late, and these must have been foundation children starting their break or something.

I guess, realising that this was too much distraction, Margaret let the children out of assembly. However, Margaret had sent the kids out early, only to realise that there was no TA out there – so I was asked. As soon as I got outside I encountered an argument. Kilcott has a new set of tyres attached to the ground which the children play on. It is obviously highly popular as (unbeknown to me) only one group can use it at a time. So I initially worsened things by saying 'can't you all use it together'. The other noteworthy incident was some kind of argument which led to two Year Two girls coming over to me, one with a cut knee. Not knowing either of these girls, and feeling a bit lost for useful words, I sent them down to the school office.

Back in class after break time, I was introduced to one of the TAs, Marjorie, who didn't ordinarily work in Year One, but who Sarah had asked to come and help for the PPA in the afternoon. We were talking generally about the school and some of the children in the Year One class. One of those we talked about was Andrew. She said that she knew the family quite well and that the men in it were all quite aggressive and violent, and she saw this as a partial explanation for his behaviour problems. I commented that in my first visit I had been surprised by how tame much of Andrew's behaviour was, she immediately replied that this was because I was a man and so understood better.

The exact nature of this comment did not materialise in the conversation, but clearly everyone is always just waiting for poor Andrew to slip up at any time.

Towards the end of lunch I came back into the Year One classroom from my car where I had been writing a fieldnote. Sarah was alone in the classroom, and we had a chat about the morning's work and about my experience so far. Sarah gave me a list of 'ones to watch' who she thought I may be interested in following.

# APPENDIX V

## Sample of fieldnotes from Alderley Primary

### Year One, day four 18 October 2006

In the staff meeting this morning there was talk of a child protection training day which might be interesting. Also a springboard meeting on 1 November, when I'm in school anyway, and Sue said that I would find that interesting. Sue closed the meeting by saying that she had decided to sack off the sheer amount of bureaucracy she was facing and would be spending more time in the classroom – she acknowledged that she could get in serious trouble about this but seemed serious about her intentions – some of the staff seemed less than enthusiastic about the idea of Sue hanging around classrooms, but . . .

8.55 in class. Registration and sandwich and dinners went by with few minor disruptions. It's assembly with parents of special mentions and PE this morning so interesting to watch Ben and how he gets on. Heather is currently in the class, supporting Chris.

Sitting beautifully is James, who is asked to hold the door open. Jane and Lisa register and Kyle walks hand in hand with Miss Chapel (MC), who has a quiet word with Kyle that I do not hear. MC enjoins all children to walk in silence looking smart and keeping a smart line.

Assembly is the usual, Sue stands at the front and presents the special mentions, everyone sings a song and everyone troops out again. Sue gave everyone in Key Stage 1 a little congratulations at the end of assembly for being so much better behaved in assembly. On the way out Kyle is messing around, by spinning around and making himself giddy, and earns a little talk from Sue.

9.30 back in class. Andrea comes in and removes Kyle, Chris and Sam to go to Mrs Archer to do pottery making – the rest of the class will be doing this this afternoon. There is much more restlessness and noise in class now. Lewis has brought in some kind of flashing key ring and some cars, which are causing distraction and disruption, Marcus looks upset and tells MC that he is very tired after not much sleep – know how he feels, I was awoken at 5.30 by the squawkings of the parrot next door . . .

9.35 Everyone should now be getting changed for PE, and this causes some excitement – Daniel is brought up for running around and not getting changed. Lewis was also messing around I think with Josh and has ripped his PE bag – 'Oh! me PE bag's ruined . . . MC, me PE bags ruined, I need a new PE bag!' Meanwhile Andrew and Greg are on the carpet messing around – they are reprimanded on the end of a general request for quiet from MC.

9.37 Andrew, Marcus, Chris and Josh are all now messing about on the carpet in various states of undress. Robert sits quietly next to them fully changed and ready – he is the only boy who is in this state, though Jane and a couple of the girls are ready. Maggie has been sat in the corner of the carpet – on MC's chair telling various boys off for their disruption, but now Lewis has managed to engage her with his flashing keyring.

9.39 Ben seems to be getting changed without incident, I've not heard his name mentioned in anger at all. MC is alerted to the disruption over on the carpet and gives a sharp 'boys!' and threatens to confiscate the cars and keyrings if they cause further distraction. MC now goes back to Daniel who she has started counting down from ten for each item of clothing to try and speed him up. Greg is still fully dressed and doesn't seem to be doing PE today.

9.41 Andrew and Ben come over to me – Andrew does his usual 'Hello Mr Bailey', he's quite proud that he's remembered my name all the way from last week – I try to look suitably impressed. I say something to Ben and he is shocked that I know his name – 'I know everything' is my response.

9.44 MC asks me to put Lewis's shoes on – I fail miserably and MC has to do it (apparently I can't do laces from the other side!).

9.45 Predictably enough, the cars are confiscated – 'Other boys just can't leave them alone!' MC says, then starts going over the meaning of the whistle once the PE session starts.

9.46 MC 'We're still fussing, we've already taken 15 minutes, Lewis! Come and sit over here and James and Liam open the door, Richard take the basket, Josh take two hoops, Ben take the other two.'

9.47 Still talking, Tom and Spence. The class files out.

# NOTES

## 1 Introducing ADHD

1   A pseudonym. All names have been changed and no detail has been provided sufficient to identify people or places.

## 2 Time, space and possibility

1   See Appendices IV and V for samples of fieldnotes from each school.

## 3 Children, schools and families

1   All data gathered August 2008 from: http://neighbourhood.statistics.gov.uk.
2   All data gathered August 2008 from: http://ofsted.gov.uk/reports.
3   See Appendix I.
4   A 'natural' supplement containing cod liver oil and reported to have calming effects on children.
5   See Appendix II.
6   See Appendix III.

## 4 Routine conduct

1   An earlier version of this chapter was co-authored with Pat Thomson and published by Taylor & Francis as: Bailey, S. and Thomson, P. (2009) 'Routine (dis)order in an infant school'. *Ethnography and Education*, 4, 211–27. The analysis is reproduced here with permission from both publisher and co-author. The fieldwork and analysis were all conducted by me. However, Pat's contributions were of great value in helping me organise the analysis and situate it within the discourses of the school. I acknowledge this contribution in retaining the collective authorial pronoun throughout this chapter. Interestingly, where this involves referring to myself in the third person, this helps 'objectify the objectifying distance' (Bourdieu, 1990, p. 14) of the participant–observation role of teaching assistant, which is discussed in Chapter 2.
2   fn = fieldnote, all dates in this chapter refer to 2005.

3 Preparation Planning and Assessment, under the National Agreement for raising standards, from September 2005 teachers were to be entitled to 10 per cent of their timetabled teaching hours out of class planning. At Kilcott the attempt was to give teachers this time together.

## 5 Boys will be boys

1 Retrieved 21 August 2008 from: http://home.earthlink.net/~mishal/phil1.html.
2 Int = interview. Dates refer to the period I worked in Alderley, September 2006 and June 2007. Fieldnotes in this chapter are presented with the regular recordings of time which I was able to take, free of the demands of participation. Direct quotations within fieldnotes are marked with double quotation marks, all other reference to speech or conversations is paraphrased. Where I present several sections from a longer passage the gaps of missing time are marked (...).

# BIBLIOGRAPHY

Abikoff, H. *et al.* (2002) Observed classroom behavior of children with ADHD: Relationship to gender and comorbidity. *Journal of Abnormal Child Psychology*, 30, 349–59.

Able, S.L., Johnston, J.A., Adler, L.A. & Swindle, R.W. (2007) Functional and psychosocial impairment in adults with undiagnosed ADHD. *Psychological Medicine*, 37, 97–107.

Alderson, P. (1995) *Listening to children: Children, ethics and social research*, Barkingside: Barnardo's.

Allan, J. (1996) Foucault and special educational needs: A 'box of tools' for analysing children's experiences of mainstreaming. *Disability & Society*, 11, 219–33.

Allan, J. (1999) *Actively seeking inclusion: Pupils with special needs in mainstream school*, London: Falmer.

Alvesson, M. & Willmott, H. (2002) Identity regulation as organizational control: Producing the appropriate individual. *Journal of Management Studies*, 39, 619–44.

Anderson, S.L. & Teicher, M.H. (2000) Sex differences in dopamine receptors and their relevance to ADHD. *Neuroscience and Biobehavioral Reviews*, 24, 137–41.

APA (2000) *Diagnostic and Statistical Manual for Mental Disorder: Text Revision (DSM-IV-TR)*, Washington, DC: American Psychiatric Association: http://www.ldawe.ca/DSM_IV.html.

Armstrong, T. (1997) *The myth of the ADD child*, New York: Plume Books.

Arnot, M. & Mac an Ghaill, M. (2006) (Re)contextualising gender studies in education: Schooling in late modernity. In Arnot, M. & Mac an Ghaill, M. (eds) *The RoutledgeFalmer reader in gender and education*, London: Routledge, pp. 1–14.

Arnot, M. & Miles, P. (2005) A reconstruction of the gender agenda: The contradictory gender dimensions in New Labour's educational and economic policy. *Oxford Review of Education*, 31, 173–89.

Bailey, S. (2007) So, what's all the fuss about nurture groups? Annual conference of the British Educational Research Association, Institute of Education, London.

Bailey, S. (2008) Disordered experiences – beyond myth/reality. *British Educational Research Journal*, 34, 135–41.

Bailey, S. (2009) On *being* someone *with* something. 'Improving life chances for children and young people with ADHD' conference, 30 April, Royal College of Psychiatrists, London.

Bailey, S. (2010) The DSM and the dangerous school child. *International Journal of Inclusive Education*, 14, 581–92.

Bailey, S. & Thomson, P. (2009) Routine (dis)order in an infant school. *Ethnography and Education*, 4, 211–27.

Ball, S., Macrae, S. & Maguire, M. (1999) Young lives, diverse choices and imagined futures in an education and training market. *International Journal of Inclusive Education*, 3, 195–224.

Banks, T., Ninowski, J., Mash, E. & Semple, D. (2008) Parenting behaviour and cognitions in a community sample of mothers with and without symptoms of Attention-deficit/ Hyperactivity Disorder. *Journal of Child and Family Studies*, 17, 28–43.

Barkham, P. (2012) What can athletes with ADHD teach us about the condition? *Guardian*, 1 August.

Barkley, R. (1997) *ADHD and the nature of self-control*, New York: Guildford.

Barkley, R. (2002) International consensus statement on ADHD. *Clinical Child and Family Psychology Review*, 5, 89–111.

Barkley, R. (2003) Issues in the diagnosis of attention–deficit/hyperactivity disorder in children. *Brain and Development*, 25, 77–83.

Bauman, Z. (2005) *Work, consumerism and the new poor*, Maidenhead: Open University Press.

BBC (1999) One child in five 'mentally ill', *BBC News*, 3 February.

BBC (2008) White working class boys failing, *BBC News*, 31 January.

Beck, U. (1992) *Risk society: Towards a new modernity*, London: Sage.

Becker, H. (1963) *Outsiders: studies in the sociology of deviance*, New York: The Free Press of Glencoe.

Behar, R. (1996) *The vulnerable observer: Anthropology that breaks your heart*, Boston: Beacon Press.

Benjamin, S. (2002) *The micropolitics of inclusive education: An ethnography*, Buckingham: Open University Press.

Bennathan, M. & Boxall, M. (1998) *The Boxall profile, handbook for teachers*, Maidstone: AWCEBD.

Bennathan, M. & Boxall, M. (2000) *Effective intervention in primary schools: Nurture groups*, London: David Fulton.

Bennett, R., Gottesman, R., Rock, D. & Cerullo, F. (1993) Influence of behavior perceptions and gender on teachers' judgments of students' academic skill. *Journal of Educational Psychology*, 85, 347–56.

Bennett, J. (2004) (Dis)ordering motherhood: Mothering a child with Attention Deficit/ Hyperactivity Disorder. PhD dissertation, Birkbeck College, University of London.

Bhatara, V., Loudenberg, R. & Ellis, R. (2006) Association of Attention Deficit Hyperactivity Disorder and gestational alcohol exposure. *Journal of Attention Disorders*, 9, 515–22.

Biederman, J. (2005) Attention-Deficit/Hyperactivity Disorder: A selective overview. *Biological Psychiatry*, 57, 1215–20.

Billington, T. (2006) *Working with children: Assessment, representation and intervention*, London: Sage.

Bourdieu, P. (1984) *Distinction: A social critique of the judgement of taste*, London: Routledge & Kegan Paul.

Bourdieu, P. (1987) The biographical illusion. *Working papers and proceedings of the Centre for Psychosocial Studies (University of Chicago)*, 14, 1–7.

Bourdieu, P. (1990) *The logic of practice*, Stanford: Stanford University Press.

Bourdieu, P. & Passeron, J.C. (1979) *Reproduction in education, society and culture*, London: Sage.

Boxall, M. (2002) *Nurture groups in school: Principles and practice*, London: Paul Chapman.

Bradley, C. (1937) The behavior of children receiving benzedrine. *American Journal of Psychiatry*, 94, 577–85.

Britzman, D.P. (2000) The question of belief: Writing poststructural ethnography. In St Pierre, E. & Pillow, W. (eds) *Working the ruins: Feminist poststructural theory and methods in education*, New York: Routledge, pp. 27–40.

Brook, U. & Boaz, M. (2005) Attention deficit and hyperactivity disorder/learning disabilities (ADHD/LD): Parental characterization and perception. *Patient Education and Counseling*, 57, 96–100.

Brown, J. & Duguid, P. (2001) Knowledge and organization: A social-practice perspective. *Organization Science*, 12, 198–213.

Burman, E. (2009) Beyond 'emotional literacy' in feminist and educational research. *British Educational Research Journal*, 35, 137–55.

Butler, J. (1993) *Bodies that matter: On the discursive limits of 'sex'*, London: Routledge.

Butler, J. (1997) *Excitable speech: A politics of the performance*, New York: Routledge.

Cameron, C. (2007) *Social pedagogy and the children's workforce*, London: Thomas Coram Research Unit, Institute of Education.

Cannella, G. & Viruru, R. (2004) *Childhood and postcolonization: Power, education, and contemporary practice*, London: RoutledgeFalmer.

Carpenter, L. & Austin, H. (1999) Silenced, silence, silent: Motherhood in the margins. In Johnson, B. & Reid, A. (eds) *Contesting the curriculum*, Sydney: Social Science Press.

Carpenter, L. & Austin, H. (2008) How to be recognized enough to be included? *International Journal of Inclusive Education*, 12, 35–48.

Carspecken, P. (1996) *Critical ethnography in educational research*, New York: Routledge.

Cherkaoui, M. (2005) *Invisible codes: essays on generative mechanism*, Oxford: Bardwell.

Christensen, P. & James, A. (2000a) Researching children and childhood: Cultures of communication. In Christensen, P. & James, A. (eds) *Research with children: Perspectives and practices*, London: Falmer, pp. 1–8.

Christensen, P. & James, A. (2000b) *Research with children: Perspectives and practices*, London: Falmer.

Clark, L. (2006) Boys are being failed by our schools, *Mail Online*, 13 June.

Clifford, J. (1983) On ethnographic authority. *Representations*, 1, 118–46.

Clifford, J. & Marcus, G. (eds) (1986) *Writing culture: The poetics and politics of ethnography*, Berkeley: University of California Press.

Cline, T. (2002) Preface to Boxall, M., *Nurture groups in school: Principles and practice*, London: Paul Chapman.

Cole, D., Gondoli, D. & Peeke, L. (1998) Structure and validity of parent and teacher perceptions of children's competence: A multitrait-multimethod-multigroup investigation. *Psychological Assessment*, 10, 241–9.

Collett, B.R. & Gimpel, G.A. (2004) Maternal and child attributions in ADHD versus non-ADHD populations. *Journal of Attention Disorders*, 7, 187–96.

Colwell, J. & O'Connor, T. (2003) Understanding nurturing practices – a comparison of the use of strategies likely to enhance self-esteem in nurture groups and normal classrooms. *British Journal of Special Education*, 30, 119–24.

Comber, B. (1999) Doing schooling: Literacy and curriculum work. In Johnson, B. & Reid, A. (eds) *Contesting the curriculum*, Sydney: Social Science Press, pp. 43–58.

Condry, J. & Ross, D. (1985) Sex and aggression: The influence of gender label on the perception of aggression in children. *Child Development*, 56, 225–33.

Connell, R.W. (1995) *Masculinities*, Cambridge: Polity.

Conrad, P. & Schneider, J. (1980) *Deviance and medicalization: From badness to sickness*, St Louis: Mosby.

Cook, E. (2007) Fat mums link to hyper kids, *Mirror Online*, 3 November.

Cooper, P. (2001) *We can work it out. What works in educating pupils with social, emotional and behavioural difficulties outside mainstream classrooms?* Ilford: Barnardo's.

Cooper, P. (2003) Including students with social, emotional and behavioural difficulties in mainstream secondary schools. *Emotional Behavioural Difficulties*, 8, 5–6.

Cooper, P., Drummond, M.J., Hart, S., Lovey, J. & McLaughlin, C. (2000) *Positive alternatives to exclusion*, London: RoutledgeFalmer.

Cooper, P. & O'Regan, F. (2001) *Educating Children with AD/HD: A teacher's manual*, London: RoutledgeFalmer.

Cooper, P. & Tiknaz, Y. (2005) Progress and challenge in nurture groups: Evidence from three case studies. *British Journal of Special Education*, 32, 211–22.

Corbett, J. (1996) *Bad-mouthing: the language of special needs*, London: The Falmer Press.

Davies, H. (2008) Reflexivity in research practice: Informed consent with children at school and at home. *Sociological Research Online*, 13, www.socresonline.org.uk/13/4/5.html.

Davis, J.E. (2001) Transgressing the masculine: African American boys and the failure of schools. In Martino, W. & Meyenn, B. (eds) *What about the boys? Issues of masculinity in schools*, Milton Keynes: Open University Press, pp. 140–53.

Deleuze, G. (1988) *Foucault*, London: Continuum.

Department for Children Schools and Families (2007) *Guidance on the duty to promote community cohesion*, London: DCSF.

Department for Children Schools and Families (2008) *Building brighter futures: Next steps for the children's workforce*, London: DCSF.

Department for Children Schools and Families (2010) *Working Together to Safeguard Children: A guide to inter-agency working to safeguard and promote the welfare of children*, London: DCSF.

Department for Education and Skills (2004) *Every child matters: Change for children*, London: DFES.

Department for Education and Skills (2005) *Excellence and enjoyment: A strategy for primary schools*, London: DFES.

Department for Education and Skills (2006) *Every child matters outcome framework – version 2.0*, London: DFES.

Dermott, E. (2005) Time and labour: fathers' perceptions of employment and childcare. In Pettinger, L., Parry, J., Taylor, R. & Glucksman, M. (eds) *A new sociology of work?* Oxford: Blackwell, pp. 91–103.

Derrida, J. (1967) *Writing and difference*, London: Routledge.

Donzelot, J. (1979) *The policing of families*, New York: Pantheon.

Douglas, M. (1970) *Natural symbols*, London: Routledge.

Down, S. & Hughes, M. (2009) When the 'subject' and the 'researcher' speak together: co-producing organizational ethnography. In Ybema, S., Yanow, D., Wels, H. & Kamsteeg, F. (eds) *Organizational ethnography*, London: Sage, pp. 83–98.

Doyle, R. (2003) Developing the nurturing school: Spreading nurture group principles and practices into mainstream classrooms. *Emotional Behavioural Difficulties*, 8, 252–66.

Ecclestone, K. (2004) Learning or therapy? The demoralisation of education. *British Journal of Educational Studies*, 52, 112–37.

Ecclestone, K. & Hayes, D. (2008) *The dangerous rise of therapeutic education*, London: Routledge.

Eco, U. (2007) *Foucault's Pendulum*, New York: Harcourt.

Elwood, J. (1995) Undermining gender stereotypes: Examination and coursework performance in the UK at 16. *Assessment in Education*, 2, 283–303.

Epstein, D. (1997) Cultures of schooling/cultures of sexuality. *International Journal of Inclusive Education*, 1, 37–53.

Fairclough, N. (1992) *Discourse and social change*, Cambridge: Polity Press.

Fairclough, N. (2000) *New Labour, new language?* London: Routledge.

Fine, G. (1993) Ten lies of ethnography: moral dilemmas of field research. *Journal of Contemporary Ethnography*, 22, 267–94.

Fine, M. (1991) *Framing dropouts*, Albany, NY: State University of New York Press.

Foucault, M. (1967) *Madness and civilization: A history of insanity in the age of reason*, London: Routledge.

Foucault, M. (1972) *The archaeology of knowledge*, London: Routledge.

Foucault, M. (1973) *The birth of the clinic: An archaeology of medical perception*, London: Tavistock Publications.

Foucault, M. (1974) *The order of things: An archaeology of the human sciences*, London: Routledge.

Foucault, M. (1977) *Discipline and punish: The birth of the prison*, Harmondsworth: Penguin.

Foucault, M. (1979) On Governmentality. *Ideology & Consciousness*, 5–21.

Foucault, M. (1980) Power and strategies. In Gordon, C. (ed.) *Power/Knowledge: Selected interviews and other writings 1972–1977*, Brighton: Harvester, pp. 134–45.

Foucault, M. (1981a) *The will to knowledge: The history of sexuality vol. 1*, Harmondsworth: Penguin.

Foucault, M. (1981b) The order of discourse. In Young, R. (ed.) *Untying the text: A poststructuralist reader*, London: Routledge & Kegan Paul, pp. 48–78.

Foucault, M. (1982) The subject and power. In Dreyfus, H. & Rabinow, P. (eds) *Michel Foucault: Beyond structuralism and hermeneutics*, Brighton: Harvester Press, pp. 208–26.

Foucault, M. (1984) On the genealogy of ethics: An overview of work in progress. In Rabinow, P. (ed.) *The Foucault reader*, London: Penguin, pp. 340–72.

Foucault, M. (1988) Technologies of the self. In Gutman, H. & Hutton, P. (eds) *Technologies of the self: A seminar with Michel Foucault*, London: Tavistock.

Foucault, M. (1990) *The care of the self: The history of sexuality vol. 3*, Harmondsworth: Penguin.

Foucault, M. (1991) Governmentality. In Burchell, G., Gordon, C. & Miller, P. (eds) *The Foucault effect: Studies in governmentality*, Chicago: University of Chicago Press, pp. 87–104.

Foucault, M. (1996a) The ethics of the concern for self as a practice of freedom. In Lotringer, S. (ed.) *Foucault live: Collected interviews 1961–1984*, New York: Semiotext(e), pp. 432–50.

Foucault, M. (1996b) Talk Show. L. Hochroth & J. Johnston, trans. In Lotringer, S. (ed.) *Foucault Live: Collected Interviews 1961–1984*, New York: Semiotext(e), pp. 146–70.

Foucault, M. (1996c) The concern for truth. L. Hochroth & J. Johnson, trans. In Lotringer, S. (ed.) *Foucault live: Collected interviews 1961–1984*, New York: Semiotext(e), pp. 455–64.

Foucault, M. (1997) For an ethics of discomfort. In Lotringer, S. (ed.) *The politics of truth: Michel Foucault*, New York: Semiotext(e), pp. 135–46.

Foucault, M. (2000) About the concept of the 'dangerous individual' in nineteenth-century legal psychiatry. In Faubon, J. (ed.) *Michel Foucault: Power*, London: Penguin, pp. 176–200.

Foucault, M. (2004) *'Society must be defended': Lectures at the College de France, 1975–76*, London: Penguin.

Francis, B. (2008) Teaching manfully? Exploring gendered subjectivities and power via analysis of men teachers' gender performance. *Gender and Education*, 20, 109–22.

Frank, B., Kehler, M., Lovell, T. & Davison, K. (2003) A tangle of trouble: Boys, masculinity and schooling – future directions. *Educational Review*, 55, 119–33.

Fraser, N. (1997) *Justice interruptus: Critical reflections on the 'postsocialist' condition*, London: Routledge.

Fraser, N. & Honneth, A. (2003) *Redistribution or recognition? A political-philosophical exchange*, London: Verso.

Furedi, F. (2003) *Therapy culture: Creating vulnerability in an uncertain age*, London: Routledge.

Geertz, C. (1973) *The interpretation of cultures*, New York: Basic Books.

Gershon, J. (2002) Gender differences in AD/HD: An overview of research. In Quinn, P. & Nadeau, K. (eds) *Gender issues and AD/HD*, Silver Springs, MD: Advantage Books, pp. 23–38.

Gerwitz, S., Ball, S. & Bowe, R. (1995) *Markets, choice and equity in education*, Buckingham: Open University Press.

Giddens, A. (1990) The globalising of modernity. In Williams, P. & Chrisman, L. (eds) *Colonial discourse and post-colonial theory*, Herts: Prentice-Hall.

Giddens, A. (1991) *Modernity and self-identity: Self and society in the late modern age*. Cambridge: Polity.

Gillborn, D. & Gipps, C. (1996) Recent research on the achievements of ethnic minority pupils. OFSTED Reviews of research, London: HMSO.

Gleeson, D. & Husbands, C. (2001) *The performing school*, London: RoutledgeFalmer.

Goffman, E. (1968) *Stigma: Notes on the management of spoiled identity*, Harmondsworth: Penguin.

Goleman, D. (1996) *Emotional intelligence: why it can matter more than IQ*, London: Bloomsbury.

Gore, J. (1993) *The struggle for pedagogies: Critical and feminist discourses as regimes of truth*, London: Routledge.

Gore, J. (1995) Foucault's poststructuralism and observational education research: A study of power relations. In Smith, R. & Wexler, P. (eds) *After post-modernism: Education, politics and identity*, London: Falmer Press, pp. 98–111.

Graham, L. (2006) Caught in the net: A Foucaultian interrogation of the incidental effects of limited notions of inclusion. *International Journal of Inclusive Education*, 10, 3–25.

Graham, L. (2007a) Out of sight, out of mind/out of mind, out of site: Schooling and Attention Deficit Hyperactivity Disorder. *International Journal of Qualitative Studies in Education*, 20, 585–602.

Graham, L. (2007b) Speaking of 'disorderly' objects: A poetics of pedagogical discourse. *Discourse: Studies in the Cultural Politics of Education*, 28, 1–20.

Graham, L. (2007c) Schooling Attention Deficit Hyperactivity Disorders: Educational systems of formation and the 'behaviourally disordered' school child. Doctoral thesis, Queensland University of Technology.

Graham, L. (2007d) (Re)visioning the centre: Education reform and the 'ideal' citizen of the future. *Educational Philosophy and Theory*, 39, 197–215.

Graham, L. (2008) From ABCs to ADHD: The role of schooling in the construction of behaviour disorder and production of disorderly objects. *International Journal of Inclusive Education*, 12, 7–33.

Greene, R.W., Biederman, J., Faraone, S., Sienna, M. & Garcia-Jetton, J. (1997) Adolescent outcome of boys with Attention-Deficit/Hyperactivity Disorder and social disability: Results from a 4-year longitudinal follow-up study. *Journal of Consulting and Clinical Psychology*, 65, 758–67.

Habermas, J. (1981) Modernity vs postmodernity. *New German Critique*, 22, 3–14.

Hacking, I. (1986) Making Up People. In Heller, T.C., Sosna, M. & Wellbery, D.E. (eds) *Reconstructing individualism: Autonomy, individuality & the self in western thought*, Stanford: Stanford University Press, pp. 222–36.

Hacking, I. (1995) The looping effects of human kinds. In Sperber, D., Premack, D. & Premack, A. (eds) *Causal cognition: A multi-disciplinary approach*, Oxford: Clarendon Press, pp. 351–83.

Hacking, I. (1999) *The social construction of what?* Cambridge, MA: Harvard University Press.

Halasz, G., Anaf, G., Ellingson, P., Manne, A. & Thomson Salo, F. (2002) *Cries unheard: A new look at Attention Deficit Hyperactivity Disorder*, Altona: Common Ground.

Hall, S. (ed.) (1997) *Representation: Cultural representations and signifying practices*, London: Sage.

Hammersley, M. & Atkinson, P. (1983) *Ethnography: Principles in practice*, London: Routledge.

Haraway, D. (1988) Situated knowledges: The science question in feminism and the privilege of partial perspective. *Feminist Studies*, 14, 575–99.

Hartmann, T. (1997) *Attention Deficit Disorder: A different perception*, Grass Valley, CA: Underwood Books.

Hartung, C., Willcutt, E., Lahey, B., Pelham Jr, W., Loney, J., Stein, M. & Keenan, K. (2002) Sex differences in young children who meet criteria for Attention Deficit Hyperactivity Disorder. *Journal of Clinical Child and Adolescent Psychology*, 31, 453–64.

Harvey, E., Danforth, J.S., McKee, T.E., Ulaszek, W.R. & Friedman, J.L. (2003) Parenting of children with Attention-Deficit/Hyperactivity Disorder (ADHD): The role of parental ADHD symptomatology. *Journal of Attention Disorders*, 7, 31–42.

Harwood, V. (2006) *Diagnosing 'disorderly' children*, London: Routledge.

Haywood, C. & Mac an Ghaill, M. (2006) Education and gender identity: Seeking frameworks of understanding. In Arnot, M. & Mac an Ghaill, M. (eds) *The RoutledgeFalmer Reader in Gender and Education*, London: Routledge, pp. 49–58.

Henry, J. (2006) Failing boys put university drive in doubt, telegraph.co.uk, 27 August.

Hershel, J. & Kaye, J. (2003) Epidemiology and possible causes of Autism. *Pharmacotherapy*, 23, 1524–30.

Hjorne, E. (2006) Pedagogy in the 'ADHD classroom': An exploratory study of 'the little group'. In Lloyd, G., Stead, J. & Cohen, D. (eds) *Critical new perspectives on ADHD*, Abingdon: Routledge, pp. 176–97.

Holligan, C. (2000) Discipline and normalization in the nursery: The Foucaultian gaze. In Penn, H. (ed.) *Early childhood services: Theory, policy and practice*, Buckingham, PA: Open University Press.

Holstein, J. & Gubrium, J. (1995) *The active interview*, London: Sage.

Hunter, I. (1994) *Rethinking the school: Subjectivity, bureaucracy, criticism*, Sydney: Allen & Unwin.

Hyland, T. (2006) Vocational education and training and the therapeutic turn. *Educational Studies*, 32, 299–306.

Jackson, P. (1960) *Life in classrooms*, New York: Teachers College Press.

Jackson, P., Boostrom, R. & Hansen, D. (1993) *The moral life of schools*, San Francisco: Jossey-Bass.

James, A., Jenks, C. & Prout, A. (1998) *Theorizing childhood*, Cambridge: Polity.

Jeffrey, B. & Troman, G. (eds) (2012) *Performativity in UK Education: Ethnographic cases of its effects, agency and reconstructions*, Stroud: E&E Publishing.

Jeffrey, B. & Woods, P. (1998) *Testing teachers*, London: Routledge.

Jenkins, R. (1973) *Behavior disorders of childhood and adolescence*, Springfield, IL: Charles C. Thomas.

Johnson, K. (2000) Research ethics and children. *Curriculum Perspectives,* November, 6–7.

Jones, L., Macrae, C., Holmes, R. & Maclure, M. (2008) Eccentric performances and disorderly conduct: The pathology of difference. Annual conference of the British Educational Research Association, Herriot-Watt University, Edinburgh.

Kelso, P. (2008) Judge by the weight in gold – Michael Phelps stakes his claim for title of greatest Olympian. *Guardian,* 14 August.

Kenway, J. (1990) Education and the right's discursive politics: Private versus state schooling. In: Ball, S. (ed.) *Foucault and education: Disciplines and knowledge*, London: Routledge, pp.167–206.

Kenway, J. & Fahey, J. (2009) Imagining research otherwise. In Kenway, J. & Fahey, J. (eds) *Globalizing the research imagination*, London: Routledge, pp. 1–40.

Kenway, J. & Fitzclarence, L. (1997) Masculinity, violence and schooling: Challenging 'poisonous pedagogies'. *Gender and Education*, 9, 117–33.

Kenway, J., Willis, S., Blackmore, J. & Rennie, L. (1997) *Answering back, remaking girls and boys in schools*, Sydney: Allen & Unwin.

Kewley, G. (1999) *ADHD: Recognition, reality and resolution*, Horsham: L.A.C Press.

King, P. (2012) *ADHD magazine – debut issue coming soon – The Unexpected Guest* [Online]. Accessed: 14 December 2012. Available: http://www.purplerevolver.com/bulletin/news/122753-adhd-magazine---debut-issue-coming-soon---the-unexpected-guest.html#68O89TOyhTCWBmz2.99.

King, R. (1978) *All things bright and beautiful?* Chichester: John Wiley.

Klein, R.G. & Mannuzza, S. (1991) Long-term outcome of hyperactive children: A review. *Journal of the American Academy of Child & Adolescent Psychiatry*, 30, 383–7.

Kutcher, S. *et al.* (2004) International consensus statement on Attention-Deficit/Hyperactivity Disorder (ADHD) and Disruptive Behaviour Disorders (DBDs): Clinical implications and treatment practice suggestions. *European Neuropsychopharmacology*, 14, 11–28.

Lacan, J. (1966) *Ecrits*, New York: Norton.

Laing, R.D. (1969) *The politics of the family and other essays*, London: Tavistock.

Laurence, J. (2008) ADHD: The end of the problem as we know it? *International Journal of Inclusive Education*, 12, 99–111.

Laurence, J. & McCallum, D. (1998) The myth-or-reality of Attention-Deficit Disorder: A genealogical approach. *Discourse*, 19, 183–200.

Laurence, J. & McCallum, D. (2009) *Inside the child's head: histories of childhood behavioural disorders*, Rotterdam: Sense.

Lefebvre, H. (2004) *Rhythmanalysis: Space, time and everyday life*, London: Continuum.

Lingard, B. (2003) Where to in gender policy in education after recuperative masculinity politics? *International Journal of Inclusive Education*, 7, 33–56.

Lloyd, G. (2005) 'EBD girls' – a critical view. In Lloyd, G. (ed.) *Problem girls*, London: RoutledgeFalmer, pp. 129–45.

Lloyd, G. & Norris, C. (1999) Including ADHD? *Disability & Society*, 14, 505–17.

Lloyd, G., Stead, J. & Cohen, D. (eds) (2006) *Critical new perspectives on ADHD*, London: Routledge.

Lupton, D. (ed.) (1999) *Risk and sociocultural theory*, Cambridge: Cambridge University Press.

Mac an Ghaill, M. (1994) *The making of men: Masculinities, sexualities and schooling*, Milton Keynes: Open University Press.

MacNaughton, G. (2005) *Doing Foucault in early childhood studies*, London: Routledge.

Mandell, N. (1991) The least-adult role in studying children. In Waksler, F. (ed.) *Studying the social worlds of children*, London: Falmer.

Marcus, G. (1998) *Ethnography through thick and thin*, Princeton, NJ: Princeton University Press.

Mauss, M. (1973) Techniques of the body. *Economy and Society*, 2, 70–88.

Mayall, B. (2000) Conversations with children: Working with generational issues. In Christensen, P. & James, A. (eds) *Research with children: Perspectives and practices*, London: Falmer, pp. 120–35.

Maynard, M. (1993) Feminism and the possibilities of a postmodern research practice. *British Journal of Sociology of Education*, 14, 327–31.

McWilliam, E., Lather, P. & Morgan, W. (1997) *Headwork, fieldwork, text work: A textshop in new feminist research*, Brisbane: Centre for Policy and Leadership Studies, Queensland University of Technology.

Meadmore, D. & Symes, C. (1996) Of uniform appearance: A symbol of school discipline and governmentality. *Discourse*, 17, 209–25.

Meyenn, B. & Parker, J. (2001) Naughty boys at school: Perspectives on boys and discipline. In Martino, W. & Meyenn, B. (eds) *What about the boys? Issues of masculinity in schools*, Milton Keynes: Open University Press, pp. 169–85.

Millard, E. (1997) Differently literate: Gender identity and the construction of the developing reader. *Gender and Education*, 9, 31–48.

Miller, J. (1993) *More has meant women: The feminisation of schooling*, London: Tufnell.

Miller, T. (1993) *The well-tempered self*, Baltimore: Johns Hopkins University Press.

Miller, T. & Leger, M.C. (2003) A Very Childish Moral Panic: Ritalin. *Journal of Medical Humanities*, 24, 9–33.

Moeran, B. (2009) From participant observation to observant participation. In Ybema, S., Yanow, D., Wels, H. & Kamsteeg, F. (eds) *Organizational ethnography*, London: Sage, pp. 139–55.

Moreno, C., Laje, G., Blanco, C., Jiang, H., Schmidt, A. & Olfson, M. (2007) National trends in the outpatient diagnosis and treatment of Bipolar Disorder in youth. *Archives of General Psychiatry*, 64, 1032–9.

Murphy, E. (1999) 'Breast is best': Infant feeding decisions and maternal deviance. *Sociology of Health & Illness*, 21, 187–208.

Nayak, A. & Kehily, M.J. (2001) 'Learning to laugh': A study of schoolboy humour in the English secondary school. In Martino, W. & Meyenn, B. (eds) *What about the boys? Issues of masculinity in schools*, Milton Keynes: Open University Press, pp. 110–23.

NICE (2006) *Attention Deficit Hyperactivity Disorder (ADHD): Final Scope*. London: National Institute of Health and Clinical Excellence.

NICE (2008) *Attention Deficit Hyperactivity Disorder: Diagnosis and management of ADHD in children, young people and adults*, London: National Institute for Health and Clinical Excellence.

NIMH (2006) *Attention Deficit Hyperactivity Disorder*, Bethesda, MD: National Institute for Mental Health.

Noblit, G. & Dempsey, V. (1996) *The social construction of virtue*, Albany, NY: State University of New York Press.

Noblit, G., Flores, S. & Murillo, E. (2004) *Postcritical ethnography: An introduction*, Cresskill, NJ: Hampton.

Nolan, E., Gadow, K. & Spafkin, J. (2001) Teacher reports of DSM-IV ADHD, ODD, and CD symptoms in schoolchildren. *Journal of American Academy for Child and Adolescent Psychiatry*, 40, 241–9.

O'Connor, T. & Colwell, J. (2002) The effectiveness and rationale of the 'nurture group' approach to helping children with emotional and behavioural difficulties remain within mainstream education. *British Journal of Special Education*, 29, 96–100.

Osler, A. & Vincent, K. (2003) *Girls and exclusion: Rethinking the agenda*, London: Routledge.

Palmer, S. (2007) Boys must be boys – for all our sakes. *The Sunday Times*, 18 November.

Parkin, J. (2007) Stop feminising our schools – our boys are suffering, dailymail.co.uk, 31 January.

Parsons, T. (1961) The school class as social system. In Halsey, A., Floud, J. & Anderson, C. (eds) *Education, economy and society*, New York: The Free Press.

Patai, D. (1994) Sick and tired of nouveau solipsism. *The Chronical of Higher Education*, Point of view essay, 23 February.

Pillow, W. (2003) Confession, catharsis, or cure? Rethinking the uses of reflexivity as methodological power in qualitative research. *International Journal of Qualitative Studies in Education*, 16, 175–96.

Pollard, A. (1985) *The social world of the primary school*, London: Holt, Rinehart and Winston.

Popewitz, T. (2003) Governing the child and the pedagogicalisation of the parent: A historical excursis into the present. In Bloch, M., Holmund, K., Moqvist, I. & Popkewitz, T. (eds) *Governing children, families and education: Restructuring the welfare state*, New York: Palgrave Macmillan, pp. 36–61.

Prosser, B. (2006) *Seeing red: Critical narrative in ADHD research*, Teneriffe, Queensland: Post Pressed.

Quinn, P. & Nadeau, K. (eds) (2002) *Gender Issues and AD/HD*, Silver Spring, MD: Advantage Books.

Raphael Reed, L. (1999) Troubling boys and disturbing discourses on masculinity and schooling: A feminist exploration of current debates and interventions concerning boys in school. *Gender and Education*. 11, 93–110.

Reid, R. & Maag, J. (1997) Attention Deficit Hyperactivity Disorder: Over here, over there. *Educational and Child Psychology*, 14, 10–20.

Reid, R., Maag, J. & Vasa, S. (1993) Attention Deficit Hyperactivity Disorder as a disability category: A critique. *Exceptional Children*, 60, 198–214.

Renold, E. (2001) Learning the 'hard' way: Boys, hegemonic masculinity and the negotiation of learner identities in the primary school. *British Journal of Sociology of Education*, 22, 369–85.

Renold, E. (2007) Primary school 'studs': (De)constructing young boys' heterosexual masculinities. *Men and Masculinities*, 9, 275–97.

Rodriguez, A. & Bohlin, G. (2005) Are maternal smoking and stress during pregnancy related to ADHD symptoms in children? *Journal of Child Psychology and Psychiatry*, 46, 246–54.

Rodriguez, A. et al. (2008) Maternal adiposity prior to pregnancy is associated with ADHD symptoms in offspring: evidence from three prospective pregnancy cohorts. *International Journal of Obesity*, 32, 550–7.

Rose, N. (1989) *Governing the soul: The shaping of the private self*, London: Routledge.

Rose, N. (1998) *Inventing our selves: Psychology, power, and personhood*, Cambridge: Cambridge University Press.

Rose, N. (1999) *Powers of Freedom: Reframing political thought*, Cambridge: Cambridge University Press.

Rose, N. (2007) *The politics of life itself*, Princeton, NJ: Princeton University Press.

Rose, N. & Miller, P. (1992) Political power beyond the state: Problematics of government. *The British Journal of Sociology*, 43, 173–205.

Rose, S. (2005) *The 21st-century brain*, London: Vintage.

Rousseau, J.-J. (1762) *The social contract*, Herts: Wordsworth.

Rudd, B. (1998) *Talking is for kids: Emotional literacy for infant school children*, London: Sage.

Said, E. (1978) *Orientalism*, London: Penguin.

Saltmarsh, S. & Youdell, D. (2004) 'Special sport' for misfits and losers: Educational triage and the constitution of schooled subjectivities. *International Journal of Inclusive Education*, 8, 353–71.

Sanders, T. (2007) Helping children thrive at school: The effectiveness of nurture groups. *Educational Psychology in Practice*, 23, 45–61.

Sayal, K., Taylor, E., Beecham, J. & Byrne, P. (2002) Pathways to care in children at risk of Attention-Deficit Hyperactivity Disorder. *British Journal of Psychiatry*, 181, 43–8.

SCIE (2004) *ADHD – background, assessment and diagnosis*, London: Social Care Institute of Excellence.

Sellman, E. (2009) Lessons learned: Student voice at a school for pupils experiencing social, emotional and behavioural difficulties. *Emotional and Behavioural Difficulties*, 14, 33–48.

Sharp, P. (2001) *Nurturing emotional literacy: A practical guide for teachers, parents and those in the caring professions*, London: David Fulton.

Simons, H. & Usher, R. (eds) (2000) *Situated ethics in educational research*, London: Routledge Falmer.

Singer, J.B. (2006) Making stone soup: Evidence-based practice for a suicidal youth with comorbid Attention Deficit/Hyperactivity Disorder and Major Depressive Disorder. *Brief Treatment and Crisis Intervention*, 6, 234–47.

Singh, I. (2002) Bad boys, good mothers, and the 'miracle' of Ritalin. *Science in Context*, 15, 577–603.

Singh, I. (2003) Boys will be boys: Fathers' perspectives on ADHD symptoms, diagnosis and drug treatment. *Harvard Review of Psychiatry*, 11, 308–16.

Singh, I. (2004) Doing their jobs: Mothering with Ritalin in a culture of mother-blame. *Social Science and Medicine*, 59, 1193–205.

Singh, I. (2005) Will the 'real boy' please behave: Dosing dilemmas for parents of boys with ADHD. *The American Journal of Bioethics*, 5, 1–14.

Singh, I. (2007) Clinical implications of ethical concepts: Moral self-understandings in children taking methylphenidate for ADHD. *Clinical Child Psychology and Psychiatry*, 12, 167–82.

Sinn, N. & Bryan, J. (2007) Effect of supplementation with polyunsaturated fatty acids and micronutrients on learning and behavior problems associated with child ADHD. *Journal of Developmental & Behavioral Pediatrics*, 28, 82–91.

Skeggs, B. (2003) *Class, self, culture*, London: Routledge.

Skelton, C. (1996) Learning to be tough: The fostering of maleness in one primary school. *Gender and Education*, 8, 185–97.

Skelton, C. (1997) Primary boys and hegemonic masculinities. *British Journal of Sociology of Education*, 18, 349–369.

Skelton, C. (2001) *Schooling the boys: Masculinities and primary education*, Buckingham: Open University Press.

Skelton, C. (2002) The 'feminisation of schooling' or 're-masculinising' of primary education. *International Studies in Sociology of Education*, 12, 77–96.

Skelton, C. & Francis, B. (2005) *Reassessing gender and achievement*, London: Routledge.

Slee, R. (1995) *Changing theories and practices of discipline*, London: Falmer.

Slee, R. (1997) Imported or important theory? Sociological interrogations of disablement and special education. *British Journal of Sociology of Education*, 18, 407–19.

Smart, B. (1986) The politics of truth and the problem of hegemony. In Hoy, D. (ed.) *Foucault: A critical reader*, Oxford: Blackwell.

Smith, A. (1776) *An inquiry into the nature and causes of the wealth of nations*, Chicago, IL: University of Chicago Press.

Smith, D. (1975) Women and psychiatry. In Smith, D. & David, S. (eds) *I'm not mad I'm angry: Women look at psychiatry*, Vancouver: Press Gang, pp. 1–20.

Smith, D. (1987) *The everyday world as problematic: A feminist sociology*, Boston: Northeast University Press.

Smith, D. (1990) *Texts, facts and femininity: Exploring the relations of ruling*, London: Routledge.

Smith, D. (2005) *Institutional ethnography: A sociology for people*, Lanham, NY: AltaMira.

Solberg, A. (1996) The challenge in child research: From 'being' to 'doing'. In Brannen, J. & O'Brien, M. (eds) *Children in families: Research and policy*, London: Falmer.

Southall, A. (2007) *The other side of ADHD: Attention Deficit Hyperactivity Disorder exposed and explained*, Oxford: Radcliffe.

Still, G. (1902) Some abnormal psychical conditions in children. *Lancet*, 1, 1008–12, 1077–82, 1163–8.

Swadener, B. & Lubeck, S. (eds) (1995) *Children and families 'at promise': deconstructing the discourse of risk*, Albany, NY: State University of New York Press.

Tait, G. (2010) *Philosophy, behaviour disorders, and the school*, Rotterdam: Sense.

Taylor, E. (1994) Hyperactivity as a special educational need. *Therapeutic Care & Education*, 3, 130–44.

Thomson, P. (2002) *Schooling the rustbelt kids: Making the difference in changing times*, Stoke-on-Trent: Trentham Books.

Thornberg, R. (2007) Inconsistencies in everyday patterns of school rules. *Ethnography and Education*, 2, 401–16.

Timimi, S. (2005a) *Naughty boys: Anti-social behaviour, ADHD and the role of culture*, Basingstoke: Palgrave Macmillan.

Timimi, S. (2005b) The rise and rise of ADHD. In Newnes, C. & Radcliffe, N. (eds) *Making and breaking children's lives*, Ross-on-Wye: PCCS Books.

Timimi, S. & Leo, J. (eds) (2009) *Rethinking ADHD: from brain to culture: international perspectives*, London: Palgrave Macmillan.

Torgersen, T., Gjervan, B. & Rasmussen, K. (2006) ADHD in adults: A study of clinical characteristics, impairment and comorbidity. *Nordic Journal of Psychiatry*, 60, 38–43.

Train, A. (2005) *ADHD: Attention Deficit Hyperactivity Disorder. How to deal with very difficult children*, London: Souvenir Press.

Tyler, S. (1986) Post-modern ethnography: From the document of the occult to the occult document. In Clifford, J. & Marcus, G. (eds) *Writing culture: The poetics and politics of ethnography*, Berkeley: University of California Press, pp. 122–40.

Valencia, R. (ed.) (1997) *The evolution of deficit thinking: educational thought and practice*, London: Falmer Press.

Vincent, C. (2000) *Including parents? Education, citizenship and parental agency*, Buckingham: Open University Press.

Wagner, J. (1993) Ignorance in educational research or, how can you not know that? *Educational Researcher*, 22, 15–23.

Walker, S. (1998) *The hyperactivity hoax*, New York: St Martin's Press.

Walkerdine, V. (1984) Developmental psychology and the child-centred pedagogy: The insertion of Piaget into early education. In Henriques, J., Holloway, W., Urwin, C., Venn, C. & Walkerdine, V. (eds) *Changing the subject: Psychology, social regulation and subjectivity*, London: Methuen, pp. 153–202.

Walkerdine, V. (1986) Post-structuralist theory and everyday social practices: The family and the school. In Wilkinson, S. (ed.) *Feminist social psychology: Developing theory and practice*, Milton Keynes: Open University Press.

Walkerdine, V. & Lucey, H. (1989) *Democracy in the kitchen*, London: Virago.

Wallace, I. (1999) *You and your ADD child: Practical strategies for coping with everyday problems*, Sydney: HarperCollins.

Weber, M. (1930) *The protestant ethic and the spirit of capitalism*, London: Routledge.

Wender, P. (2000) *ADHD: Attention Deficit Hyperactivity Disorder in children, adolescents, and adults*, Oxford: University Press.

Willis, P. (1977) *Learning to labour*, New York: Columbia University Press.

Wolcott, H. (1999) *Ethnography: A way of seeing*, Walnut Creek, CA: AltaMira.

Wolcott, H. (2002) *Sneaky kid and its aftermath*, Walnut Creek, CA: AltaMira.

Wolcott, H. (2005) *The art of fieldwork*, Walnut Creek, CA: AltaMira.

Ybema, S. & Yanow, D. (2009) Making the familiar strange: A case for disengaged organizational ethnography. In Ybema, S., Yanow, D., Wels, H. & Kamsteeg, F. (eds) *Organizational ethnography*, London: Sage, pp. 101–19.

Young, I.M. (1990) *Justice and the politics of difference*, Princeton, NJ: Princeton University Press.

# INDEX